Praise for
The Age of

T0245009

"A wide-ranging and deeply intelligent investigation . . . Howsare makes it clear that the human relationship with deer has always been in flux, a mysterious give-and-take with this crepuscular, liminal creature, thriving where the wild meets the tamed."
—MAX WATMAN, *The Wall Street Journal*

"A masterpiece . . . Howsare's hands-on approach keeps her storytelling vivid and personal." —MICHAEL SIMS, *The Washington Post*

"Fascinating . . . A splendid document of intellectual and emotional growth." —LORRAINE BERRY, *Los Angeles Times*

"Howsare engages thoughtfully with big ideas, from classical art and old myths of deer and deer-gods to the long, intertwined history of human beings and deer in North America, from pre-Columbian Indigenous folkways that shaped and affected deer population to the near-extinction that occurred after white settlers arrived."
—KATE TUTTLE, *The Boston Globe*

"*The Age of Deer* blends Howsare's personal story with literary analysis and in-depth reportage . . . It is this tension between kinship and stewardship that shapes Howsare's book, a conflict that produces a third way that collapses the traditional hierarchy. What if deer have something to teach us, not just to give us in the forms of their beauty and their bodies?"
—ANNIE BERKE, *Washington City Paper*

"An engaging and thoughtful look at what matters to deer and what they mean to us. Howsare is fascinated by the paradoxical status of an animal we all think we know: not tame, but not quite wild either; fetishized by some, resented by others; all too common, and yet impossible to ignore. I highly recommend it!"
—NATE BLAKESLEE, author of *American Wolf*

"*The Age of Deer* is a wonderfully perceptive and rewarding exploration of life in all its interconnected forms."
—MICHELLE NIJHUIS, author of *Beloved Beasts: Fighting for Life in an Age of Extinction*

"Extraordinary and absorbing, *The Age of Deer* proves John Muir's notion that when we pick out one thing in the universe, we find it hitched to everything else. Howsare understands that we live in an age of numbness when 'few of us are willing to really feel,' and suggests, through the lives of deer and her experience with them, an elemental antidote."
—DAVID GESSNER, author of *Return of the Osprey* and *All the Wild That Remains*

"A brilliantly researched book on deer. Howsare has an ear for the contradictions of our entanglements with these creatures, who increasingly occupy a middle ground between wild and domestic, survivors of our species' worst predations. This is also a book about nature, culture, and nationhood—an interrogation of the American project as it continues to unfold across our deer-happy landscape."
—ALISON HAWTHORNE DEMING, author of *A Woven World*

"*The Age of Deer* joins a growing canon of fresh treatments of wild creatures that are anciently enmeshed in the human story. And as Howsare reminds us in her warm, relaxed style, we will always have such a relationship with deer. The next one you see is going to intrigue you in a whole new way."
—DAN FLORES, *New York Times* bestselling author of *Coyote America*

"I carried *The Age of Deer* in my pack for a few days through a canyon in Colorado, and it was a great complement to the lopsided slopes of fallen trees and the sound of roaring water. The deer is due its storyteller, and Howsare takes the role with smartness and grace."
—CRAIG CHILDS, author of *Tracing Time* and *The Secret Knowledge of Water*

The Age of Deer

The Age of Deer

TROUBLE AND KINSHIP
WITH OUR WILD NEIGHBORS

Erika Howsare

CATAPULT 🦌 NEW YORK

First Catapult edition: 2024
First paperback edition: 2025

"Long Hair," by Gary Snyder, from *Regarding Wave*, copyright © 1970 by Gary Snyder. Reprinted by permission of New Directions Publishing Corp.

Full image credits appear on page 337. Deer fur © Roman Pyshchyk/Adobe Stock; deer silhouettes © jan stopka/Adobe Stock and © elvil/Adobe Stock; antler silhouette © NikolaM/Adobe Stock; hoof silhouette © Roi_and_Roi/Adobe Stock.

Hardcover ISBN: 978-1-64622-134-9
Paperback ISBN: 978-1-64622-250-6

Library of Congress Control Number: 2023936804

Cover design by Nicole Caputo
Cover art courtesy of Index of American Design
Book design by Olenka Burgess

Catapult
New York, NY
books.catapult.co

Printed in the United States of America

10 9 8 7 6 5 4 3 2

To my dearest: John, Elsie, Rosa

Landscapes are ephemeral compared to species.
ANNA LOWENHAUPT TSING ET AL.

As all hunters know, the deer is the sweetest of game.
PAUL SHEPARD

Contents

Introduction

SUMMERTIME: THE LIGHT WAS FULL AND GREEN. I SAT IN
a camper in the woods, writing, facing a steep hillside. And here
came twin fawns; one, then the other.

They couldn't see me, despite my easy view of them. They
made their way down through beech and oak trees along a flank
of the hill, on a pathway I'd often seen deer use—that I myself
have often used, walking with my daughters.

The fawns were a few months old, still spotted along their
sides, but past the newborn stage when their mother would have
left them curled on the ground while she went off to find food.
At this age, they'd be spending much of their time roaming along
with her, learning how to move through her home range and
what to eat.

But where was the mother? The twins had arrived at the bottom of the hill, where there's a gate between stone pillars and
a place to cross the quiet one-lane road. They loped across the
pavement and into the tangle of weeds and boulders on the other
side.

I kept writing. Maybe fifteen minutes passed. Then I looked
up and she had materialized, a little uphill of the gate: not walking, just standing. She faced the way her fawns had gone, her
head raised high. I watched her for a second or two—some fleeting mother-to-mother understanding in my mind: *You're looking
for them, aren't you?*—before the fawns burst into view, galloping back across the road and straight toward where she stood.

They were so much like human children as they ran, just like
when I come home and my own girls rush right at me. It was that

same unadulterated bond. There was no slowing down as they reached their mother. They crowded under her and jabbed their faces into her belly and began to nurse.

I laughed out loud. I'd never seen deer nursing before! They were just like baby goats or calves, the lusty way they went at it, bumping their mother's hindquarters backward as they latched on. Being half-grown, they had to crouch to fit into the space under her body, their back legs folded and their forelegs outstretched; I could see the nearer one pawing the ground repeatedly with a front hoof, and again I was reminded of my own children, how they used to stroke my shirt with a hand as I nursed them. And I remembered that mix of sensations—patience and immense satisfaction—that, now, I imagined I could see in the stance of the doe, stoically waiting while her babies drank her down.

A car approached; I could hear it coming over the rise. The three weren't in danger where they stood, but the doe would not want to keep nursing as the car went by. My mind flicked to the driver, wondering if that person would get to see what I was seeing, wondering if they'd be delighted, too.

The mother leapt, as lightly as a dandelion seed; no disentanglement, no pulling or tugging; she just seemed to float up and over her fawns as she moved away up the hill, calm and self-contained. The white broom of her tail whisked the air once or twice.

The fawns followed. The car passed. And the moment was done.

⚘

I live in rural Virginia, on a narrow road that noses against the austere, forested wall of the Blue Ridge. My yard backs up to thousands of acres of woods. White-tailed deer are a constant in these introverted mountains, almost as elemental as the trees. Just in the last week, I've had two encounters with small groups of deer, found tracks in my garden, and discovered two of their bodies decomposing in the woods.

Yet half an hour away there are big suburban housing developments where residents spot deer just as often as I do. And in Charlottesville, the place we mean when we say we're going "to town," deer also thrive, in the pockets between busy bypasses and leafy residential warrens and dry cleaners and bakeries. However strongly we might associate them with wilderness, there are deer who spend their whole lives in cities, and for the most part, they do fine.

Species like dogs have a special relationship to humans that has evolved over millennia, one based on mutual benefit. Others, like big cats and whales, would be much better off without humans in the picture at all. But deer—in their quiet way—occupy a middle zone between those extremes of domestication and wildness. Far from tame, they are nonetheless experts at living with people, and in many ways, they actually prefer to share habitat with us. All across North America, as in many other parts of the world, we exist in intimate proximity to deer. Like any family member, they stir knotty feelings.

🦌

In my earliest memory of deer, my friend's father is dragging a carcass toward me. It's late fall in rural Pennsylvania—probably overcast, brown and gray. I'm standing in their yard, looking across a ravine to where he and another man, both wearing coveralls, have emerged from the woods with a deer they've shot.

The powerline cut where they're walking is a brushy no-man's-land, running up and over ridges in a straight line. Behind me is the road my friend and I both live on. Nearby is her house, chocolate brown, where we spend a lot of time playing dress-up and pretending to be detectives. Downhill are the ammonia-smelling pens where her father keeps his hunting dogs.

He is a frightening, bad-tempered man. His words for us are always harsh. I remember him in this moment much more clearly than the deer; like the sky on that day, his presence is oppressive, and I don't want to be there when he enters the yard. The memory ends when he's still far away; we must have skedaddled inside.

My uncle Jim hunted, too. I was bookish and shy of these men, and unlike them, I had little connection to the woods. In Boy Scouts, my brother learned how to make a fire and pitch a tent, but in Girl Scouts we wove sit-upons from wax paper and made Christmas ornaments out of different pasta shapes. I don't ever remember seeing a deer in our yard, and though it seems impossible, I have no memories of seeing living deer anywhere. They must have been there, but it was the dead ones that left an impression.

We lived south of Pittsburgh amid the small-town ruins of extractive industry. Pulling things out of the land—coal and natural gas—had a long legacy there. The Pittsburgh rivers, Monongahela, Allegheny, Ohio, are big and muscular, and the industries had been too, but during my childhood in the 1980s, the general feeling was one of embitterment and loss. Many steel mills had closed; jobs had disappeared; downtowns had hollowed out, leaving only lawyers' offices and hearing-aid stores. Driving around, we saw gravel pits, junkyards, moldering industry and raw-looking farms. People lived modestly and carefully because they had to. The folks who tended to talk about the loss of prosperity were the same ones who had gun racks in their basements.

My parents weren't in this category. Both their fathers had hunted, but they didn't; our house contained no trophy heads but lots of LPs, books, and art. Culturally, if not geographically, my mother and father had moved some distance away from their roots. When I came of age I took another big step, to urban California, and began to see Rust Belt ruins with more detachment. Looking at photos from this time, I see I was also drawn to the caricatures we make of living things: dolls in a junkshop window, decals of spring fawns and bunnies. I made ironic trophies of these places where our relationship to beings had been stretched beyond the realm of myth and snapped, becoming grotesque and candy-sweet.

After some time in California, where I met my now-husband, John, I returned to the East Coast and landed in Virginia, outside Charlottesville. This was not the Rust Belt; it felt gentler and cleaner. We lived in deep woods, learned to identify bird calls, and started a garden. I worked on a small farm for three summers, harvesting vegetables and observing as other workers dealt with live and slaughtered Berkshire hogs. We moved to a rented cottage on a large estate and, wandering its acres, found a spot where many deer bones had been dumped. I know we saw living deer too, though again, I don't specifically remember them—except one, a white doe that we spotted from the car one Halloween at dusk.

We were becoming more attuned to the land. We bought a house at the foot of the Blue Ridge, kept chickens, and studied the trees. I also worked as a writer and was asked to produce a column on homesteading and "green living," then a phrase much in circulation. My subject matter boiled down to dilemmas. There were the minutiae: Should we rip out invasive brush if it's sheltering songbirds? Is it better to buy hybrid seeds from the local hardware store, or mail-order heirloom ones from Maine? And there was the big picture: What does stewardship mean? What was done to this place in the past and how should that inform our actions?

These questions spilled outside the boundaries of the column and into longer and longer essays and manuscripts of poetry. What is natural, and is natural behavior necessarily more ethical? Our ties to animals were the thorniest dilemmas of all. Human concepts framed their lives and deaths in deeply unsettling ways. The questions about them looked back at me with eyes of their own.

Life among the ruins, the biology of artifice: These were still my habitat.

All this time, deer had been lurking at the edges, as they do. In the background of our wedding photos was a deer skull we'd picked up at that dump site and hung on the wall of the farm cottage where we married. In our conversations with neighbors, there was talk about deer eating people's gardens. We saw them leaping fences or lying crumpled along the road on our long commute. Gunshots pierced the quiet in the fall; a neighbor brought us the tenderloin from a whitetail he'd shot on the edge of our land. The door handle on our old shed, installed by some former owner, was made of an antler. Now and then, I'd hear about my brother getting a deer back in Pennsylvania; six years younger than me, he'd learned to hunt from Uncle Jim after I left for college.

⚘

A lot of roads led to this book. I don't remember one moment when I decided to write it; it must have been an ordinary one, like spotting a deer on an evening run, or dusting off the deer bones we'd found in the woods. My understanding of the human place on earth, shaped by post-industrial rupture, scented by tomato plants, was profoundly uneasy. And deer were a single node where many of my questions—about damage, repair, myth, nourishment, and the things that divide us—might come together.

Deer speak to our twin American obsessions with death and its denial. But being in Virginia had given me an awareness of deer as *living* beings, fellow inhabitants of the landscape who are not rare, but familiar. They are animals whose impossible beauty plays against their commonness, their constant abundance. Deer sightings are most interesting to me when they're in some kind of half-human zone: a backyard, a roadside. I note their scat on trails, or look up to find them watching me from among young trees and the rusting chassis of a pickup truck.

⚘

I'm writing this in winter. These last few months have seen the annual fall rutting period for deer, which coincides with both hunting season and the highest incidence of deer–vehicle collisions. In general, deer act a little crazy in the autumn before settling down to survival mode in winter, and their interactions with people reflect that cycle. Fall is a good time to observe the more contentious, fraught aspects of our modern relationship to them—the signs that, whether we think of it or not, we are living in an age of deer.

In America, just during these last few months, people have debated the ethics of baiting deer with food or doe urine in order to shoot them, of hunting deer using dogs, and—in a number of communities around the country—of culling programs that reduce urban deer herds. We've celebrated young children who have managed to kill big bucks, and punished an eighteen-year-old who filmed himself riding one in the backyard. We've encouraged hunters to kill coyotes, so that the coyotes won't kill as many deer, so that hunters will have more chances to kill deer.

We like it when people with some perceived disadvantage—little girls, old women, wounded warriors—successfully bring down deer. But we also like it when deer become victims for people to save: from icy rivers, from storm drains, from fences and clotheslines in which they get tangled. One woman from Colorado posted a video of a mountain lion attacking a deer; off-camera, her distressed voice asks, "Oh, the poor thing—what should I do?" as though humans have some responsibility to stop predators from eating.

On Vancouver Island, Canada, deer started turning up with BB gun injuries; conservation officers suspected homeowners had been shooting them to protect their shrubs. Mule deer dangled from helicopters in Utah, where scientists studied their health.

While officials reminded the public that feeding deer is a bad idea, stories nonetheless surfaced of people using food to lure deer onto their porches and even into their homes. The town of Pulaski, New York, announced that it would install a bronze statue commemorating Bella, a deer that had become the town's unofficial mascot. Raised by a farmer after her mother was killed by a car, Bella lived her adult life in town and was unusually comfortable with people; a local newspaper called her "a special member of the Pulaski community."

Several people were gored by deer; in Michigan, a hunter was killed by a deer he'd just shot.

As in most years, vehicles in the U.S. killed well over a million deer, and hunters killed nearly six million.

Chronic wasting disease, which is fatal to deer, was confirmed in more than twenty-five states and kept on spreading; this continued to fuel debate over the sale and transport of deer raised on game farms.

A deer crashed through the storm door of a home in Edmond, Oklahoma, running wildly through several rooms before (according to *Newsweek*) "locking itself in a bathroom." The homeowner described the scene inside his house as being like "a bomb, an explosion, a crash." Animal control officers pulled the deer out of the house by a rope tied to its antlers. Then they euthanized it, citing its "numerous cuts."

Etsy offered more than eight thousand products whose designs incorporated deer skulls, including window decals, cornhole boards, and hip flasks. A new game came onto the market called Deer Pong, in which players toss balls into plastic cups hanging from the antlers of an electronic buck's head.

At least two deer were spotted with Christmas lights tangled in their antlers.

⚮

Despite all the commotion, deer remain, living their lives—usually with a quieter sort of drama.

A few months ago, I bent down to photograph some pink plastic flowers that were piled in the corner of a little cemetery near my house. They must have blown off a headstone and been caught by the fence; they were half-buried in dead leaves from the monstrous oak nearby. My daughter, who often spots things the rest of us miss, called me over to see something.

It was a dead fawn, trapped by one rear hoof near the top of the fence, the rest of its body draped downward, head and neck resting on the ground. Though its snared leg still looked much as it had when the fawn was alive, with tawny fur and a pert black hoof, the body became progressively more decomposed as our eyes followed it down, down, all the way to the dark leathery skin that clung to the hollow-eyed skull.

We couldn't tell how exactly the foot had gotten tangled. But it was easy enough to imagine what must have come next: the awful struggle, the exhaustion and starvation, the likelihood that the fawn's mother had been nearby, unable to help, forced at some point to leave her baby to die.

Like the well-meaning woman asking "What should I do?" while the mountain lion pinned its prey, I had the urge to help the fawn; I wished it were still alive and I could free it. Unlike the mountain lion, however, the fence was not a natural predator. It was one of the many, many lines that humans have drawn across the land, enclosing and dividing space in human terms.

But calling the fence an unnatural threat to a native animal would be too simple. This fawn was part of a deer population that, in itself, has been profoundly shaped by people. Virginia and other eastern states actually imported deer in the mid-twentieth century, restocking herds that had been depleted by human hunting and habitat destruction.

In places where wolves and big cats are largely absent from the picture, humans are now the most significant predator of deer. Where humans once acted to raise their numbers, now wildlife managers rely on hunters as a sort of volunteer army, keeping the deer population in check.

This fawn was a victim of a human artifact. But then, the fawn itself was a human artifact. It owed its existence in part to the laws that restrict hunting, the landscaping plants that likely made up some of its diet, the lack of predators. This is the biology of artifice. And the fawn's quality of life, too—the experiences it had while it was alive—was massively shaped by human action. Undoubtedly it crossed roads many times in its life; was barked at by pet dogs; ate non-native plants; drank from compromised waters; chose bedding spots away from all-night lights; followed its mother along paths whose courses tracked or avoided human driveways, property lines, powerlines, fields. Perhaps, before it died, it had even managed to jump a few fences.

I am not a deer hunter, deer tracker, or deer scientist. Before I wrote this book, I'd never even touched a live deer, unless you count the two times I've collided with them while driving (or that snapshot of me as a preschooler, feeding a fawn at a petting zoo).

But like so many people, I see deer almost every day, mostly in the middle distance. They usually move away, in a mood of caution but not panic.

There's a curious quality to these sightings: a mixture of interest and habituation. We almost always remark on deer when we see them, an acknowledgment that we don't often grant crows, vultures, or squirrels. Deer are bigger and more charismatic than any of these by an order of magnitude, and it just feels odd to let their presence go unremarked.

Too, there's something about how a deer *looks back*. A squirrel or a vulture seems quite oblivious to my presence, whether I'm watching or not, whereas deer are clearly attuned to my arrival and my intentions. Knowing that deer are primed to react makes each one seem like more of a live wire.

Yet deer are too familiar to be surprising. They don't appear right underfoot, strike from the underbrush, or lurk on shelves in the toolshed. They usually receive nothing but a matter-of-fact "There's a deer"—yet they receive this almost every time they appear.

The human relationship to large animals has historically been a destructive one; as we fanned over the globe, megafauna mostly disappeared. Deer are the largest wild animals we still live with in any widespread way, one of the signal species of our time, as firmly established in our cities as in our national parks.

More simply, their size is like our size: an eerie analog for our own physical presence. If you wrapped your arms around a deer of any North American species, it would be much like embracing another human adult.

The prey status of deer makes them "good" by default, and perhaps that appeals to a certain side of the human self-image:

we like to think we're innocent, just doing our best to get along. Watching deer, we see a picture of what we might be like if we were wild, eating our food right off the stem, subject at every moment to predation.

⚜

Around the world and through the ages, from the Argentinian pampas to the Siberian steppes to the Scottish Highlands, deer have provided people with meat. (In the main, they haven't given us milk, though the notion is oddly persistent, chasing itself through various mythologies and legends.) Our bodies have been entwined with theirs in deep and sometimes troubling ways. We've used their skins to cover our skin; they've furnished us with clothing and tools, often in greater quantities than any other game animal. They are dependable yet wild providers. For complex reasons, they've mostly stayed out from under the roof of domestication. They remain uncowed.

They've also given us ideas: stories, icons, and imagery that begin in our deepest artmaking past and continue through to the present. A Nlaka'pamux story from British Columbia tells of a human hunter who marries a deer woman and learns, from her family, to always throw the bones of his quarry into water, so that the deer can come back to life. He soon realizes he has been hunting the woman's own brothers, but the ritual restores them. "Thus these Deer people lived by hunting and killing each other and then reviving." By the end of the story, he has hunted, killed, and resurrected his own wife and son. It's a complex interspecies alliance, as though deer and people are metaphorical in-laws, shocking and harmonious all at once.

Other myths tell of women who shapeshift into deer, or deer who steal the sun and carry it away in their antlers. Their profiles—slim and shapely—are like letters of the alphabet, initials that stand for wilderness, grace, and hunters' quarry. They have been—they still are—what is desired, what flees, what is pursued, and sometimes what gets caught.

⚜

Unlike other species with whom deer have key interactions—predators, food sources—humans bring *ideas* to the relationship. We carry inside us images and narratives that tell us how to look at the deer before us. They're a screen upon which we project our conflicting concepts about nature. They exist somewhere between what we believe about nature and what's actually true.

Given all that, deer may not only be a great historical species with long, tangled, essential ties to humanity. They may also be the species that perfectly symbolizes the way we live with nature now, and the way we will carry on into whatever weird, paradoxical future awaits.

Many mythical heroes have followed deer away from the familiar and toward new destinies, glorious or tragic. This is true for Rama of the *Ramayana*, King Arthur, Herakles, warriors and saints. Once I began to trace their paths—trained my sights on them like a hunter would do—deer led me, too, to a world of surprises.

To look at our modern relationship with deer, as I found, is to step into some of the discomforts—political and social—of how people live with each other. And it means asking the biggest question of all: How will we live on this planet?

𑁦

There is a long-standing tradition in certain American yards of displaying life-size artificial deer. These may serve as targets for shooting practice. Just as often, plastic deer are purely for decoration.

If landscape painters have often placed deer in bucolic wilderness settings in order to symbolize purity and abundance, then imitating that look in one's yard seems to broadcast "Here is a peaceable kingdom." It's a message of coexistence, as though our dwellings were no disturbance at all to wild animals, and might even be favorite landmarks along their routes.

In the case of deer, this can be a version of the truth, especially if we've planted some tasty hosta or lettuce nearby. Not so for the unfortunate buck who approached a plastic doe in an Illinois yard a few years ago and tried to mate with her.

Humans watching from indoors filmed the whole thing: how the buck sauntered near, mounted, did his best to copulate (here some strategic blurring was added in postproduction), and only gave up when the doe's head—this must have been a down-market product—popped right off her body.

In the video, the buck jumps away in confusion, then comes back to give a forlorn sniff at the fallen plastic head. It's the wrong texture, scent, temperature; unresponsive and stiff; but nonetheless, enough like the idea of a deer to have substituted, briefly, for the real thing.

The Age of Deer

Part I
Standing

CHAPTER 1

Dancing

IT WAS THE NIGHT OF WINTER SOLSTICE, AND HERE WERE all the trappings of a school play: music stands, metal risers, handmade banners. The battered stage was hung with garlands of evergreen. My family and I, among several hundred others, sat with our coats draped over the backs of our plastic chairs.

Two mothers whispered—"Oh, is that Evelyn?"—"Yes." A baby coughed.

Christmas would barrel over us in just a few days, but there were no mangers or Magi here. This was the annual winter play presented by a small private school near my home. We'd come again that year to soak up its bohemian patchwork of song and chant: pagan Yule traditions, solstice rituals, and medieval Christmas overtones. Kids were dressed as aproned villagers, as avatars of the four elements, as Saint George and Father Christmas, and as Holly and Ivy, the beloved evergreen leaves of winter.

In the audience, I spotted a woman I know and nodded to her. She leaned against the wall, wearing deer antlers on her head and a long cloak of dark green, like a hemlock forest at dusk.

Some elements of the performance change from year to year, but the Abbots Bromley Horn Dance stays the same. Abbots Bromley is a village in the West Midlands of England, and the program hinted that the dance originated there nearly a thousand years ago. As the first notes of the tune cut through the murmur and movement of the audience and seven dancers entered in a stately single file, the Horn Dance did carry an unmistakable sense of antiquity. It had the feel of an artifact older than the red cross on Saint George's breastplate. This dance felt almost prehistoric, and it was the antlers the kids held to their heads that made it so.

The music was a halting, minor-key tune played on recorder by a lone eighth grader at the corner of the stage. The antlered dancers wore plain tunics, the color of deerskin. The choreography was very simple: The dancers slowly crossed the stage, pausing to lift a foot behind them every few paces, the toe pointing backward just like a deer's hoof when it strolls through grass. Some of the girls' legs were nearly that slender.

A dignified melody, almost a dirge. The dancers formed two lines and approached each other, then retreated and bowed; the lines interlaced. In a diagonal across the stage, they arranged themselves by height and by antler size: the old obsession with status, manifested in bone.

In Abbots Bromley, the dance is one of a number of traditional European "hoodening rituals," in which people once donned animal skins or heads, dancing or marching to ensure a successful hunt. As far back as the fourth century, Saint Augustine is said to have condemned these practices and called them "filthy," both their antiquity and their pagan power seen as threats by the ascendant church.

Gradually, as the dancers and the tune looped around on themselves, the audience settled into a hypnotic hush. If a shabby auditorium in Virginia was not the Horn Dance's native habitat, it carried power nonetheless, even when its vehicles were nervous middle-schoolers. That naked, shaky music felt to me like the struggle of any human, striving within a matrix—family, community—and these ritualized movements conveyed a common need for the good luck of sustenance.

Here in Virginia, the deer season was mostly behind us. Some people in the room had killed does or bucks that fall. Some would go home to venison backstrap in their freezers, venison stew in Crock-Pots on their counters, racks of antlers on their walls or porches. Some may have given meat to hungry neighbors. Surely there are households in this county where people pray to kill deer in the fall, so that throughout the winter they'll have enough to eat.

ⅱ

When Europeans encountered Indigenous people on the edges of North America, they must have understood the importance of deer to the Native population. Such a connection was part of their own cultural foundation, too. Throughout much of what would come to be called the Old World, people had lived with and made use of deer for generations.

Across cultures, deer are frequent actors in stories and myths. But in truth, our intimate involvement with deer is older than any of these artifacts. We've been bound by mysterious ties since before any story we remember.

Deer keep company with some of the oldest human graves in the world. A tomb found in Qafzeh Cave—a rock shelter in the Yizrael Valley in Israel—contains the bones of at least twenty-seven people, which have rested on this rock ledge for nearly a hundred thousand years' worth of days and nights. The people lie among hearths and various animal remains, including red and fallow deer. Archaeologists point to ornamentation with ocher and seashells as evidence that these were deliberate human burials.

The people at Qafzeh did another remarkable thing: They seem to have spent many years caring for a child with a terrible brain injury. After a blow to the head around age five, the child, known as Qafzeh 11, would likely have suffered "significant neurological and psychological disorders, including troubles in social communication," yet lived until age twelve or thirteen. After death, he or she was laid supine into a pit, in a ceremonial burial that apparently indicates "a unique case of differential treatment"—extra honor, as it were, as though to make up for such a compromised existence. It's a pair of deer antlers that signals this distinction. They're held in the child's folded hands, near the face.

Antlers keep company with other prehistoric remains, too, or-
namenting hearths, or forming beds or roofs inside tombs.

We can only speculate on what such offerings meant at the
time, but we do know that more recent mythologies cast deer
as psychopomps: escorts to the afterlife, a part of nature that
breaks off to soften nature's deadly force. It's a wish for someone
to take care of us on the journey to the hereafter—to oversee us,
forgive us, keep us company. Vikings, for example, believed that
a deer with oaken antlers, called Eikthyrnir, wandered Valhalla
and accompanied fallen heroes on the journey across the river
to the land of the dead. The stag's antlers dripped water into a
spring that fed all the rivers of the world: a connection between
deer, water, and renewal that infuses many myths.

I once saw a reference to deerskin burial shrouds, too. Certainly this idea exists in legends—like in the *Chansons de Roland*,
when Charlemagne has the bodies of Roland and two other heroes prepared for burial: "The barons' bodies they then take up
and wind / Straitly in shrouds made of the roebuck's hide."

It's a tantalizing idea, that people wrapped the dead in soft,
warm skins as they laid them into the earth. Something about it
is tremendously comforting.

There's an old Siberian-Turkish story about a hunter who recon-
structs the skeleton of a deer he's just killed, substituting a piece
of wood for the rib his arrow had broken. Later, he kills a different deer and discovers the wooden rib inside its body.

Hunters in both Eurasia and the Americas felt bound to treat
their quarry as a respected interlocutor, a sort of dance partner
in the ritual of survival. A deer was not just a target, but a conscious being who participated in the event of its own demise.
Though its meat would transmute into human life, bones were
the undestroyed basis by which deer life, in a larger sense, could
continue. To carefully lay out a deer's skeleton after cleaning and
butchering its body was a gesture of honor and atonement. In
turn, one *became* one's prey. In some places, eating venison was

thought to make one swift and wise; in others, it was said to breed timidity.

Some cultures propose a single, eternal figure who represents all deer: Awi Usdi is a white deer who oversees Cherokee hunters, making sure that each slaughtered deer is properly asked for forgiveness. If a hunter neglects the ritual, Awi Usdi will cripple that person with rheumatism.

Different groups made different rules for hunters. Some banned boastful talk; others made it taboo for hunters to cook or consume certain parts of a deer, like stomachs and tongues, or to hunt while one's wife was pregnant. Before the hunt, hunters around the globe might dress in deerskins or make deer sounds. In North America, hunters purified themselves in steam or with special elixirs, called or sang out to their prey, and set off on the hunt carrying charms sewn into deerskin pouches: crystals, pigments, or the foot of a fawn.

Even the stags galloping across the walls of Paleolithic cave art sites have been understood this way—as an address to the animal other. In Europe's most significant cave galleries, Lascaux, Chauvet, and Altamira, deer are one of the four most frequently depicted subjects.

We are still finding more ancient deer on the rocks. In 2003, archaeologists discovered more than twenty figures inside a cave called Church Hole, one of many caves in a limestone gorge in England named Creswell Crags. The images are the first Ice Age art identified in Britain; they are engraved, not painted, which helped them go unnoticed even during many decades of excavating the cave floor.

"We know that Neanderthals were here, fifty thousand years ago," said the paleontologist Angharad Jones as we crossed a tiny bridge and followed a path into the gorge. To one side, a group of schoolkids were throwing spears at a rubber bison. Jones, tall and elegant in a trench coat, had already shown my family and me a reindeer mandible found here, perhaps 57,000 years old, maybe

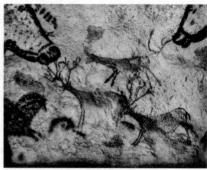

Deer at Lascaux

dragged into a cave by hyenas. Now she led us through a metal gate and into the mouth of Church Hole, where Ice Age *Homo sapiens* had summered, hunting wild horses and mountain hare.

We squinted as she angled a flashlight at the wall, then moved a laser light along the rough stone just above eye level, tracing a stag. "Here's the nose . . . you see the ear . . . the antler . . ." And as the red dot moved toward the stag's front hoof, we all said *Ohhh* at the same time: it was such a *leg*, muscled and real as our own. A profile known to earthlings, as meaningful as that of the waxing moon.

Any theory about cave art is speculative. Were the figures made by bored teenagers? Were they the anchor of a ritual, an expression of an eternal dreamtime, or storytelling props? Jones told us that the species this figure depicted—red deer—was not known ever to have lived in this area. Like the flint used to carve it more than twelve thousand years ago, knowledge of these animals was an import from elsewhere. As the artists migrated in and out of mainland Europe, this deer had ridden here with them, inside their minds: a memory from some other place.

Outside, in the gorge, couples walked lapdogs on leashes, and a man flew a drone over the lake—fringed with green now, though a film in Creswell's museum had shown us that during the Ice Age, it was too cold for trees to grow here. It was breathtaking to think about how easily this communication could have been missed: the thinness of that tensile thread, connecting us across millennia to people who had stood here in a different world, like a line on a family tree.

◖◗

In the Americas, deer weave in and out of Indigenous stories as easily as they thread through human life.

Cree people tell stories about the trickster Wesucechak, who grants language to the people but sometimes steals it back. When he turns into a deer and causes a woman named Two Loons to forget how to say "deer," they both understand that a vital food source is at stake: If she can't call the deer, no one will have venison. She recovers her memory, though, singing a beautiful song to the deer ("You who stands sideways / looking at us / You who flick your tail / up . . ."). Wesucechak ends up frightened and foolish, his false antlers tangled in trees, hungry for venison that the people won't share.

The word, then—the name of the deer—is not just a label; it is a sacred bond. It encloses the whole, intensely physical relationship between humans and an essential animal.

In the Sonoran Desert, on both sides of the U.S.–Mexico border, deer dances, or *pahko*, are still an active part of Yaqui culture, and the image of the deer dancer, a human head topped by an antlered deer head, peppers the region. The *pahko* are intimately tied to hunting, but really they seem to encompass an entire metaphysics of being and relation. Reenacting a hunt, the dancer plays not hunter but animal—glancing around for danger, twitching and stepping nervously. Loudly shaking a rattle in each hand, the dancer weaves those movements sonically, seamlessly, into the human music that undergirds them.

Meanwhile, the lyrics of the songs, recursive as a mantra, constantly shift between human and deer perspectives. So a person says "There he comes out" and the deer replies "I come out from there." The songs ask permission to hunt through profound acknowledgments: that the animal has its own point of view, and that deer minds and bodies correlate to those of humans. Flowers tangled in his antlers, the deer enters the human realm in which he may be asked to give his life for human survival. But the very songs used to ask for this gift are said to have been translated from the language of the deer themselves, by hunters who had crept close enough to hear their talk, using deerskin disguises.

◆◆

Our fascination with the shimmering line between *alive* and *dead* makes it an essential borderland, and it's expressed in the way relics like skins, bones, and antlers carry their inherent potency into art and ritual. Maybe the fact that deer have been food for so long, in so many places, explains the way people have linked them equally with death and life.

If deer are border dwellers in the human imagination, that's entirely fitting with their place in the physical and ecological world, where they are in fact denizens of the edges. They skirt the fringes of forest and clearing. They are most active at dawn and dusk, the twilight hours when day and night shade into each other. Their natural home is analogous to what the Greeks called *eschatiai*—lands of transition, the places where civilization and wilderness meet and interlace.

The boundary is also a pregnant zone of possibility. The deer is the sacred animal of Artemis, the Greek goddess who leads a retinue of nymphs on nightly hunts. In a strange way, through her vow of chastity, Artemis encompasses the *potential* for procreation—the gift of life that also means the death of maidenhood. For Artemis (Diana to the Romans), this change is always deferred, never actually realized. As wild land could someday be cultivated, Artemis embodies *becoming*, just like the deer, her familiar.

In fact, all humans—even in the more settled periods of our lives—are profoundly unsettled creatures. Trout belong to the stream and owls to the treetops, but humans are constantly in and out of the ecotone, venturing forth, retreating to shelter; seeking water, then an overlook, then the privacy of a thicket, always on the move and on the make. Evolutionarily, our descent from trees to ground level coincided with the fixture in our character of a certain perpetually juvenile quality, as though we can never quite call ourselves finished. Animals of the margins, like deer, may be icons not only of life transitions but also of our very nature as people.

They embody binaries: victim and transgressor. Elusive and ubiquitous. Symbols of life and *memento mori*.

𝄯

For a long time Europeans thought of deer not only as symbolic, but also as magic. Medieval bestiaries claimed that when ill, deer could delay death by swallowing snakes or eating crabs. Stags were said to purge the snakes' venom from their bodies by drinking large amounts of water, after which they would shed their antlers, making way for new ones to grow. The bestiaries also described deer as having life spans of a hundred years or more, according to one legend that proposes Alexander the Great as a sort of proto-biologist, capturing and marking deer for experimental reasons.

This vital energy could carry through to people: One could find protection from fever by eating venison, or drive away snakes with the smoke of burning antlers. Medea was supposed to have revived the slain King Aeson by infusing a decoction of deer's liver into his veins. Ancient Egyptians may have used antlers as a remedy for headaches.

One English folk legend tells of King Richard's gamekeeper, Herne the Hunter, who during one fateful hunt heroically throws himself in front of the king to save him from being gored by a cornered stag. Herne, who managed to knife the deer to death even as it speared his own body, knows he is mortally wounded, saying alliteratively to the king, "A hurt from hart's horn bringeth to the bier." Then he faints.

Fortunately, he's soon revived when a mysterious man steps out from among the trees, cuts off the deer's head, and affixes it to Herne's own head. But the cure comes at a terrible price: The healer has caused Herne to lose all his skill in horsemanship and archery. Several embarrassing hunts later, the king is forced to fire him. Herne hangs himself from an oak tree with the hart's skull again lashed to his own head. The magic of resurrection-by-deer has proven no more than temporary, and the antlers have become a death mask.

Herne's ghost haunts Windsor Forest through the reigns of seven more monarchs, his "great ragg'd horns" earning a nod from Shakespeare in *The Merry Wives of Windsor*. He's still well-known enough to turn up in modern media from comics to pop songs, a story laced with that old idea: that deer are a guide to death.

⁂

Some of the old deer images are fundamental enough that they keep arising in our present reality. D. H. Lawrence was captivated by images of deer and predators in ancient Etruscan tombs. One day I was reading his meditations on these paintings when I heard the snort of an alarmed whitetail and looked out the window to see a doe being chased through the yard by the neighbor's German shepherd. Neither was running at top speed; the doe easily outflanked the dog without breaking out of a trot, and it was obvious that the dog was playing, just passing the time on a mild June afternoon. Each carried out a role prescribed by evolution, even if blunted by the conditions of our time, in which the predator is Purina-fattened and the prey knows there's no real danger.

I turned back to Lawrence: "Above the false door in the angle of the gable is a fine design: two black, wide-mouthed pale-maned lions seated back to back . . . They each one lift a black paw against the cringing head of a cowering spotted deer, that winces to the death-blow."

He finds a yin-and-yang interdependence in this vision, which spans dozens of cultures. Homer tells us that the brooch Odysseus wore on his cloak, when he first left Ithaca, was engraved with a dog attacking a fawn. Wolves, dogs, and lions sinking teeth and claws into deer is a motif that endlessly recurs in Old World art, from prehistory into antiquity and beyond. Always the victim is shown in the high relief of the terrible moment when it succumbs to the predator.

Take, for example, an exquisite silver gilt amphora, found in Ukraine and made in the fourth century B.C., on which griffins attack an antlered stag. The predators may be fantastical, but the deer itself is almost more realistic than a photo. We see perfectly its ribs, its cloven hooves, its finely expressive face. This is allegory, not history, but the loving attention to the anatomy of the deer speaks to an intimacy with real animals.

The amphora "must have been used for koumiss, a fermented juice based on mares' milk," says the monograph, *Scythian Art*, in which I found it. *Scythian* is a term that archaeologists apply not only to a group of tribes who lived on the steppes near the Black Sea, but also to a broader world of shared culture that stretched across much of Central Asia for nearly a millennium before the Common Era.

The Scythians themselves, nomadic herdsmen and fierce warriors, did not rely on deer for survival; their domesticated cattle were their main source for meat and hides. Yet their artwork is obsessed with deer. Stags decorate their scabbards, their bridles, their vessels and jewelry. What did deer mean to these people, so utterly distant from us, who got drunk on fermented horse milk?

Maybe just victims who yield to greater force. But then, some of these images inspire sympathy for the hunted. Though their people were often the victors, there was something about victimhood that the Scythian craftspeople were drawn to mentally inhabit. They got inside the pain of the defeated, as though asking what agony might have to do with dignity.

Somehow it's antlers that embody this paradox. Antlers in Scythian art are a party: They loop back on themselves, they form repeating series of hooked crescents; they make flame shapes, tree shapes, wave shapes. They go beyond visual hyperbole to the purely fanciful: Another stag has antlers that extend for what must be six or eight feet above and behind its head, and

each tine ends in the plumed head of a bird. This animal, too, is being ravaged by a griffin.

⚮

One spring day in 1891, a crew of peat-cutters in a Danish bog unearthed something astonishing. Their irons turned up an exquisite piece of metalwork, an ancient cauldron more than two feet wide—a true buried treasure.

Archaeologists have more questions than answers about the vessel that would come to be called the Gundestrup Cauldron. We don't know exactly how old it is (best guess: around two millennia), who made it, or how it ended up in Denmark. But it clearly depicts a man, or a god, with an imposing rack of antlers.

This figure, like the dignified Scythian stags, is serene and authoritative, akin to a meditating Buddha. Next to it, a deer with identical antlers seems to echo and amplify whatever the human figure represents.

Which is—what? If this vessel was made for the Celts in the workshops of the Thracians, as many scholars believe, the antlered man is probably Cernunnos, a mysterious Celtic/Gaulic deity. His divine purview is uncertain—perhaps he's a god of animals and fertility?—but his antlers give him great gravity (and the name Cernunnos itself may derive from an ancient term for

"horn," from which we also get the word *cornucopia*). In some images he holds a sack issuing a river of grain. In other images, it overflows with coins: money as the life force itself. One related, and not very subtle, stone sculpture from Luxembourg even depicts a stag vomiting coins.

It's tempting to make one other connection—between the patriarchal symbolism of a figure like Cernunnos, crowned with antlers, and the actual crowns worn by human monarchs. Could it be that the idea of adorning the heads of powerful people arose, millennia ago, from awe at the beauty of deer's bony crowns?

The loveliness of deer might go without saying, but still, there it is: The more you look, the more they seduce. Their forms are luscious, pulling the eye in an endless pathway, from haunch to fetlock, from ear to antler, line to swell to shadow. They're lean as knives, but they're curvy, too. The whole of a deer's being, every atom of its body, expresses its animal awareness, its aliveness and presence. From far away, deer look stamped onto the hillside, as perfect as the outline of a fern or a seashell. Fleeing us at close range, they spring over fences like water flying from a fountain.

They can mean so many different things, but the easiest one is just this: Deer mean beauty. For that, they've earned a specific type of human loyalty. Few wild animals are treasured so quietly, yet so often, from Lascaux all the way to the desk of the modern copywriter.

I live near a national park whose website plugs its proximity to Washington, D.C., and then conjures its "protected lands that are haven to deer." Even in an age when many city dwellers are familiar with deer to the point of contempt, the well-worn rhapsody still has power. There's no doubt that many Washingtonians do make the pilgrimage to the park, and that for at least some of them, spotting deer is part of the thrill.

⬤

The very etymology of *wilderness* links it to deer. The Old English word *deor* meant "animal," and so *wild-deor-ness* was a place of wild animals. That deer lurk in the center of our modern word *wilderness* suggests that deer are thoroughly baked into our idea of nature at its purest, and perhaps that deer are such a fundamental presence in human life that they, of all species, took over the word we once used for animals in general.

On another island, Aeaea, Homer's Odysseus is relieved to bring a fresh deer to his men after they land; not only is it food, but it succors their grief after various bloody disasters. It is a sign of hope. "The kill was so immense!" Odysseus marvels; he is talking about the deer, but he could equally be speaking of the loss of many comrades, slaughtered by the Laestrygonians, the Cyclops, and the Cicones. He drags the beast back to where his men, "bent with pain and bone-tired," are waiting. As they catch sight of him, "Heads came up from cloaks and there by the barren sea / they gazed at the stag, their eyes wide—my noble trophy. / But once they'd looked their fill and warmed their hearts, / they washed their hands and prepared a splendid meal." Feasting follows, and wine and sleep. But it's the looking—Odysseus's first glimpse of the stag drinking from a stream, and then his sailors' long gaze upon its carcass—that seems to fill a deeper need. Violence, and a certain brutal competence ("Treading on him, I wrenched my bronze spear from the wound"), is the hinge between seeing and consuming.

Deer mean abundance for the taking, by eye or by weapon. In existing, they prove that the world is not barren. And even when the facts of history and ecology suggest otherwise, we continue to look to deer for a promise of stability.

🦌

In 1834, the American painter Thomas Cole embarked on an ambitious cycle of five paintings he would eventually title *The Course of Empire*. Each image represented a distinct stage in the growth of a mythical civilization, and the first one pictured a skin-clad hunter pursuing a deer within a wild and turbulent landscape. Cole called this painting *The Savage State*, and like other Romantic works, it diminishes the human; rather than culture, nature looms. Clouds wrapping a mountain easily outweigh the little drama of a man chasing a meal. Yet it's a timeless story: the hunt and the kill.

The *Empire* series expressed Cole's deep ambivalence about wilderness and civilization. Its third painting, *The Consummation of Empire*, shows the allegorical civilization at its peak; it has almost totally obscured the land on which it rests. But things fall apart. In the fifth and final image, *Desolation*, the human presence is moldering back into the earth, overgrown and forgotten, and deer return to the canvas. "Art is again resolving into elemental nature," Cole wrote, and painted a buck and doe near a ruined temple.

Deer turned out to be the survivors: the bookends to Cole's vision of the human rise and fall, the outward expression of a nature that could be subdued for a time, but would always come back in the end. They were the truth that exists before and after human fictions.

Cole was an American painter in the age of Manifest Destiny.

The pessimism of his cycle's end was out of step with the national mood at the time, but these days, it seems more prescient. He conjured a fantasy that blurred the distinctions between Indigenous people and settlers: In that last image, *all* the humans—even that original hunter—have been erased by the empire's collapse.

◖◗

It's a trope that repeated in the early days of the COVID pandemic. Amid the headlines of plague and chaos, there appeared a little subgenre of news stories about how, with so many people sheltering indoors, wild animals were emboldened to move about in cities. Among photos of coyotes in San Francisco and jackals in Tel Aviv, there were images of deer strolling sidewalks in Poland and grazing London lawns. In a moment of collective horror at the invasion of our lives by a virus, we clutched at the idea that nature was sending in ambassadors of beauty, too. Yet what made room for the deer was the withdrawal of people.

We need images of a stability that humans can tend to by our presence, not our absence. We need images of coexistence.

◖◗

It was early on a September Monday, and the Abbots Bromley Horn Dance would begin as soon as the vicar blessed the horns. I sat in a pew and listened to villagers murmuring. Black robes swirling, the vicar had just appeared from some secret part of the thousand-year-old church, hoisting a wooden ladder—*Even that looks ancient,* I thought—against the wall where the antlers rested on pegs. The dancers were milling around in their short pants, woolen shirts, and vests. "Blimey, we are early this morning!" said the jester. Someone climbed the ladder and carefully lifted down the first set of antlers—polished with age, attached to a small wooden deer's head.

I'd crossed the ocean to be here, hoping to see a living link between deer and human history. Now it occurred to me that the Horn Dance tradition also connected this place to my home: in both small towns, it's an annual event.

Of course, in Abbots Bromley, it had been so since the year

1226. And it was an all-day affair. Soon the dancers set off from the church at a swift clip: six of them bearing antlers, plus the jester, a man playing Maid Marian, two accordion players, a teenage Hobby Horse, and several young boys, one playing a triangle. A small crowd of us trailed them down the lane until the jester gave a signal and the dance began. The music was livelier here than it was at home, but I recognized the choreography. Interlacing, spiraling lines.

For the next twelve hours, this eccentric parade would wind its way through town, out into the Midlands countryside, and back to the high street, stopping at intervals for rest and sausage pasties and ale. An entourage would follow; for many onlookers, this was an annual pilgrimage. I hadn't realized that being a dancer is something one must be born to do: A young woman explained that most dancers come from the same two families, and start in the children's roles before working their way up to wearing the antlers, as her father and brother were doing.

"I overindulged last night," I heard another man say. He was wearing the costume but wasn't dancing. "That's why my son is doing the Hobby Horse. He started out on triangle and then he was the bowman until the outfit didn't fit him anymore." Something fairly new for Abbots Bromley: one set of antlers was carried by a woman.

In Virginia, the dance had made me think about hunting, and individual survival. In Abbots Bromley, I found myself attuned to the collective. We trudged down hawthorn-fringed lanes, chatted outside pubs, exchanging bits of lore. *The oak-leaf pattern on the dancers' pants comes from when the vicar's daughter made costumes from old curtains.* And: *In World War I, four soldiers were allowed to come home from the Western Front to perform in the dance.*

The fact repeated most often was that the antlers themselves— grown by reindeer and supported by iron props—had been carbon-dated and were at least a millennium in age. They were sacred civic objects, not allowed to leave the parish, and they turned the people not into deer but into icons of their home, and of kinship. The antlers' age seemed to authenticate both the dance itself, said to be the oldest such tradition in Britain, and the way it had been shepherded through time, long after its origins were obscured. *In 2020, the dance was canceled, but they still did a quick version at dawn just to say they'd done it.*

The young dancer playing the bowman—he seemed about seven—wore a tam-o'-shanter and looked utterly bored all day. But I envied him. He'd been born into something rare and gentle. Queen Elizabeth had died four days before; in church the vicar had proclaimed, "We are passing from the second Elizabethan age into the third Carolean age." Here was rootedness, constancy, both life and death as givens. Bowmen would become hobby horses; princes, kings.

I followed the tall, bobbing antlers from a distance. "Do the dancers rehearse very much?" I asked someone. "Oh no," he replied. "They just grow up knowing it."

CHAPTER 2

Goods

I WAS A LITTLE LATE TO MEET THE WOMAN WITH THE hide, so I jogged past the turnoff for the West African village and the English farm. I bypassed the German farm and followed the signs for the New World, toward the Cracker Barrel sign that stabbed up from the horizon. It was October, and the sky was a blameless blue. The interstate was a few hundred feet away through the trees, and I could hear it roaring.

Around the corner I spotted the Native American village, and Mary Kate Claytor—cross-legged under a catalpa tree, with a soggy deer hide spread out on the ground in front of her, flesh side up.

This was the Frontier Culture Museum in Staunton, Virginia, an outdoor complex that sprawls over two hundred acres of former farmland in the Shenandoah Valley. The museum attempts to tell the story of how a panoply of cultures—from Europe, Africa, and North America—amalgamated over hundreds of years to create a new, American way of life. It's interactive: You can try on wooden clogs in the German farmhouse and chat with a blacksmith at work in the Irish forge. You can brush past banana trees growing in West Africa and pull a crosscut saw outside a 1740s log cabin, like the dwellings white settlers cobbled together on the forested frontier.

As I approached Claytor, she was pressing the deer hide down over the sharp point of an awl made from deer bone, trying to poke a hole. The hide had been waiting in a freezer since it was peeled off a whitetail by a hunter last fall. Early that morning she'd taken it out and soaked it in water to help it thaw.

Claytor was tall and rosy-cheeked, with black overalls, tat-tooed arms, and hair hidden by a dark knit cap. As she worked, her outgoing and ponytailed colleague, Misti Furr, explained to some visitors that this village represents Indigenous cultures across a huge swath of territory: from Canada to Florida, from the Mississippi River to the Atlantic Ocean—the "Eastern Woodlands" nations, an impossibly large and varied world to be contained in just a handful of wigwams. "We're in this weird place—non-Native people interpreting Native culture," Claytor would later tell me. But the hide-tanning technique she demon-strated was at least one common thread shared by many groups in pre-contact North America.

The awl balanced on its handle, pointing straight up, and Claytor wiggled the hide down over it. Finally the point punched through. She'd already made most of the holes she'd need, at five-inch inter-vals all around the edge of the skin. In front of her on the ground was a wooden frame with dozens of handmade nails pounded into it, and her next step would be to lace jute through the holes and around the nails, so as to stretch the hide evenly over the frame.

I was mesmerized by the hide itself. It lay fur side down, its mostly smooth surface marbled with pinks, whites, and light browns in irregular patterns, like an aerial view of the desert floor. This side of the skin had been next to the body of the deer—the live side, you might say. Most of the flesh had already been removed. I asked if I could touch it. It was rubbery and slightly slimy, like raw chicken.

"That's the membrane, this goopy part," Claytor said. She'd need to scrape that away, and on the hide's other side, all the fur and the "grain"—the top layer of skin—had to come off too. "If you don't, it's harder for the oils from the tanning solution to penetrate," she said. "You'll end up with crusty spots."

As she began stretching, she tossed me a piece of finished buck-skin so I could see the end result. As soon as I touched it I wanted to take off my jeans and acrylic sweater and wrap my naked skin in this instead: It was seductive and velvety under my fingers and much finer and more pliable than I'd imagined. It felt like the best possible way to clothe the human body. Its color was a subtle yellowy-brown, and its irregular edges were slightly crispy, with small holes here and there. It had been preserved from decay, but it retained the feel of something organic and alive.

Now Claytor wound and knotted jute around the nails and worked it through the holes in the hide. She'd begun with the neck of the deer, where the hide was thicker—maybe, she explained, because it's the part of the body predators tend to latch onto with teeth or claws.

She pointed out the place on the flank where a projectile had torn through. "It's hard to tell if it was a gun or a bow," she said, poking her fingers into the hole. "Arrow holes are usually triangular." But this one had a weird shape—it was actually two holes, eerily like the split-heart print a deer hoof makes in snow.

⚌

Stretching the hide was an unhurried process. Every time Claytor threaded another hole, she had to carefully pull the jute tight with one hand while massaging the hide outward with the other. Her fingers moved and shifted under the skin, persuading it to lengthen toward the frame. Sometimes the jute snapped— far more likely to break than the hide itself. Then she grabbed the hide at both shoulders and stretched it crosswise, her hands straining in opposite directions. I thought of clay, or maybe pizza dough. But a small spot of blood on one edge of the skin reminded me that this was part of an animal.

The strength of deerskin is part of what made it so useful to Indigenous peoples. As Claytor worked her way around the skin, Furr explained to two nearby couples that hides also became an important export from the American colonies back to Europe, where buckskin was used to make gloves and rawhide served as pulley cables. "These skins help fuel the Industrial Revolution, and they make a lot of money for the mother country," she said.

"It's one of the colonies' most stable exports"—more reliable year to year than cash crops like tobacco.

That trade changed life for Native Americans; they acquired European goods, and they hunted more deer to satisfy European demand. Furr wove a tale of interlocking changes that stretched from the woods of eastern North America to the shores of West Africa and down to the sugar plantations of the Caribbean. The usefulness of deer hides—their size, their pliability, their toughness and abundance—made them a valuable resource in the early global economy. But before that, they were a basic life material for people all over this continent.

Claytor kept lacing down one flank of the hide. She was still less than halfway done stretching, and making finished buckskin would take days. She'd dry it and scrape it on the frame. Then she'd soak it in a tanning mixture, wring it out, soak, wring, soak, wring, maybe half a dozen times altogether. After that, she'd dry it again, while stretching and handling it repeatedly to keep it soft and pliable. In the end she'd smoke it over a smoldering fire to waterproof and preserve it.

It's the tanning mixture that holds special importance in the history of deer in North America. Europeans too had long hide-tanning traditions, but their standard recipes for tanning solutions involved urine or rotting bark, making a stiff, shiny leather. In North America, said Claytor, "Brain tanning was used more than any other method." Brains are full of fats and oils that lubricate the tiny fibers in the skin. Egg yolks can also work, or even Dawn dish soap. But in most mammals, the brain contains the right amount of material to tan the animal's own hide—an elegant, and practical, correspondence.

Native Americans long used buckskin to make wrap skirts for women, breechcloths for men, dolls for children, and bags and moccasins for everybody. Buckskin was a basic material like cotton is today, though people's sense of how it arrived at hand was surely more nuanced.

Deerskins could be used in other ways, too. With some hides, people tanned only the flesh side, left the fur on, and used them as blankets. They sewed whole skins into flasks for storing oil and honey. And they took rawhide—skin that is dried but not softened—and cut it spirally into one enormous length of tough, narrow cord with as many uses as duct tape has now.

Some hides ended up playing fairly exalted roles. Furr showed me a picture on her phone: Powhatan's Mantle, a four-hundred-year-old hanging made of several buckskin hides sewn together and embellished with thousands of white marine snail shells. The shells form three figures—a human and two animals, one of which has cloven hooves like a deer—and a series of circles that probably represent settlements.

The Mantle may have belonged to the seventeenth-century Powhatan leader Wahunsenacawh, the father of Pocahontas, in what is now Virginia. But like millions of other colonial-era buckskins, it too crossed the ocean to Britain. By 1638 it had arrived in London, and if you wanted to see it in person today, you'd have to visit the Ashmolean Museum in Oxford.

The jute broke again. Claytor, nearly finished lacing, patiently cut another length of twine and spliced it together, walking her fingers along the edge of the hide to find the next hole.

We'd been sitting on the grass, in the October sun, for almost two hours, as she pulled and stretched and knotted. A green catalpa worm dropped from the branches above and made its way across the tightening hide, where a few bits of grass clung to the membrane.

Tug and knot; tug and knot. I asked whether, in Indigenous American communities, hide-tanning had been women's work. Claytor said yes and explained that—although every group had its own mores and traditions—in many communities, women served as the domestic constants. To provide food, clothing, and shelter was a crucial, and honored, role. Processing a deer into its many parts and materials complemented the labor of hunting, and women's work was their own sovereign domain.

So much was lost in a fog of erasure, as European colonists worked deliberately to separate Indigenous people from their lifeways—the songs or stories, say, that might have accompanied this communal labor, as women passed hours under trees. Claytor and Furr saw their work as a kind of ongoing engagement with half-obscured knowledge; they'd try things, examine archaeological evidence and oral histories, experiment and learn and then try something else. Their ways were a mix of old and new, undertaken in twenty-first-century clothing, with no pretense of reenactment, and sometimes with frank anachronisms. I was enchanted, for example, by the hide scraper Claytor made from a deer leg bone, but she readily offered, "I had to make it quickly, so I used a Dremel tool."

Non-Native interpreters like her and Furr get information when they can from contemporary tribal members, but they also try to avoid undue prying and, especially, failing to properly attribute knowledge to its sources. Even more important, the old ways changed over time and geography. They weren't the same everywhere, and as in all cultures, they evolved. If brain-tanning a deer hide in the 2020s is a niche skill, it's still part of a long, ragged line of human knowledge transmission. And the deer, and the hands, are still real.

At the time the deerskin trade between Native Americans and Europeans began, each side brought to the table its own long history with deer. For the Europeans, that was a story in which deer had gradually become like diamonds—luxury goods out of reach for most people.

Herds of fallow deer may have been kept in enclosed spaces in Britain during the Roman occupation, but it wasn't until after the Norman conquest in the eleventh century that the practice of keeping a deer park—a large acreage attached to a castle and reserved for the production of venison, sometimes harvested by the resident lord in elaborate, ritualistic hunts—really took off. Deer parks soon became a widespread phenomenon: By their heyday in the fourteenth century, parks in Britain may have numbered as many as three thousand. There were a number of parks in France as well.

For a nobleman to enclose land as a deer park was, first of all, a way of showing off his money. The construction of a fence or wall to keep deer contained was, says one source, "an elaborate and expensive" undertaking. (Such barriers had a special name—*pales*—from which we take our expression for someone out of bounds: They are *beyond the pale*. And if they try and fail to leap the fence, they may become *impaled*.)

Building the park was only the beginning of the expense. One needed a gamekeeper to manage the herd, a legion of groundskeepers to mow and tend. The average park was about a hundred acres in size, but some were much more sweeping; a deer park in Lincolnshire, for example, grew to encompass 4,600 acres. The pales were constantly in need of repair, and poachers had to be dealt with. In the winter, deer sometimes required feed; at least one deer park included a shelter for the animals.

All this flagrant spending occurred against a general background

of scarcity. Still, the aristocracy saw deer parks as essential stages
on which to demonstrate skill in the art of hunting. Hunts were
occasions of pomp and pageantry, replete with horse and hound,
and the successful killing of a deer provided the climactic moment when the lord and his retinue confirmed their power over
the weak. In other words, whereas the Scythians might have allowed a lion to symbolize their dominance over other people,
medieval English and French lords preferred performance art:
They became, in real time, the lions.

Deer parks also let nobles show off their good design taste.
A certain well-groomed yet naturalistic look prevailed. In particular, medieval aristocrats liked their forests free of undergrowth, to make for easier riding. That inviting, human-friendly
structure—with trees separated by open ground—foretold what
we still expect a public park to look like today.

Even the choice of deer species had an aesthetic aspect: Fallow
deer, which were deliberately stocked in the deer parks, boosted the
lord's image because they were exotic imports. They also made good
decorations—they tended to stick together in large herds, a picturesque scene when observed from afar by the lord and his attendants.

More materially, to fence deer in was to fence people out. In creating a deer park, a noble showed not only that he had been granted special hunting rights by the king but also that he in turn was denying those rights to nearby commoners. There would be a steady supply of venison on his table, while his tenants could be punished by blinding, castration, or death for taking a deer from inside the pale. Feudal obligations might even force tenants to help maintain the very fence that kept them out.

Among hungry people, it was a source of great resentment. The wealth that Robin Hood redistributed stands for venison as much as anything. In Howard Pyle's telling of the Robin Hood legend, Robin's career as an outlaw commences with the shooting of a deer ("the noblest hart of all the herd") in an archery contest.

"Knowest thou not," says a forester, "that thou hast killed the King's deer, and, by the laws of our gracious lord and sovereign, King Harry, thine ears should be shaven close to thy head?" One thing leads to another, Robin kills a forester, and suddenly he's living on the fringes of society. Many of his compatriots, like him, are on the run for poaching deer, and yet theirs is a life in which deer are freely and defiantly used. The merry men rest on "couches of sweet rushes spread over with skins of fallow deer" and "shoot the dun deer, and feed upon venison and sweet oaten cakes, and curds and honey." This is a fantasy version of social unrest that really occurred, not only in Britain but in France, Prussia, and other places. The elite control of forests and game became intolerable to the peasantry and even sometimes to the nobles' well-to-do neighbors. In 1642, for example, an unruly confederation of commoners and gentlemen poachers mounted a rebellion that involved the massacre of more than six hundred deer belonging to the Earl of Middlesex.

The Robin Hood tales are one echo of the deer park system. There are other marks, too: physical traces of park pales can still be identified in Britain, and many place names (like Richmond Park in London, still famous for its deer) recall the parks' long-ago importance.

The social underpinnings of the deer park carry through to modern society, too, on both sides of the pond. When the rich and powerful mix business and pleasure while hunting on a Texas ranch, where oversized bucks of impressive size roam inside tall fences, they are re-creating in a modern way the ritual of a medieval deer park. But even golf courses—highly manicured landscapes that cater to an elite aesthetic of nature—might descend from that long-ago age, when a special slice of the countryside became a set piece where powerful people showed off, and reinforced, their status.

When Europeans landed in North America, these were their associations with deer. They encountered all kinds of novel animals, but in their minds, deer had a significance all their own.

⚹

Finally Claytor had the hide fully stretched. With its lacings and vaguely round shape, it looked like something from a Warner Bros. cartoon about a grizzled backwoods trapper. Claytor stood the frame on end and turned it around so I could see the fur side. It was dark brown along the spine, lighter on the flanks, fading to white at the edges. The sun was behind it, and just for a moment it shone through the skin, making it glow pink and alive.

Claytor leaned the frame against the catalpa tree and sized up her array of scraping tools. Besides the bone scraper she had made, she had a couple of palm-sized seashells and some steel tools, representing the access to metal that Native Americans gained through trade with Europeans.

She tried a bone tool first. It was made from a deer's cannon bone—on a person, it would come from the hand—with little teeth carved into one end. When she pulled it along the flesh side of the skin, the membrane began to peel away. "It's doing it!" she said, excited. A young guy in Carhartts and a sleeveless shirt wandered over to watch. He asked a few questions about making deer hide blankets and then wondered, "What else can you do with deer parts?"

Claytor showed him her bone scraper. "You can also use hooves, and scraps from the hide-scraping, to make glue. You can use the backstrap tendon"—which runs along the spine— "for bowstring and cordage and fasteners."

These examples just barely began to answer the question. Almost every part of a deer has utility, and when Native hunters returned home with a deer carcass, they carried far more than meat. If the work of hunting was married to the reciprocal work of processing, the body of a deer could offer everything from food and clothing to music, insulation, and paint.

Furr gave me a tour of the wigwam village to show me other deer parts in use: a rake made from a four-point antler lashed to a pole, a shovel made from a scapula. She showed me how the corner of a deer's jawbone can make a blunt tool that flakes off larger pieces from a chunk of stone, and how the point of an antler can then make finer, strategic subtractions. She pointed out rawhide used to lash together the frame of a wigwam. She handed me a buckskin bag in the shape of a snowman, sewed shut and filled with sand, which people used to throw and catch in a game called double-ball.

And still we'd only scratched the surface. When I got home that night, I'd find a package waiting for me: half a dozen back issues of the *Bulletin of Primitive Technology*, which I'd ordered hoping they'd hold more secrets of a deer's utility. I found the mother lode in the Spring 2000 issue, which contained a hand-lettered list entitled "101 Things to Do with a Deer."

It began by listing edible parts and ways to preserve them, including pemmican (defined as "pounded jerky with fat"). Furr had also talked about making venison stew with corn and dried pumpkin from the museum gardens.

But most of the 101 uses on this list were not for food. The left column named parts of the animal: hair, hide, fat, sinew, organs, bones, antlers, hooves, teeth, eyeballs, blood, even scat and urine. And the right column read like a list of human needs, from essentials to enrichments, each need matched with a body part on the left.

That list helped me imagine a life in which I could stuff my child's pillow with deer fur, use the fluid from an eyeball for pigment, make a sack from the membrane that surrounds a deer's heart. The longer I stared at it, the more it seemed to diagram a relation: human and world, person and animal. The complementarity of it all—the sense that for every item people wanted, there was a corresponding resource at hand, offered by an animal or a plant—felt so utterly different from our own world, in which Dremel tools are made from fossil fuels and mined metal, Dawn dish soap comes from a lab, and they both are acquired using a debit card in a big-box store. The list was the opposite of abstract, the opposite of outsourced. It outlined an existence firmly anchored to a local, self-generating reality. And it represented an entirely different paradigm of waste: If every part of animal was used, there was little waste to begin with, and any minor scrap that did go unused would simply return to the earth, feeding small creatures and the soil.

Whitetails are an abundant resource in the landscape around my home. There is nothing to stop me from harvesting and using that resource except my own lack of knowledge and skills—from hunting on through skinning, tanning, butchering, carving, sewing, making cordage. Up to that moment, about the only thing I'd managed to do with deer parts was eat venison chili cooked by my brother and set a rack of antlers on my porch next to the potted geraniums.

In truth, there was a missing third column on this list. It would appear in the center, and it would name the skills—and hint at all the ingenuity and tenacity they require—that marry the animal parts to the human needs. It takes culture to turn a deer into a life-sustaining resource. The more I contemplated it, the more it seemed like a major miracle that a deer's body—which exists first for the sake of the deer—was also such a complete package of life-supporting gifts for humans. The miracle materialized in that invisible center column.

⚊

Back under the catalpa, Claytor and Furr were absorbed in picking away at the membrane with tools and fingernails. It clung and resisted like strong tape. When it pulled away in bits and swaths, each fiber let go with an audible *zziiiip*, leaving behind a whitish, velvety surface like that of the finished buckskin I'd handled earlier.

Before I left, Claytor wanted to show me something—an old scar on the flesh side of the deerskin. "Maybe it went through a barbed-wire fence and got snagged," she said. She'd also found a clump of half a dozen ticks embedded in the neck fur. "When you get through all those layers, you can see the deer's life."

⚊

In 1786, Thomas Jefferson and John Adams went on a tour of English gardens and found deer still playing a prominent role in that country's loftier outdoor settings. Jefferson, ever the data geek, recorded two to three hundred deer at an estate called Hagley and two thousand at Blenheim. Meanwhile, back in the infant nation the two tourists had helped to found, deer had played a key part in a meeting of cultures already underway for several centuries.

There's a famous image that survives from the dawn of that colonial era. Picture a winding stream, and on one bank, a group of five deer. On the other side, three more deer—but wait; these

have too many legs. And they have arms, and their hands are holding weapons. As the real deer on the right bank have just started to figure out, the deer on the left bank are human hunters in disguise, the skins of bucks draped over their backs.

Deer legs dangle over their human hips and shoulders, hooves brushing the ground. The hollowed-out heads of the skins fit like helmets over human heads, with heavy racks of antlers. The coup de grâce of the disguise is the perfect alignment of the deerskins' hollow eye holes over the keen, predatory eyes of the men.

All three of them are poised to shoot. In disguise, they've been able to creep forward to point-blank range. Two deer are already leaping away, alarmed, but the three big remaining bucks seem to have a fraction of a second left to live.

Hunters—even today—talk about the importance of getting inside the mind of the deer. These hunters inhabit not only the minds but the bodies of their targets: taking on their appearance, emulating their habits, adopting a four-legged posture. Their method is a Möbius strip of transfiguration: become a deer in deer's eyes by looking through the actual eyes of deer.

This engraving was published in a 1591 book by Theodore de Bry, a European artist who never left Europe. His images of Timucuan people in Florida reflected the European mind as much they did any sort of North American reality. Regardless, they became important seeds for early European notions of what Native Americans, and North America itself, were like.

The Timucuans may in fact have used deerskin disguises; some tribes certainly did. Either way, de Bry's book as a whole clearly suggests that deer were a major feature of the Florida landscape. In its pages, deer appear as reliably as trees—frisking near the river, arranged among trees heavy with fruit, being hunted and butchered. Posing no threat to human safety, they place themselves near human settlement and get busy with the task of accumulating calories, ready for harvest.

Along with alligators, deer are the standout animals in the book. But its most searing images concern people; the Native people are depicted as cannibals, limb-hackers, flesh-roasters. It's clear that immersion in this volume, for a sixteenth-century European, would have produced two major impressions of the New World. One, that it hosted an utterly foreign and blood-thirsty culture. Two, that it was a wilderness fat with food.

⚵

Just like de Bry, colonists on both coasts noted the way Native people relied on deer, and they exuberantly described the American continent as replete with game. The colonist George Percy noted a "great store of deer" in Jamestown in 1607. Five deer showed up to the party we mythologize as the First Thanksgiving—along with fowl, the only meat source mentioned by name in Edward Winslow's description of the 1621 festivities in Plymouth. In what we now call California, Sir Francis Drake went for the word "infinite" when estimating the number of deer he observed, adding that the animals were "very large and fat."

In Indigenous America, the work of culture had interwoven human activity with cosmology and myth—a warp and weft of meaning in which an animal could be honored even at the moment of its killing. But settlers saw the New World as just that—a world, a boundless universe, provided by God for their exploitation. Compared with the tight controls over deer and other resources they'd long known in Europe, settlers found this place giddily abundant.

Meanwhile, in the eyes of the European leather industry, the North American colonies were a vast storehouse of raw material. Manufacturing acted as a gravitational pull that eventually extracted millions of deerskins from the continent.

The hide trade started small, but in Virginia, it was ample enough to warrant government regulation as early as 1630. By the turn of the eighteenth century, British merchants in particular had established the deerskin trade as a key industry in several southern colonies. In a one-year period in the 1740s, for example, Carolina exported something like 150,000 deerskins. The rapid growth of several colonial cities—including Augusta and Charleston—was largely due to their role as hubs in the deerskin trade.

After being harvested by Native hunters, skins went on to be processed, most often, by Native women. Their labor added significantly to the value of the skins. It was a little like the way people value Navajo rugs today: tradition and generational expertise—plus, perhaps, an idea of authenticity—are part of what non-Native customers pay for. The Indigenous brain-tanning method produced a superior and malleable leather. In exchange, traders offered manufactured goods like fabric, metal tools, kettles, beads, and muskets—and, eventually, rum.

The leathermakers wanted deerskins because, for one thing, they were versatile. Buckskin—a term which, then as now, was a general moniker that didn't necessarily denote the deer's sex—found its way into everything from footwear to harnesses and saddles.

Fashion played a role too, just as it famously did in the over-hunting of North American beaver, their pelts used to make gentlemen's hats. In the case of buckskin breeches, though, it was the British working classes that started the trend; from there the craze moved to the upper classes and to men abroad. "Buckskin breeches, it seems, served as the eighteenth-century equivalent of modern denim jeans," writes the historian Kathryn Braund.

Some of the products made from those hides in Europe eventually found their way back to the colonies—so a deerskin harvested from the southern Appalachians may have crossed the ocean twice before winding up as a pair of breeches or gloves worn by a Virginia planter or a Massachusetts lawyer.

Four days after watching Claytor stretch the hide, I was back at the museum. In the meantime, she'd been working hard on drying and scraping—in fact, she had to take a day off to rest her aching hands. "I went too hard," she said. "I couldn't sleep." A loose pile of fur under the catalpa tree attested to her labors.

It was another sunny afternoon, and we were now up the hill in an open area where two fork-shaped sticks standing in the ground supported a horizontal pole, over which the hide was now draped. Claytor, in blue latex gloves, was pulling and squeezing the skin, making liquid drip from it into a tin tub below. It held a couple of inches of what looked like dirty milk.

This was the brain-tanning solution. It was a little anticlimactic—I'd pictured something much gorier. Claytor assured me that when she'd first started to work with it that morning, it really did look like a brain, but now it had been mashed into a slurry and mixed with warm water.

I'd heard Claytor and Furr repeat the maxim to a number of guests by now: that any animal's brains are adequate to tan its hide. But they didn't actually use deer brains anymore at this museum. Chronic wasting disease, a fatal neurological ailment, had been found in deer nearby; although the affliction has never been known to jump to humans, the interpreters weren't taking any chances. Instead, they were using pork brains from a local butcher.

Sore hands aside, Claytor was feeling very satisfied. "This is the part I just think is so stinking cool," she said. "The structure of it doesn't feel like skin; it feels like fabric. This is looking really good."

She and Furr had a go at stretching together, grasping the edges of the skin and leaning their weight backward away from each other. I could actually see the hide expanding as they did. For a minute, their bodies made a symmetrical shape: two women on either side of a skin. A truly ancient tableau, and one that could have become a visual icon just as easily as the analogous form of a hunter, squinting down an arrow shaft. But the women's work has not carried through into our modern consciousness in that way.

I'd been reading about how trading furs and skins to Europeans brought deep change to Indigenous societies. It spurred competition among tribes and rewarded those who had acquired guns. It sometimes encouraged families to compete within their villages too, as a more individualistic mindset came in alongside the traditional communitarian ways. At some sites, the objects people buried with their dead show that in the colonial period, they were beginning to emphasize social differences through possessions more than they had in the past.

People let go of certain traditional crafts, as metal tools replaced stonework and fabric gradually took the place of buckskin. Gender roles changed, though not in any straightforward way. Europeans tended to approach Native men, not women, when they wanted to bargain. On the other hand, traders also frequently took Native wives, giving those individual women influence in their positions as mediators.

Sometimes women gained autonomy when their men left home to hunt for long periods of time; other times they found themselves pushed to the margins by a new economic system that rewarded men's activities more than their own. Cherokee women, writes the historian Theda Perdue, "now needed deerskins— and the men who provided them—to purchase the very hoes with which they cultivated their corn." This was a subtle shift, because men had always provided the deer. But the deer used to furnish—directly—skins to wear and bones to make hoes. Now their meaning became one step removed, as they provided, instead, a currency used to *purchase* clothes and tools.

Native people even changed their diets: They now ate more venison compared to pre-trade years, when lots of calories had also come from elk and bear. One can imagine that with many deer being killed primarily for their skins, there was plenty of extra venison around.

Deer, always significant, became even more so: an answer not only to people's need to survive in the present but also to their need to deal with the presence of foreigners in a way that—they hoped—could carry them into a tenable future.

It was ultimately too great a charge for the deer population to answer. The numbers simply weren't there. Hunters in the deerskin trade spent more and more time away from their villages, ranging across greater swaths of territory, killing more and more animals. During the peak decades of trade, Native hunters across the Southeast killed around a million deer every year.

People had already noted that whitetails were getting scarce near the coasts. By the end of the eighteenth century, even parts of the American interior were marked more by the absence than the presence of deer. But these losses were only the first wave of what would be a repeated phenomenon in American history. Wherever deer became a commodity, their numbers would dive.

The deerskin trade was a locus both for competition between European nations and for the expansion of colonial power along every line from economics to culture to politics. It was like a wedge that helped colonizers drive farther and farther into the continent. It also caused Indigenous groups to go into debt—and that debt was part of what eventually separated them from their land. Two and a half million acres of Cherokee and Creek land, for example, were ceded to Georgia in 1773 to cover debts. In one particularly sinister move as president, Thomas Jefferson caused his administration to extend credit to Creek Indians "beyond their individual means of paying"—knowing that land cessions would end up being the Native nations' only way to make good, and that loss of hunting grounds would pressure them to take up farming instead.

Eventually, the market shifted, overhunting took its toll, and demand for deerskins waned. The American Revolution put a final end to the business. But just as the colonies had now launched themselves on a new trajectory, the long-standing trade in deerskins had helped to set Native people on a path that led, inexorably, toward an utterly unfamiliar future.

⁙

Claytor folded the hide in quarters and plunged it into the brain solution, which I now saw was chunkier, chalkier, than I'd thought. There would be several more rounds of soaking and wringing today; she had hours of labor in front of her. Clearly, her work demanded patience, endurance, and a very specific type of curiosity that went well beyond the idle interest of a wandering museumgoer. It occurred to me that, in watching Claytor as she processed this deerskin, I had become another in a long line of white people—going back to the 1500s—who have arrived out of an alien context and observed, in its brilliance, this Native art.

⁙

Even after the deerskin trade ended, Europeans continued to believe that in some way, America was infinite. And deer continued to quietly embody the continent's uniqueness. Even as late as the 1870s, if we are to believe that beloved account of Wisconsin frontier life, *Little House in the Big Woods*, there were American forests of seemingly endless dimensions: "As far as a man could go to the north in a day, or a week, or a whole month, there was nothing but woods . . . There were no people. There were only trees and the wild animals who had their homes among them . . . Deer roamed everywhere."

This is mythology, of course (a million white people had immigrated to Wisconsin by then), but it was true in the minds of many, and it persists today. I grew up poring over the Little House books, and for all the problems I can see in them now, I still read them to my own kids. And it only recently occurred to me how deer lurk in the opening chapter of this series that has shaped the image of the frontier for so many people.

Deer meant many different things to the Ingalls family. Right off the bat, deer are food: "Every morning as soon as she was awake Laura ran to look out of the window, and one morning she saw in each of the big trees a dead deer hanging from a branch . . . That day Pa and Ma and Laura and Mary had fresh venison for dinner." Deer also mean labor. In a series that will go on to detail hundreds of different practical tasks of living, from cabin construction to dressmaking, the very first work Wilder describes is the processing of deer: skinning, stretching hides, and smoking meat over a hickory fire. (The first chapter also mentions—twice—the family's need to keep deer out of the garden.)

Subsistence hunting of venison was a given for settlers. Writing of the early Pennsylvania frontier, the pioneer Joseph Doddridge named deer as a key food source that kept settlers from starving, and provided them with their only form of currency besides: "It was no uncommon thing for families to live several months without a mouthful of bread. It frequently happened that there was no breakfast until it was obtained from the woods. Fur and peltry were the people's money."

Just as Native peoples had for generations, colonial-era whites learned to view deer as suppliers of many necessities, not just food. The ubiquity of deerskin clothing in Indigenous communities served as a powerful example. Though many settlers didn't relish wearing buckskin—despite my swooning at its touch at the Frontier Culture Museum, Doddridge complains it was actually "very cold and uncomfortable in wet weather"—they often had few other choices, especially in the earliest years when families

Buckskin hunting shirt, late eighteenth century

were too poor or isolated to buy manufactured textiles. And it was practical in other ways: a buckskin "hunting shirt" and leggings could make the difference in being able to push through thick undergrowth while hunting or scouting. Frontier women learned to make hunting shirts—which were really more like long jackets, and represented an early fusion of Indigenous and European dress—along with leggings and shot pouches. If they could possibly manage it, the women dressed in cloth garments, but wore "buckskin gloves, if any."

Footwear was another matter. "As much as backwoods settlers disliked wearing buckskin on their backs, they showed an
actual fondness for wearing it on their feet," writes one historian. Another reports that moccasins were "much more comfortable and waterproof than stiff, moldering English boots."
Stuffing them with deer hair made them even better. Moccasins
were made using an awl with a buckhorn handle, and constantly
needed mending; backwoodsmen carried a roll of buckskin with
them for nightly repairs.

All these sartorial choices were coded in terms of race. Settlers were not aiming to become Native Americans; they saw Indian dress as a temporary stop on the way to greater prosperity,
even if that took several generations to achieve. But Doddridge
describes how young men of a certain generation—in effect,
eighteenth-century punks—adopted buckskins-only as a rebel-
lious fashion statement, wearing hunting shirt and leggings but
nothing underneath.

A more serious embrace of Native-style dress was undertaken
by George Washington when, during the American Revolution,
he ordered ten thousand hunting shirts be provided as uniforms
for some regiments under his command. "The General," he
wrote, "also recommends it to the Colonels, to provide Indian
Boots, or Leggings, for their men." The shirts were often decorated with fringes at the hems and on the arms.

This wasn't a new idea; Washington had been talking about
outfitting his soldiers like Native people for almost two decades. "Were I left to pursue my own Inclinations I would
not only cause the Men to adopt the Indian dress but Officers
also, and set the example myself," he'd written back in 1758,
during the French and Indian War. It wasn't just that such
clothes were practical. It was also a way of signaling to the
redcoats that they were facing wilderness-hardened guerrillas,
men who'd learned how to fight the Indian way. Such clothing, he remarked, "is a dress justly supposed to carry no small

terror to the enemy, who think every such person a complete Marksman."

Though not all the Indian-style uniforms were necessarily made of buckskin, the phrase "Virginia buckskin" may have come to denote the white-by-birth, Indian-by-influence, all-American frontiersman and fighter, exemplified by Washington himself. Surely his inspiration included colonial-era hunting clubs whose members adopted Native dress (and celebrated venison as a quintessential American food). George Rogers Clark, and Ethan Allen and his Green Mountain Boys, built buckskin-clad reputations, too, forged in the crucible of the Revolution; soon the new state of Georgia would issue bills featuring a buckskinned hunter, and the first statue of Meriwether Lewis, made in 1807, would show him wearing buckskins. One maudlin account written in 1870 has Lord Fairfax, a Virginia aristocrat, receiving news from Yorktown of the British general Cornwallis's surrender to Washington: "The old nobleman groaned. 'A British general to surrender to a Virginia buckskin!' he exclaimed. In faint tones, he added, to his old body-servant, 'Take me to bed, Joe. It is time for me to die!'"

⚬

As the new American culture became more settled, the stage was set for nostalgia to arise. Like an elderly married couple reminiscing about their lean early years, the American mainstream would come to look back fondly on the frontier period, and deerskin clothing was part of that story.

The mythology of the wilderness helped America erase and ignore the continent's original inhabitants, and it also formed a backdrop for the exploits of conquering heroes. Eastern (and European) audiences didn't even wait for the frontier to close before they started romanticizing it; Buffalo Bill Cody wore buckskins in the late 1800s when his Wild West Show peddled an entertaining fantasy of the American West—even as the actual West still churned with conflict. George Armstrong Custer wore buckskins when mugging for photos around the same time. Later, Davy

LEFT: *Buffalo Bill;* RIGHT: *Fess Parker as Davy Crockett.*

Crockett and Daniel Boone dressed in buckskins for the television age. Clothing made from deerskin remains the pop culture sign par excellence that denotes a white male settler navigating the frontier. Buckskin symbolism has been invoked at every turn in American history from the Revolution through the Boy Scouts to Grateful Dead shows.

Yet by the time all this nostalgia took hold, deer themselves had become scarce, and the human cultures had inextricably mixed. Native society had changed forever, even as Native influences had made a permanent mark on a white-dominated America.

In the birth of a new American culture, deer took on the roles they still play today. They symbolize the continent's enduring (if dated) promise of bounty. They anchor hunting traditions associated with everyday people. And they stand in for the parts of American history—exploration and survivalism—that still lie at the heart of the country's bootstrapping self-image.

Even as late as 2020, a Trump-supporting county commissioner from New Mexico knew just how to present himself when making a stink over COVID restrictions. (Couy Griffin had founded a group called "Cowboys for Trump" and would later be tried for his role in the January 6 attacks on the U.S. Capitol.) Laboring under some warped idea of personal freedom, he protested by riding a horse through the streets of Manhattan, dressed in a buckskin-style jacket and leggings, with extra-long fringes.

CHAPTER 3

The Graph

SOMETIMES WHEN FAMILY COMES TO VISIT US AT OUR house, if they're up for a vigorous hike, we'll suggest walking out our back door and trekking straight up the mountain. We step over the moribund barbed wire that marks the rear line of our land, and the slope quickly cranks up to an angle that gets everybody panting. Among the poplar and oak trees that form a perforated ceiling, a series of fin-shaped granite outcroppings support fringy colonies of ferns. If it's spring, we step carefully over bluets and pennywort in bloom, and I like to spot the fierce-looking new shoots of black cohosh, unfurling darkly from the duff. When we gain enough elevation and turn around to look at the view, the lime green of new poplar leaves is laced by the frothy mauve of flowering redbud trees in the understory.

Here we brush—I catch myself believing—against something more basic. There is great satisfaction and comfort in the fiction that beneath the seasonal round, this place is always the same, an Eden on the mountain. On the small acreage of our property, my children grow older, we build and tear down, we adopt new habits and technologies. But beyond that barbed wire, I look for things to continue in a cyclical dreamtime. I know I rely on this notion because when anything does change in the woods—like the new gravel road, lined with lots marked for houses, that we reach at the top of our climb—I take it as a desecration.

I stand apart from myself in these moments, observing my own reaction. Look at the indignation, look at the wounded possessiveness! Some part of me is offended by evidence of human history's linear arc. Another part of me knows that timelessness is a worn-out trope. Longing for Eden might even be dangerous, if it blinds us to the history that's currently unfolding around us.

Every tree in these woods is a product of history. When my house was built, in 1932, there may have been tall trees on the mountainside, or no trees at all, or brushy young saplings filling in a space that had been logged. Our amnesia about how such places used to look is striking, given how well most of us could distinguish, say, ladies' fashions of the Depression from those of the '60s. Whatever were the conditions on this mountain when our house was new, they were probably different from what I see now on our walks.

There are plenty of clues about the contingencies of time here: ATV trails, aging deer stands, rusting midcentury truck beds lodged above the creek. Fallen, rotting trunks. A new picnic table installed near a waterfall by a developer hoping to sell parcels of land for vacation homes. Game cameras strapped to trees. Day-old deer pellets. The bleached shell of a box turtle. The slow shapes of the rocks.

⬩⬩

The woods are bigger than we are, older than we are, with their own internal doings. But they are neither original nor eternal.

The history of the Earth starts with a billion years of nothing but rock and very few of the sights or sounds we now would label "natural"—not blue sky, or wind through trees; not even the twenty-four-hour rhythm of the days and nights. In the beginning, it might have taken only two and a half hours for the Earth to spin.

The story continues through billions of years of unicellular life found only in the oceans, and only sees the arrival of land-dwelling plants when nine-tenths of Earth's history was already past.

Trees in any form—with true roots and leaves, and the ability to grow tall—took another seventy-five million years to evolve. Our planet had reached perhaps 97 percent of its current age before flowering plants appeared. Those poplar trees behind my house are a relatively old species: They've been around for the last 2 percent of the Earth's history, while the oaks and maples are a more recent innovation.

As for the animals who live among them, the arrival of large mammals had to wait until after the demise of the dinosaurs. That was 99 percent of the way through Earth's history, and the more recent geological epochs have seen a parade of mammals that, in artists' renderings, look familiar and alien at the same time—the wolflike *Sinonyx* with its oversized jaws, or *Cervalces scotti*, the 1,500-pound stag-moose, which roamed North America during the last Ice Age.

Some of deer's earliest ancestors sported tusks, which in most species gradually gave way to a different weapon: antlers. Modern deer possess a remnant of their evolution—the misnamed dewclaws, which are actually unused toes, a few inches off the ground, on the backs of their legs. These are a throwback to the ancestors that had not yet begun to walk only on their middle two toes, as deer do today.

The world now contains more than forty deer species. As for the deer whose paths we sometimes briefly follow along the flanks of this mountainside—the whitetails, by far the most numerous species of deer in North America—they appeared during the Pliocene, perhaps three to four million years ago, destined to persist through a host of changes in the landscape around them. At the end of the last Ice Age, just 11,700 years ago, they discovered a new ecological space opening to them when large mammals like cave bears, mammoths, and ground sloths died out (likely, in part, because of human hunters).

To put that another way: deer are survivors. They may not be quite as exciting as saber-toothed cats, but they've outdone them in staying power. Long before the disruptions to North American ecology wrought by Europeans, deer had a history of surviving, adapting, changing where and how they lived: exactly what they're still doing now.

Received wisdom about nature always interests me, not only because it so often goes unquestioned but also because it forms the basis of so much of our behavior. As Edward Abbey put it, we tend to confuse "the thing observed with the mind of the observer"; our beliefs are like jackets that insulate us from the weather of reality. Believing certain things about deer—as with many animals, plants, nature as a whole—leads us to proceed from certain starting points, to choose particular paths. And to feel certain ways.

When Americans today talk about deer populations, the first thing they're likely to say is that there are too many deer. This is taken as a bedrock truth, and the feeling that goes with it is exasperation. Most people see deer as overabundant, and if they go on to explain why that's so, they'll likely talk about how quickly deer populations have grown.

The older the person is, the more sharply they've probably seen deer numbers go up in their own lifetimes, at the edge of the yard, on the roadside. Deer have multiplied, clearly, and in a way that unsettles us. But that's only in comparison to their extremely low numbers of the late nineteenth and early twentieth centuries.

I remember, years ago, my mother telling me about a newspaper clipping from the 1940s or '50s, displayed at her local historical society in Pennsylvania—an article reporting that someone in the area had spotted one deer. That this had once been newsworthy was my first clue that recent history had seen radical changes. But the growth of deer populations in the twentieth century is only one of many dramatic shifts they've experienced. To fully explore this history would prove to be a much more convoluted journey than I'd expected.

How many deer were here before Europeans arrived? That would seem to be the next important question. I found plenty of graphs showing deer populations over time, and what first jumped out was their dramatic V shape, with the nadir around 1900. But the next thing I noticed was that these timelines invariably began in the fifteenth century, just before European contact. Just as I like thinking (falsely) that the woods behind my house have ever been the same, many Americans are invested in the belief that the original, proper, or true state of our landscape—its baseline, that is—was that which existed right before European boots stepped onto the soil. We're very prone to name-drop virgin forests and untouched wilderness and perfect harmonies between Native Americans and their environments. We love imagining that Eden once existed, and that it was located right here under our feet.

But there was no time without time; there was no unchanging perfection. We may not know as much about deer populations before Europeans arrived, and we may not be able to fill in that graph to the left of Columbus, but that doesn't mean there was nothing to plot. Various groups of Indigenous people came and went over the continent for thousands of years, practicing different ways of life in varying landscapes, with all kinds of effects on plants and animals. Many writers and scientists, for example, have explained how Native Americans practiced controlled burns to create openings in the forest. (They did this for many reasons, one being to improve deer habitat.)

The land hosted waves of dynamic interplay between climate, humans, ecosystems, cultures—in short, a hugely complex give-and-take that wasn't static at all. But that picture has trouble dispelling the image of Eden. For one thing, it asks us to diversify our wildly reductive view of Native Americans, which in turn disrupts a lot of national ideologies that resist movement as stubbornly as those fins of granite on our mountainside.

Paradoxically, the myth of the lost Eden also comforts our ambivalence about this technological world we've wrought. We carry a misty vision of the past: a younger Earth, a sort of natural bosom that once nurtured us, and this vision soothes us when we confront the costs of our own power. During the twentieth century, as environmentalism became part of our national consciousness through issues like nuclear waste, water pollution, and endangered wildlife, we quickly accepted the idea that humanity had sullied what was once pure—that modernized people *themselves* are an invasive species, a type of pollution, a weed or alien.

Maybe we were primed for this story because it chimed with other beliefs that had long been part of the European psyche. Eden itself, after all, was perfect without—*until*—Adam and Eve. Guilt and shame, the Fall as history's first event: These are neatly echoed by the narrative in which Europeans entered the Eden of North America and, not only by their actions but also by their very presence, spoiled what had been a timeless wilderness.

The myth of Eden comes not only from religion but also from science, and the unexpected entwining of the two. It was a search for the hand of God in nature that led Carl Linnaeus, in the mid-1700s, to describe a cyclical pattern of interactions between Earth and its creatures. Although it fluctuated, nature always returned to the same reliable starting point. In drawing this portrait, Linnaeus echoed the classical Greek naturalists before him.

Darwin upset that apple cart a century later with his picture of natural selection and evolution, but the concept of permanence found other ways to hold on. The early twentieth century ushered in the theory of the ecological climax community. Left to its own devices, this theory posited, nature would create assemblages of plants and animals living in balance and stability—a deer population, for example, supporting and being limited by a wolf population. Significantly, humans had no real place in this ecological scheme. We were a wrench in the gears, disobeyers of natural law.

Later thinkers began to seriously question that underlying belief in balance. The wildlife biologist Dale McCullough wrote in 1997 that the idea of the "balance of nature," as understood by the public at large, functions as a "quasi-religious myth." He went on to suggest that stable equilibrium in nature, appealing as it might be, is just another human concept, adding, "It would be better if we recognized that change is ubiquitous."

I found McCullough's piece in an anthology of scientific papers that examine deer ecology from numerous angles. Many of them support his vision of ecology as a stage on which both characters and set are always shifting. Just in the time since Europeans arrived in America, the climate has fluctuated (settlement happened during a cool period, the so-called Little Ice Age) and key species, like chestnut trees and passenger pigeons, have disappeared. As part of this dynamic history, deer might be expected to go through changes of their own. Hunting by Indigenous peoples, on an evolutionary scale, could be seen as a disturbance that animal and plant communities had not yet had time to integrate when Europeans arrived and set the boat rocking even harder.

"Managing deer populations to presettlement levels has little biological justification," the book states bluntly. Around the same time, the historian Gordon G. Whitney seemed to wash his hands of the old dream: "Few ecologists subscribe to the 'balance of nature' concept today."

A quarter century later, the rest of us have kept on renewing our subscriptions. Climate change and the sixth extinction are raging all around us; being able to grasp and respond to complexity is our one thread of hope. But we still habitually think in terms of a simplified paradigm—traceable to Linnaeus, the Old Testament, or beyond—in which nature is a perfect clockwork mechanism, and we just need to let it run.

Nothing is trickier than questioning our own master narratives; they keep popping up, adding their flavor to everything. The big problem with the myth of Eden is that it leaves no real place for humans.

◖◗

Personally, I can feel keenly how much conscious effort it takes to strip away my belief system, to stop looking for a baseline. I can read evidence of ecological instability all day long, but some part of my mind keeps looking for a simple, conclusive answer.

In the case of deer, the assumption that their numbers were

always the same prior to Columbus—and that only when white people arrived did they begin to seesaw up and down, too few, too many—is a seductive one because we'd really like to know how many deer would be the "correct" number for North America now. The thinking goes thus: If we knew how many deer were here before, we could plug in some numbers to account for changes in the landscape (like the conversion of prairies to agricultural land, or the growth of cities and suburbs), and come up with a population level that would be appropriate for today.

But nothing about deer is that simple, starting with that hypothetical pre-Columbian deer population. Estimates have ranged from 10 per square mile in the eastern U.S. to as much as 100—a rather wide margin of error. Even the most careful guesses tend to rest on cascades of assumptions about numbers of Native Americans and how many deer they would have required. But those factors themselves are shifty: There may have been considerably greater Indigenous populations than has long been believed. In any case, to envision any of these numbers as static makes as little sense as referring, without any date stamp, to "the population of England." Before Columbus, there were several big fluctuations in the deer population. (And even before Native Americans, climate and predators caused other swings.)

What we can say with certainty is this: For thousands of years, people and deer existed together. And after Europeans arrived, deer nearly went extinct. Surely this was a difference not just of action but also of mind. Those deer population graphs track numbers of animals, but they also map human thought.

⚊

In 2021, a reporter quoted a local politician in a Pittsburgh suburb: "We have ten times more deer in Pennsylvania than when it was founded by William Penn." His complaint evoked an image of unbridled abundance, a pestilential tsunami of deer. But his numbers were simply untrue. Pennsylvania is now home to about a million and a half whitetails; no scientist would estimate its precolonial population at only a tenth of that figure. What is true is that Pennsylvania now has orders of magnitude more deer than in, say, 1910—a time when wildlife populations were unusually low, having been slashed by a couple centuries of very aggressive hunting.

We suffer from amnesia about the history of the land we walk. In truth, European colonists and their descendants in America—right down to Americans of all stripes today—have almost never had a chance to observe deer populations free from our own influence. The earliest European explorers touched off epidemics that raced around the continent ahead of the actual colonizers, decimating many Indigenous groups before they ever had direct contact with the Europeans. This in turn deeply affected the ecosystems that Native peoples had been hunting and stewarding for generations; without their presence, many wildlife populations, including deer, suddenly burgeoned. When more European colonists began to arrive and settle along the Eastern Seaboard in the early 1600s, they found what seemed to them like incredible numbers of deer in an untouched wilderness; they assumed this was the natural state of things in North America, never realizing that they had stumbled upon a historical anomaly, a landscape in crisis.

They also may have exaggerated what they found. "References to vast numbers of wildlife frequently appear in early travel accounts and county histories," writes Whitney. "Many of these, however appear to be stock pieces, i.e., traditional themes repeated without verification." North America was indeed more abundant in game than Europe, as many settlers had already learned from the promotional tracts that descended from early reports like Theodore de Bry's and drew them to the New World colonies. (A typical one promised "millions of Elkes, Stags, Deer, Turkey, Fowl, [and] Fish," and another called Virginia "Earth's only paradise.") But maybe colonists, Whitney thinks, were just so happy to make it safely to shore that they tended to overstate the bounty of their new home. Well-known biblical and classical imagery supplied the metaphors.

The abundance encouraged the settlers' attitude toward the unfamiliar continent. There was little scientific curiosity about what was here. Rather, there was an energetic interest in what could be used. The newcomers came garbed in a belief that North America was a larder so vast and well-stocked it could never be depleted. Over the next three centuries, the actions of American colonists and citizens—driven sometimes by greed and fear that amounted to a kind of madness, other times simply by the math of an exploding human occupation—would batter the deer population, inadvertently support its recovery, then squeeze it again, hard enough to drive it down to almost nothing. The current age of deer comes after a time of sustained growth in numbers that lasted most of a century. Meanwhile, the landscape itself has been thoroughly remade, from the proliferation of human spaces and systems to the shifting mix of plants and animals, from total removal of predators in many places to changes in the climate itself.

Whatever was actually going on before Europeans arrived is no recipe for what we should want today. That precolonial state of things has long since been chopped, charred, and simmered into an entirely different stew.

⚎

There's a photo from the 1880s, taken in West Virginia's Canaan Valley, a stretch I've driven through many times. I know it as a lonely place, where isolated farms claim their bottomland spaces against a stolid backdrop of thickly forested hills. The human touch feels light there, almost tenuous. But that is another amnesia, as the photo clearly shows.

A log cabin squats in the center, its front yard squared off by a picket fence, a taller split-rail fence marking pasture behind it, the lines of its log walls and stone chimney handmade and wayward. Two rather separate groups of people are posing near the house. On the left, five men display their guns and the deer those guns have killed. On the right stands a family of eight, parents and their brood of young children. In the background, another log building, and a raw mountainside completely shaven of trees.

All the figures are small, but the cocky satisfaction of the hunters burns through like neon. One has a deer slung over his shoulders, another sits with a deer's head draped over his lap. When I try to count the deer, I find at least three, but there are other forms scattered at the hunters' feet that could be either deer or big rocks, and their helter-skelter ambiguity makes me feel a little sick; somehow it's worse than looking at the other common type of photo from this era, in which deer carcasses are hung in a line from a hunting-camp pole.

The lack of standing trees, juxtaposed with wooden house walls, fences, firewood, and gunstocks, is a perfect illustration of living things transformed into resources: plucked like summer berries, then consumed. These deer couldn't have been able to live on this brutal hillside, so the hunters must have ventured elsewhere, to some nearby creek draw or ridgeline, with a sense that they were taking the meat out of a place that would itself soon be raided for lumber. Everything looks temporary, scrappy, a landscape of churn.

Under a vague sky, these people are wresting their existence. The deer are dead; the children are many. Humans are subtracting animals and adding themselves; beings that wear fur or bark are cut down by those in cotton. There is something so familiar about the scene—it is pure Americana, from the cabin to the caps—and yet so unearthly, like a tornado's aftermath. It is a holocaust scene and an emblem of energetic pride, all at once.

◆

That Canaan Valley photo freezes one moment from a few centuries of New World death and fecundity—a fast-moving era in which deer functioned like a living ore.

As we saw earlier, the deerskin trade, especially in the southeastern American colonies, made the deer harvest into a commercial mission rather than a way to survive. A killing frenzy drove deer numbers sharply downward until around the time of the American Revolution.

Farther north, populations had suffered for other reasons.

Early New England settlers cut down forests and killed white-tails for meat. With deer harder to find, and Native hunting on English land newly restricted, some Indigenous groups began keeping livestock instead. This decreased habitat and forage for deer even further. By 1642, the Narragansett leader Mian-tonomo lamented the rapid loss of deer alongside other staples of survival: "Our fathers had plenty of deer and skins, our plains were full of deer, as also our woods, and of turkies, and our coves full of fish and fowl. But these English having gotten our land, they with scythes cut down the grass, and with axes fell the trees; their cows and horses eat the grass, and their hogs spoil our clam banks, and we shall all be starved."

The devastation in New England wasn't only a collision of different economies. It was also a matter of the spirit. The Pu-ritans were cloaked in a belief that wilderness was a dismal hell that God had ordained they should tame and transform. Like sin itself, wildness came at them in dangerous measure, its very abundance a kind of disorder. Accordingly, they attacked for-ests and wild animals with religious fervor, like early Christian missionaries in Northern Europe who'd cut down sacred groves. The word *wilderness*, "place of wild animals," links with other European terms having to do with confusion. A loss of bearings. Be*wilder*ment.

⚌

Nonetheless, it's too simple just to say that the activities of set-tlers harmed deer. Human disturbance can often be helpful to them. I see this just up the road from my house, where a large acreage was recently logged. As a human neighbor, I recoiled at my first sight of the stumps and muddy ruts made by heavy machines. But, like a classic demonstration of successional vege-tation, weeds and vines are glorying there in the sudden wash of sunlight, and in turn, so are deer.

This brings me to a key fact about deer that, culturally, we can't seem to grasp. We cherish an enduring image of deer in the forest; elusive bucks and does, in our minds, are firmly paired with tall trees and quiet groves. A brand of beer we often buy in my household has a label printed with exactly this image: shafts of sun through the straight trunks of trees, their forms as majestic as the solitary buck who stands among them.

Certainly deer do inhabit wooded lands; they like eating acorns, the seedlings of certain kinds of trees, and some of the wildflowers and plants (what ecologists call "the herbaceous layer") that pop up on the forest floor. But mature woods generally have less to offer deer than certain other environments. (The very word *forest* came into English signifying not woodland but simply "place of deer.")

The habitats that can support deer in the greatest numbers are less celebrated, less picturesque. They don't even have a name in common parlance, nothing as simple as "forest," though ecologists call them early-successional habitats. They're places with a lot of brushy, leafy vegetation below six feet in height. What does that mean in an undisturbed landscape? If by *undisturbed* we mean "untouched by humans," then it could mean a place where lightning recently caused a forest fire, opening the canopy and inviting lower-growing plants to rapidly fill in the space below. If by *undisturbed* we mean "prior to Columbus," then that fire could well have been set by Native Americans in a controlled burn.

In the last few centuries, the places most full of deer food have taken many forms, like logged forests where brush proliferates. Or lately abandoned farms, where infant trees and fast-growing shrubs are roiling upward from what had been a pasture or hayfield. Or the cuts under powerlines, where nearby trees offer shelter, and there's a vigorous supply of bushes and small plants in the sunny spaces below the lines. Or suburban neighborhoods: a tight patchwork of trees, shrubs, and the narrow zones where the woods meet the shoulders of roads.

Such places, to a strolling deer, are rich with food in the form of leaf and stem, as well as cover, one of their other key requirements. In these environments, deer live easy and reproduce

quickly. Take away the predators, too, and you've created a cervid nirvana.

These conditions did boost deer numbers, but they were always in a tug-of-war with other factors that caused their decline.
Soon enough, the forces of death proved much more powerful.

As I read about the plight of deer in early American history,
I found my eyes sliding over certain recurring phrases. They repeated again and again, as numbing in their way as the sound of
gunfire when it rings out too many times. "Seriously impaired by
human encroachment." "Sharp decline." "Slaughter." "Nearly
total demise." "Within a single generation of men, the deer became scarce." "Continued and intense exploitation." "Without
mercy or forethought." "In 1880 . . . more than 100,000 deer
carcasses were shipped to market by railroad in Michigan." "A
profitable but devastating episode." "Almost total extirpation of
white-tailed deer by the early 1900s."

Deer are our neighbors now, and it's hard to grasp: Americans
of the past came incredibly close to wiping them out.

The killing was done to provision markets for both meat and
leather. The European market for deerskins had long since closed,
but in midwestern cities like Milwaukee and Chicago, hide buyers acquired skins and shipped them to tanners in Philadelphia
and other eastern manufacturing hubs. The leather was turned
into a panoply of products that we, in our world of plastic, have
forgotten to associate with animals: snowshoe netting, bellows,
boot linings. Deerskin was used for bookbinding, upholstery fabric, wall coverings, and even as a covering for windowpanes in
lieu of glass. If this were the nineteenth century and you were
reading this book on a sofa near a window, you could be holding, sitting on, resting your feet on, looking at, and even looking
through deerskin.

Maybe you would have also eaten deer for supper. Today, in a
culture where people rarely eat venison unless they, or someone
they're close to, personally hunted the deer, it's easy to forget
that their flesh long served as a staple food. At least through

the nineteenth century, Americans generally ate a wider range of meats than we do today: venison, elk, bear, goose, opossum, turtle, pheasant, tongue of buffalo. In the late 1800s, the new technologies of repeating rifles and refrigerated rail cars drove a brisk trade in venison killed for market; even East Coast urbanites of the time had ready access to venison, harvested from places like Michigan and Minnesota.

I use the word *harvest* both deliberately and with reservation. If *hunting* has come to imply some measure of ethical fair chase, then the killing of deer for market resembled a hunt much less than the reaping of a crop in a field. It was nearly that total and methodical. But it was orgiastic, too. Single hunters took thousands of animals, using whatever means—including poison, pitfalls, and baiting—were most expedient. They slaughtered the animals when they were gathered together for warmth in the coldest days of winter. They even mounted guns in trees; when a deer walked into a tripwire, it would fire the gun on itself.

It was a clear-cut; it was the removal of a mountaintop. It's a forgotten national wound.

Learning about all this left me baffled. I grew up in a place where hunting is big and the state animal is the white-tailed deer; I thought I had a decent grasp of American history. How had I never known about the near-extinction of deer in my own country? Why had this never come up in any conversation, any passing mention? How could this narrative be so absent from our national story?

The passenger pigeon and the bison make it into our history textbooks, but deer—and many other animals—fade into the background, their dramatic histories absorbed into a cultural sleepiness about the past. It's an episode on which we have closed memory's door. But from our current perspective, if we do pause to contemplate it, this collective act was—if not quite evil—a crime. Native people saw it as the waging of environmental war, and found it unconscionable.

What were these killers thinking? Some assumed that humans could never cause extinction, no matter how hard we hunted. This was the same society in which settlers would clear forest for fields, use the soil until it was exhausted, then simply move on and repeat the process. This delusion of limitless resources correlated with wasteful early American practices in lumbering, milling, house-building, fence-building, even the generous size of the fires in fireplaces; the overuse of wildlife was simply one more item on this list. Intellectuals of the time were no more clear-eyed: Thomas Jefferson expected the continent to support a settlement way of life for a thousand generations to come.

The Lewis and Clark expedition had gone through about four deer per day procuring food for its members, which sounds like a lot. But it was nothing compared to what followed. It was the masses of ordinary pioneers and market hunters, surging in waves over ridges and into valleys, clothed in the expectation of a bounteous natural larder, that steadily wore away at deer populations.

It took a very long time for Europeans and their descendants to get over their amazement at freely available game and to outgrow the old saw about American resources being practically infinite. No one had to contemplate too deeply the depletion in more settled places when there was always another wilderness just over the next hill.

But some of those who were clearing and killing, who were up to their elbows in weeping stumps and bleeding carcasses, took a more realistic view. They knew, because they were seeing it happen, that in fact they *were* driving deer populations down to nothing. There was a finders-keepers mentality toward land itself (legally ratified by the Homestead Act, which gave away land to those who settled on it), and that attitude extended to animals as well. It was seen as Americans' right to clear land and use whatever was found there. If the decline of deer was an inevitable part of taming the wilderness, people sometimes took that as a reason to kill even faster—because the overall project of settlement was the master moral narrative of the age, and individuals wanted to get a decent piece of the pie while they still could. Only later would hunting be defined as "sport," implying an ethic of fair chase.

At the same time that white settlers were gobbling up the bounty of wildlife in the New World, they themselves were proliferating wildly—from a few hundred in the early 1600s, to more than two million at the time of the American Revolution, to seventy-six million by 1900.

The assumption that any population needs an external control—a predator or a human manager—to prevent it from overrunning the Earth is still with us in the way we talk about deer today. Then and now, we picture ourselves as the last line of defense against a threat of brimming fecundity. Yet what species has burgeoned more rudely, with deeper repercussions, than humans?

⁑

And was there grief about all this? Thoreau called the American landscape "a maimed and imperfect nature," but his was a lonely voice in mourning the changes. It's very unlikely that the Canaan Valley homesteaders of the 1880s saw themselves as witnesses to (much less perpetrators of) an ecological tragedy.

Yet just a generation after the photo was taken, the problem had become impossible to ignore. By the early twentieth century, deer populations had gone down to zero in many areas, with isolated herds holding on in the swamps of Virginia, the mountains of Kentucky, the remote river bottoms of Iowa. Kansas was declared deer-free in the 1930s. Ohio's herd had been extirpated for three decades by then. Vermonters hadn't seen a deer for two generations.

"They are so gone now, the great beasts, that we have no sense of them left," wrote the naturalist Donald Culross Peattie in 1938. I don't know whether many other white people mourned the deer, but there are certainly hints that Native Americans grieved. "In my day," an Eastern Oklahoma Delaware elder wrote in 1984, "I used to see the elderly women cry and wipe the tears from their eyes with their aprons because there were no deer anymore. Every place the hunter went there were 'No Trespassing' signs. Nevertheless, the hunting songs were still sung."

Whatever their emotional state, Americans began to make room for a new and very distinctive idea—the forerunner of the save-the-Earth imperatives that are now so firmly woven into our awareness. (It was a new idea for America, anyway; according to Marco Polo, Kublai Khan established no-hunting seasons for deer back in the thirteenth-century Mongol empire. "This is that they may increase and multiply," Polo explained.) At the moment when the North American deer population was at its lowest ebb came the dawn of a new conservation ideal. For deer, it was a powerful savior. During the early twentieth century, most states severely restricted deer hunting, with many places outlawing it altogether. States officially began to manage wildlife. And a new federal law, the 1900 Lacey Act, outlawed the interstate sale of poached meat. This was the big hinge—the point where that deer population graph begins to creep back up.

It wasn't the first time that Americans had tried to protect deer; laws restricting their killing had gone on the books as early as 1646, but due mainly to lax enforcement, they hadn't worked. Perhaps the failure spoke to the lack of a cultural foundation for "saving" wildlife: The idea was just not rooted in enough people's minds to outweigh the pillage.

But now American culture was changing. More people were living in cities, buying meat from butchers, and this allowed them the luxury of viewing hunting as a relic, maybe even somewhat barbaric. Industrialization allowed many people to move away from the natural world in their daily lives, even as art and science invited them to regard it as an interesting object of study—so while they might tolerate hunting, they could easily see why it had to be limited.

Meanwhile, science organized itself around a utilitarian view of land and wildlife. Both trees and deer had been overexploited, and the country could no longer ignore the damage. What's been called "nature's second coming" relied on heavy-handed human assistance. In saving deer and trees, Americans began to view both like a farmer views corn: as crops.

In 1933, the American ecologist Aldo Leopold articulated the philosophy behind a brand-new profession. "Like all other agricultural arts," he wrote, "game management produces a crop by controlling . . . environmental factors." In this system, behind-the-scenes manipulation (of predators, hunting seasons, and bag limits) would maximize the number of mature deer available to be taken by hunters. Habitat would still appear "natural." Yet the quality and abundance of deer themselves would be, in large measure, a product of human actions. Coming as it did at a time when deer populations were so badly decimated, this idea must have seemed self-evident. Good hunting in the future clearly depended on Americans making wise decisions in the present.

Since Europeans first arrived in North America, there had been a swirl of conflicting ideas about what wilderness meant, about how wildlife should be regarded. There was the myth of a timeless Eden; the Puritans' hatred of the forest; North America as a paradise of abundance. There was the idea that humans could never truly harm places or species; the idea that since harm was inevitable, one should take what one could get; and the idea that nature's profligacy demanded human control. There was a growing sense that nature was worth careful study, and a mounting suspicion that animals deserved human sympathy and protection. And there was the new view of wildlife as a crop.

Maybe, in the end, the most salient force wasn't any one of these concepts in its own right. Maybe it was the very fact of confusion—the modern person's deep, abiding uncertainty about who we are on the planet, and the way we cast about for answers, trying and discarding one after another, like ill-fitting jackets.

CHAPTER 4

Value

ONE DAY LAST DECEMBER I DROVE PAST AN ABANDONED old farm in my county, with a quirky white farmhouse that overlooks a wide sweep of river bottom. It's a place I often pass, and when I do, my eyes habitually scan that grassy bottomland for deer. On that day, as sometimes happens, I was rewarded with the sight of a herd: five or ten animals, widely scattered, heads down as they fed.

I'm always reassured to see them there; from the surrounding trees they've come, into the open, bringing with them a hint of wildness. Their forms are so much lighter, their bearing so self-sufficient, compared with the Angus cattle I see in many other fields. And yet, in a sense, they are artificial.

Of course white-tailed deer (*Odocoileus virginianus*) are a native North American species. Historically, they ranged across much of the continent, with as many as thirty subspecies, including small local populations (*O. v. nigribarbis*, from Georgia's Blackbeard Island) and widespread varieties like *O. v. borealis*, which inhabited a vast quadrant of the northeastern U.S. and southeastern Canada. Meanwhile, mule deer (*Odocoileus hemionus*) were the dominant species in the West, though they rubbed shoulders with whitetails at the edges of their ranges, differing only in relatively minor ways.

These were America's deer. But the destruction of the animals by around 1900 was so extensive that it constituted a genetic watershed. Besides hunting restrictions and the establishment of refuges, there was another tool used to help deer recover. In at least thirty states from Florida to Vermont and from Montana to Texas, game managers deliberately restocked whitetails, often moving them from one state to another, as a way of seeding future populations. My own state of Virginia is one where deer were restocked, and so any deer I see in my daily life are likely to have descended from animals placed here by people.

Even if they hadn't been restocked, deer probably would have skirted extinction; in the early 1900s they were holding on in isolated pockets, and new conservation laws were coming into play. But without the restocking programs, it's doubtful that we would have nearly as many deer now as we do. Over a period of decades, restocking supercharged the resurgence of deer like fertilizer on a crop, in Aldo Leopold's terms. As far as wildlife restoration, it's one of the planet's great success stories. It made it possible for those of us living now to take deer pretty much for granted. And it was driven in great measure by the desire to hunt them.

The first restocking efforts depended partly on private funding—they were bankrolled by sportsmen and landowners—but public monies increased after 1937, when the federal Pittman-Robertson Act started cash flowing from taxes on guns and ammunition, to be funneled into wildlife restoration and management. Bigger deer-stocking programs got underway and continued through the 1960s, with deer being trapped and released in some places as late as the 1990s.

Restocking was an exercise in human domination. Deer were baited into traps—large wooden boxes with doors that suddenly slid downward, guillotine-style, creating a dark enclosure. When the doors opened again at the touch of human hands, they led into smaller crates or nets. The task, one manager wrote, was to let no more than ten seconds pass between approaching a trap and removing the deer; otherwise, animals would injure themselves by thrashing against the trap's walls. Once the people had their hands on the deer, they'd put its head in a wrestling hold in order to tag its ear, rope its antlers, or lay hold of its ears or hind legs to extend its body along the ground; sometimes they'd blindfold it, lie on top of it, hog-tie it, ignoring its cries.

Those could be death cries; a portion of captured deer, sometimes as high as one in seven, tended to die from stress or injuries. This could happen in the trap or up to a week after release. People were out to save deer, not hurt them, but saving a species entailed death for individuals. For a conservationist project ultimately driven by the desires of hunters, maybe that was perfectly fitting.

Once crated, deer would be loaded on trucks and hauled away, sometimes many hundreds of miles, to some new home chosen for them by people thinking in terms of population goals, state and county borders, wildlife regulations. The deer's concerns were less abstract; they were about to encounter in many cases an environment that looked, smelled, and tasted different from their home. Deer (who normally learn from their mothers how to navigate their home ranges) were moved from Wisconsin to Mississippi. From Maine to Pennsylvania. From Iowa to Virginia. The plants they encountered in these new habitats offered unfamiliar types of food, different structures for cover; the days may have been longer or shorter, the rocks and soils of a strange texture, the wind carrying peculiar scents of unknown animals or flowers. The water might have come from a new type of source; it may have tasted more earthy or sweet. Yet, suddenly conscripted into a type of ecological pioneering, they mostly lived.

In many places, early restocking using out-of-state deer provided the nucleus of a population that would in turn be used to seed other new herds within the state. North Carolina, Wisconsin, Texas, and Michigan were the most important source states. Oklahoma moved almost nine thousand deer around within its own borders. Texas moved more than thirty thousand.

On a diet of regrowing forests and fields, and eventually of suburban landscaping, deer did extremely well. There were well below five million of them in 1900; at least twenty million by 1950; thirty-eight million by the turn of the millennium.

If the American project was, in part, to make a pastoral land-scape out of a wilderness, deer benefited from that project in a cultural sleight of hand. We thought of them as part of the wild, but we had misconceived them. Their secret was that they, like us—like squirrels, corn, apple trees, clover, and sparrows—would flourish in our human garden.

⚶

I was on my way to a winery that afternoon, in the midst of re-searching everything from Lyme disease to car accidents. We no longer look at deer as a species in trouble; instead, we often think of them as troubling us. Calling them a commodity had almost wiped them out, while calling them a resource had helped them recover. In either case, though, we had treated deer more or less as objects.

So it's not surprising that in our world, deer are still bought and sold in many ways, most of them indirect, and many related to hunting. If we consider that hunting is a $26 billion industry, and that deer are by far the most popular game animal in the U.S., it's easy to see that the conservationists who saved the spe-cies also contributed substantially to the economy we're living in right now. Having researched the tangled history of deer and people up through the restocking era, now I was following that relationship out to many of its current endpoints, places where the old attitudes wear new faces.

I soon arrived at one of them: a cushioned chair at a winery table on a bluestone patio. Here, there was brightness: four tall gas heaters with chasing flames, and the berry-red of ribbons on Christmas wreaths. Out beyond the patio's edge, in the landscape of vineyards and woods, the colors were muted dun and sepia.

I sat and looked out at the view—the Blue Ridge's deep indigo cutting into a heavy sky. A man at a big table near me bobbed his foot up and down, a foot clad in Nikes the color of unripe mango. It was not even three; I was sipping a very nice Cabernet. A plate appeared in front of me bearing a puck-shaped portion of venison tartare, maybe two and a half inches across, served with thin wedges of toasted brioche and a garnish of micro mustard greens.

I stared at that plate for a while. I'd hardly been in restaurants at all for the last two years, because of COVID, and I felt both awkward and delighted, savoring it all, even the peculiar pleasure of overhearing conversation from the next table ("Everybody wants to quit their jobs, fine, but then what? How will they live?").

Finally I picked up my fork.

◖◗

One small community's experience with stocking reads like a fable. On Monhegan Island off the coast of Maine, which had never had its own deer population, about six whitetails were released in the mid-1950s at the request of town leaders. (It is very hard to imagine any local government taking such action today.) The deer fared well on six-hundred-acre Monhegan; they increased to one hundred over the next half century. But by the late 1990s, more than one in ten residents of the island were suffering from Lyme disease, which is carried by a type of tick that requires both deer and rodents as hosts at different points in its life cycle. In this case, the rodents were Norway rats, which had also been introduced by humans.

The people of Monhegan decided that, to correct an untenable situation, deer were the species that would have to be eliminated. (The rats were too difficult to eradicate without harming pets.) They got permission from the state to hire a professional culling outfit, White Buffalo, Inc., and within two years the job was done: the last deer on the island, a male fawn, was killed in January 1999. Once again, Monhegan was deer-free.

An island is fundamentally bordered in a way that most places are not. The increase and subsequent trouble experienced on Monhegan would ring a bell for people all around the U.S., but hardly any communities have the option of total eradication (not to mention the will).

In that it enabled the spectacular recovery of a key native

mammal, the restocking movement can hardly be condemned. But its hubris, in hindsight, is very clear. Here we were, a hundred or so years ago, on a gravely injured continent. It had been stripped of trees, emptied of predators and many other large mammals and key native birds, subject to a wave of non-native plant species, tree parasites, and diseases. It was entering an age of intensified farming and ranching, soil erosion, drought, and flood; its surface was quickly being laced with a dense network of roads, highways, houses, and commerce; its wildlands were being prevented from burning naturally, its waters dammed and diverted, its atmosphere filled with novel compounds and particulates. Ecologically, the boat had been rocking hard for three hundred years, and that rocking was about to get even more violent. And onto this chaotic stage, Americans generously applied seed populations of a large mammal—one that needs to eat nearly a ton of vegetation annually to survive, can reproduce fast enough to double its population every two years, and now had, in many regions, no predators to eat it. Which brings us to today.

◊◊

"What we do," chef Tim Moore had explained to me on the phone, "is simply slice the meat, probably about a quarter-inch thick, then go back and julienne, then turn those and dice them. Then we run our knife through it one or two more times." I had called him because his restaurant, housed in a newish winery called Early Mountain Vineyards, was one of the few I could find serving venison in my area. "Then we season it with nice kosher salt, then add a crème fraiche–based dressing and fold it all in. Tartare is something you do not want to overmix because you'll end up working the muscle a little bit too much. So you fold gently and take your time. Be very easy with it."

That was how I ate it, too: slowly, with care. The meat was raw and pink, flecked with orange zest, mild as a fawn. A Jack Russell terrier climbed onto the lap of a man with a salt-and-pepper beard while I speared a pickled cranberry and dragged it through the ultrafine leek ash dusting the sides of the bowl. There were flashes of Thanksgiving here—my mother's cranberry relish with orange zest, the fullness of the land in fall, the rituals of ripe fields, and the soil's piquant fruits. Another sip of wine; another pour of clear water into a tumbler. Cool air flowing over the patio, between the steady heaters.

The tiny bites had nearly filled me already, but a second plate appeared, a larger one: four slices of venison tenderloin on a bed of parsnip purée, with a little pond of veal glace to one side, all dotted with baby beet greens.

Moore had described his method for this choice cut of venison. "We torchon it," he'd said. "It's a technique that makes that tenderloin into a perfect cylindrical piece. Then we'll Cryovac it in a reduced oxygen bag and sous-vide it at 134.5 degrees. Then we're icing it down, then taking it out. We crust the whole tenderloin in crushed juniper berry and sear it to medium rare." It didn't sound like a process the average home cook could hope to re-create.

The winery, one of many in central Virginia, embodied the food movement that prizes all things local and seasonal; it also took part in an aesthetic—familiar to me from years of reporting on architecture and food in this region—that mixes the rural and the cosmopolitan. Or, you might say, it presents the rural *to* the cosmopolitan.

I'd asked Moore why he likes to put venison on his menu. "It's kind of a delicacy, almost," he answered. "You don't go to the Texas Roadhouse down the street and get venison. It's a very elevated protein that is not cheap and has to be done right in the right way for people to enjoy." So many people think of venison as tough and gamy, but Moore enjoyed changing their minds. "Once they taste a properly prepared, sustainable piece of venison, they're blown away."

Certainly this meal could make a convert. The color of each tenderloin slice ranged from almost black at the juniper crust to a warm pink in the center, and I could practically cut it with the side of my fork. It had a flavor very much like beef but with something slightly different about it, something specific to veni-son, interesting but reassuring. I didn't so much chew it as let it melt.

Far off, a herd of cattle moved across a hillside. There were lots of red cedar trees in sight—*Juniperus virginiana*, the ubiq-uitous fencerow evergreens that bear the juniper berries now shattering pleasantly between my teeth, a customary autumnal partner to venison.

The big table next to me had begun talking about how basket-ball has become a much higher-scoring game. One man declared he'd never worked so hard in his life. "I am consumed," he said. "It's so American."

Sitting there looking toward the mountains, it would not have surprised me if a deer—or several—had wandered out from the edge of the woods toward the vineyard. After those centuries of being overhunted first for their hides, again for their flesh, and finally protected by conservation, they are now as emblematic of this landscape as the cows and the cedar trees. But I knew the venison I ate was not from Virginia, nor even the United States. In order to anchor this small celebration of autumn in the Blue Ridge, in order to mingle on the same plate with traditional American flavors of juniper and apple and cranberry, this tender-loin had come from a farm in New Zealand: a place where the seasons are upside-down from the ones I know, a place where, at this moment, it was late spring.

What I was gazing at and what I was eating were, in a real way, the results of those acts by the early hunter-conservationists—a consequence they could never have dreamed.

For Moore to serve wild venison at Early Mountain would be illegal; the federal Lacey Act is still the law of the land and prevents the sale of wild game, a fact at odds with the winery's stated goal of using local ingredients. What if the law were differ-ent and he could offer meat from deer taken in this area, maybe even right here at the vineyard? Moore told me he still wouldn't do it. Actually, he seemed a little put off by the question.

"That's a wild animal," he said. "They could be starving, they could be hungry, they could have disease. The farmed ones are strong beautiful animals, as opposed to the deer you almost hit driving down the street. They're bred and taken care of and farmed for strictly that purpose, to be a beautiful piece of product." He'd found his reason: "That's the difference right there. There's no one taking care of the deer in the woods."

⚊

Learning about restocking had shifted my view of deer profoundly. Wild though they may be, any deer I see in my environment today likely owes its life to people. By first erasing, then redrawing the deer population, humans have permanently marked the very presence of the species. Whatever validity the previous subspecies designations had had, it was mostly made moot by the transfer of Great Lakes deer to the Appalachians, or Great Plains deer to New England. Deer scientists today still identify lingering effects of the genetic shakeup—for example, the timing of when deer go into rut. Deep within, deer's bodies remember their former homes.

If there's something unnatural about restocking, it's not only the idea of human meddling. Increasing the population of a large animal goes against the vast majority of our legacy as humans on the planet. With few exceptions, where we've gone, large animals have disappeared. So much of North America lost the native elk, bear, wolves, panthers, lynx, bison, moose. But we saved the deer—even if it meant they had to colonize new homes, like astronauts on an alien sphere. And it left them playing very odd roles in our economy.

The big party got up, gathering the terrier, slipping phones into pockets, and filtered away. Now I was the only diner on the patio. There were still some bites of venison left on my plate, this product of the globalized era, which Moore had said cost him around $28 a pound. A luxury meat that had flown eight thousand miles, crossing the equator and eighteen time zones, in order to land here in front of me.

"Everyone left us!" the server remarked to me, gathering empty glasses. The flames in the heaters still leapt; the land rolled away to the mountains. I had that same odd mix of feelings that's become the familiar response to our times: pleasure and a little subsequent guilt, an unease that's hard to place. *Bewilderment.*

But overall, I was strangely elated. I said, "I feel like I have the whole world to myself."

CHAPTER 5

Kinfolk

ANTLERS ON AN ALBUM COVER. DEER ON SHAMPOO BOT-tles. Fawn Ridge Drive on a map.

Writing about deer, I'd begun spotting them everywhere. Another winery near my house put up a new sign with an antlered buck logo. I'd learned that The White Hart is one of the most popular pub names in England. Deer turned up in coats of arms, on bottled water, on a hat worn by my kids' camp counselor.

They were ubiquitous icons, attractive but hollow. In art history, too, deer were abundant—as noble stags, bucolic ornaments, and fleeing quarry—though strangely, they almost always averted their eyes from the viewer. Their gaze implied that we, the onlookers, were not there. As though we could observe something without being noticed ourselves.

People once imagined deities in animal form. But humanoid gods have taken over, and animals themselves have been more and more commodified, their images reduced to symbolic or sentimental references. Old Anglo-Saxon surnames like Buck and Hart and Deere, originally adopted in honor of the animals, become empty signifiers, as generic as the monikers John and Jane Doe.

Our living connections to other beings have atrophied. Yet deer, themselves, are still living.

From the Song of Solomon: "My beloved is like a roe or a young deer. / Behold, he stands behind our wall! / He looks in at the windows. / He glances through the lattice."

It seemed to me, in light of all that had happened in this country between people and deer, that we'd forgotten something very important about them: that they have eyes of their own. Where, I wondered, were the deer who look in? If we were to converse with them like the beloveds they once were, what would that sound like?

⚬

One day in Charlottesville, near where I live, I noticed a mural by the artist Meesha Goldberg. Sprawling across a long, low wall, it showed a herd of running deer flanked by two limbs of a single word: KIN/FOLK.

Some months after I saw Meesha's mural, a friend sent me a photo of another of her pieces: an assemblage made of a long white dress, with two real deer legs where a woman's feet would be.

Intrigued, I wrote to Meesha, and she invited me to the farm outside town where she lives, to see her pieces and the landscape from which they grow. It was a home that felt, when I visited, as quietly intense as Meesha herself: a sprawling place of open pastures, swishing horses' tails, and sheltering woods. From a block of stone set into the ground, I stepped up into her spare wooden house, and she poured cups of tea. She was barefoot, with her black hair wound into coils.

She told me she'd grown up in about as different an atmosphere as one could find from the farm—Queens, New York—and had come to Virginia in 2017 after meeting her partner at the Standing Rock protests in North Dakota. Here she'd dived into a new life more dependent on her own labor than on the supermarket: growing vegetables, tending a milk cow, raising chickens for meat and eggs. And there was a porousness between these domestic foods and the world of beings beyond the house and barns. Crossing that ragged border, she would gather other foods, like mushrooms and berries.

"There's something special about wild food," she said. Her voice was low, unhurried; her gaze direct. "We get to participate in the generosity of the wild." There were many deer on the farm, too, and sometimes her partner would kill one for food, and Meesha would help with gutting and processing. That work, she said, "feels basic to being a human being. It reminds you of what life is."

Like many people who harvest their own food, she'd come to deeply ponder the nature of eating, and how interwoven it was with the ecological crisis. "Whatever you eat is becoming who you are," she said. "Especially coming from the city, I'm now realizing the life of our food. I feel like these experiences are really seeping into my art."

Several years earlier, she'd made a painting of two deer along with moon and sun images, thinking of them as "ancestral deer . . . part of the forest, an intrinsic energy." They were connected to a realm beneath—down under the soil, where traces of animals mingle with those of people. She was thinking about the earlier inhabitants of her land, the Monacans, who also ate venison. "For deer to be a primary food source in this area for millennia makes it an obvious relationship to be inspired by," she said. "They're kin animals." The word *kinfolk* on her mural nodded to that. It was a term she'd heard her rural neighbors use.

She continued, "One way they exist symbolically for me is that a deer could be right here, eating, and then they see you and snort and run off. They're just on the periphery of our lived world, and then they disappear. They're an ambassador from the wild."

As if on cue, she spotted two whitetails through the big kitchen window, melting in and out of the fence line at the edge of a field. An embassy. We got up and kept talking, leaning on the sink, watching for them to reappear.

She mused about how even as she consumed deer, living here had made her more aware of the seasons when they matured, grew antlers, raised young. We knelt on the floor and looked at a different piece, made of brown paper she'd drawn on with white pastel, cut patterned holes into, and sewn with white thread. A large central deer figure was surrounded by other running deer and their silhouettes and tracks: a delicate map of land, body, and material connections.

"These are tree rings," she said, pointing to a concentric pattern on the large deer's flank. "They're eating bushes and trees, so they are part tree; they're like a four-legged extension of trees." On the left was a map of the farm creek, interlacing with deer trails.

The mural project in Charlottesville included an acknowledgment of Monacan land and a donation of funds to the tribe. "Kinfolk," as a guiding principle, applied across groups of people as well as species. It seemed to take on an even greater dimension as Meesha unwrapped two other pieces—oil paintings—from a newer body of work called *Daughterland*, one that reckons with her own identity through intricately symbolic images of ceremonial Korean dresses. "My mother was born in Korea," she said, "and I realized I did have access to my own indigeneity. I can make a claim on my own ancestral culture, even though I'm displaced from it. I still come from an agrarian, shamanic culture with strong observances of the cycles of time, and sacred ways of interacting."

I thought of all the deer I'd found, in art, literature, commerce; deer who functioned as "a sight," something to view or to spot, ornaments or tokens. Meesha's white deer—"a messenger," she said, tapping into an ancient notion—gazed directly at the viewer from the dress's skirt. Here was a deer who looked back.

In these pieces, strong female hands, some of them clutching weapons, expressed resistance. But they played against the permeability of the faceless figures, with their skirts harboring animals like forests do, their arms and wombs holding babies.

"I like exploring that boundary of the wild and the domestic," she told me, "because that quality of being at home in nature is what's getting lost in humanity."

She took me out to an open-air kitchen in one end of a horse barn and fed me custard made from her cows' milk and her chickens' eggs, dotted with tiny sweet blueberries from her bushes.

The day was warm and green, and I thought of those deer we'd watched, somewhere nearby, enclosed in these environs of which they were made, and which they helped to make.

⚹

There's a growing recognition in both science and art that our centuries-old image of animals as nothing more than instinct-driven machines—that is, our denial of their capacity of mind—has been a grave mistake. Instead, we've begun to realize that animals can think, feel, plan, communicate, remember, and to some degree understand the inner experience of other beings. Biologists are documenting the fact that whales have culture. Decades of research have accumulated on the language powers of apes and parrots. But even supposedly lower animals, and for that matter plants, wind, rocks, and rivers, are being recognized as animate presences in the work of some thinkers today. In that sense, Western culture is coming around to something long considered fundamental in Indigenous traditions.

We really are relatives of deer, if we choose to remember it. Not only have we mingled our bodily lives with theirs (by eating their flesh, wearing their skins, following their paths), but we share with them, like other mammals, a deep evolutionary affinity. To be fellow warm-blooded creatures, with spines and placentas and hair, is like crouching together on a small, homey side-branch of the sprawling tree of life. Compared with bacteria, algae, even sharks and crows, hominids and cervids are extremely close cousins, much more similar than different.

In a very real sense, when we look at deer, we are looking in the mirror. So it makes perfect sense that we would be fascinated, disturbed, and aroused by their otherness.

"I have seen five necks rise like swaying snakes, a small snake-like head on each," wrote the nature writer Nan Shepherd about the hinds of her native Scotland. The alien sight inspired "some atavistic fear." But we might take our commonality with deer as a springboard in the other direction: a reason to see them as relations.

Real deer are more like Meesha's white messenger deer—with its forceful eye contact—than the deer in conventional art. Wary they may be, but they are not afraid to see us; keeping an eye on potential predators is one of their most basic survival moves.

I began to think about how that truth is embodied in the work of tracking them: If you want to get close to a deer, you need to understand its movements, but you won't gain that awareness without keeping in mind its reciprocal awareness of you. You have to stay quiet, consider your appearance, your scent, your way of moving. You have to see yourself as a deer would.

Though the art of tracking was historically a part of hunting (and still is), these days it's often studied as a pursuit in its own right. I did a quick search for tracking schools in my region and found at least four different operations offering workshops and lessons within a day's drive.

Like birding, tracking is a form of appreciation. But following animals on foot is also a basic mode of grasping that they, like us, look out at the world from inside a selfhood of their own.

Formal study aside, sometimes tracking lessons come un-sought, like one day when my daughter Elsie and I were in the creek, gathering wood nettles for tea.

They stung our hands only the tiniest bit at that time of year—mid-May, with the heavy scent of multiflora rose in the air. The creek seemed a little low. My bag was already full of nettles, so I stopped trying to spot their toothy leaves among the other low-growing plants near the water. Instead I let my eyes wander over the shards of quartz and granite in the creek bed, the basswood trees on the bank, and the spicebush that grows on the flat shelf of ground above.

And then, like a pattern emerging from a field of dots, some-thing gently announced itself to me: a series of broken plants, a slightly worn track on the ground, and a subtle thought that didn't exactly have a physical mark, but arose from this short, steep bank of the creek. *If I were a deer, I'd climb out of the water right there.* The evidence cooperated with the thought, murmuring small facts, as though the ground itself were answering. *A deer* did *climb up right here.* Elsie and I followed.

We were soon at the top of the bank. I've noticed that deer trails are often clearest on steep ground; once the track mounts to the flat, it gets fainter. Still, through some combination of visuals and instinct, we were more or less able to find our way as the deer had done.

A few months earlier, I'd asked an expert tracker how to find evidence of deer on my property. One of his recommendations was to walk bent over, with my face at about the height of a deer's face—to try to see, at least crudely, as a deer would see. Now I bent over because I remembered his advice, and also because I had no choice: the trail led uphill again through tangles of thorny greenbrier and other pricklies that forced me to duck and twist myself sideways. This was one of the corners of our land that I was pretty sure I had never walked before, a spot that didn't invite human travel at all. Maybe there was also food for deer along this route, or evidence of their browsing, though I was feeling too cramped to stop and search for it. Elsie, petite at ten years old, had an easier passage. I was relieved when I was able to stand up straight again.

And as soon as I did, I had a little revelation. I was standing next to a deer bed. And just off to my right, there was a second one. Looking at the ground in these two places—about six feet apart—it was totally obvious that these were twin spots where deer had slept within the last few hours.

Each bed consisted of an oval of flattened ground cover. One had some bare ground and a few ankle-high wingstem plants that were broken in half, recently enough to have barely begun to wilt. The other pressed into a thick mat of prolific light green weeds called, fittingly, bedstraw. It had made quite a soft place for a deer to lie: its body, curled on the ground, very similar to my own in size and weight.

On the first bed, Elsie and I spotted something else—long white and brown hairs, coarse and individual, scattered on the earth. It was intimate, electrifying, as though the deer had written its name here. I got down on my knees and sniffed at the spot, but my nose wasn't sharp enough to catch the deer's scent. I knew that if the deer returned here, though, it would certainly smell me. Suddenly I felt like I was being incredibly rude—as though I had climbed between a stranger's sheets while she was off at work.

From this spot, I could see places where my family and I often walk: a big boulder my kids like to climb on, the path we usually follow to the back corner of our land. This was part of our place and yet not ours at all. Branches and vines arched over our heads and screened us from the more open areas just a few feet away. The deer must have been so nicely hidden in here, able to see our human spots without being seen.

Like their trails, deer beds can be used by many generations of animals; they are part of a relationship between deer and land that may span a greater time scale than the life of any one animal. The beds were in a secret place I had never given a thought to before, a spot that had always been blank on my mental map, its use a minor exercise of animal genius.

❦

Humans tend to make everything into stories. In fact, it may be that the act of tracking game was the very thing that signaled the beginning of abstraction in the early human mind. Hoofprints, droppings, signs of browse—if these mean "deer" to us, it's because we have learned to make them into symbols, detached, in a way, from their context. Real and abstract: another knife's edge on which deer seem to balance.

Science is becoming more and more tuned into the symbiosis and cross-species interaction that is key to every level of life on this planet—how we are, in Aldo Leopold's phrase, "fellow-voyageurs with other creatures in the odyssey of evolution." If we can't help telling stories and gleaning symbols from the world, can we somehow put our abstractions to work in the service of connection, rather than distance? Can we avoid getting carried away from our sense of animals as subjects?

Gary Snyder writes the question in mythological terms: "Once every year, the Deer catch human beings. They do various things which irresistibly draw men near them; each one selects a certain man. The Deer shoots the man, who is then compelled to skin it and carry its meat home and eat it. Then the Deer is inside the man."

I once read an interview with the wildlife researcher Joe Hutto, who spent nine years studying mule deer in Wyoming, spending enormous amounts of time very close to the deer. He'd said, "I realized that if I crouched down next to the mule deer at eye level and scratched their necks, they would start either nibbling on me or grooming me with their tongues, as if I were family. I had known many of them since they were born." When a deer dies, he observed, "The change that occurs in the survivors is palpable. I don't know whether to call it grief or confusion or something else; it doesn't matter."

Of course deer are not humans, but perhaps we are lurching toward a readiness to acknowledge that they are persons.

⚹

No discussion of intimacy with deer could leave out hunters—a large contingent of people who, right here in the twenty-first century, know what it's like to put their hands on a still-warm deer, make a slit in the skin, cut up the meat that they'll eat. This is a form of connection as clear to the many who practice it as it is alien to others.

The continued existence of hunting, in our hypertechnological world, is one of those cultural wedges that, on the surface, breaks things very starkly: the urban cleaves from the rural, the gun owner from the vegan. But such divisions are never as simple as they seem. Hunting was adjacent to many of the living connections I was finding to deer—adjacent to tracking, to Meesha's artwork, and to Gary Snyder's words. And later, though it made me wary, I would investigate hunting directly.

First, though, there was something else I wanted to chase down.

◍

Ever since I'd watched Mary Kate Claytor tanning that hide, the image of her stretching the deerskin over her bone awl had stayed with me. It wasn't exactly that I kept seeing the action run like a film; more that I kept feeling the tool in my own hand. Then there was that list of 101 uses for a deer. It came from the *Bulletin of Primitive Technology*, not a scholarly journal but a manifestation of a strange and intriguing subculture that, like the awl, had lingered in the back of my mind.

And now here I was, sitting under a tent, feeling oddly surprised. I'd just looked down at my hand and found an awl that I myself had apparently made.

The tent was really just a piece of canvas stretched over rough wooden poles, and I sat beneath it with about eight other people. We were cross-legged on the ground in a ragged circle. For the last couple of hours, we'd been learning, from a man in buckskin shorts, how to make awls.

It was the first morning of my first-ever primitive skills gathering (also known in the movement as earthskills or ancestral skills). I'd traveled here, to the mountains of North Carolina, in order to spend nights camping in a field with hundreds of other people, and days taking classes on things that humans have been doing for millennia.

It was the most frankly countercultural scene I'd been in for a long time, a world in which fires were started by friction and my flashlight seemed out of place; everyone else found their way by moonlight. We started each day by gathering around a central fire pit, called there by blasts on a conch shell. We slept, sat, and ate on the ground. There wasn't a cell phone in sight—phones didn't work here, and anyway there was no place to plug them in. There were a lot of bare feet, a lot of buckskin, a lot of feathers in hats. The vibe was communal and joyful. If the gathering had a hedonistic edge, it mostly tended toward the wholesome: a little skinny-dipping here, some spontaneous ocarina playing there.

The talk around me was laced with mentions of native herbs and homesteading and rabbit snares. Once I overheard two people discussing supplies for very long road trips. One of them was about to travel out west, and the other seemed to live out of a car full-time. "What's your diet?" asked the latter. "Do you eat meat or dairy?"

"No," answered the first, "not unless I take part in the hunting, skinning, or butchering, and it's not often that that happens."

"Do you want to help me skin a squirrel?"

As for the class list, deer were liberally sprinkled throughout, befitting their role as all-purpose preindustrial provider. These gatherings are a growing movement, with dozens every year around the U.S. and abroad, and for those who want to taste a hunter-gatherer mode of being, chances are good they'll be dealing somehow with deer parts or their acquisition. My first stop was under this tent, in a bone awl workshop.

"Harder and sharper than wood, less brittle than stone, bone meets a material niche in ancestral skills and working with it helps us connect with the greater gifts of our animal kin," the class description said. The session began with Josh Barnwell, the instructor, spilling out a pile of bones onto a canvas sheet on the ground. They were raw-looking, in shades of ecru and mauve, and each one was really a pair—the ulna and radius from a deer's foreleg, fused by tough connective tissue.

Josh had some pretty intense visual aids for the anatomy part of the lesson: he picked up a deer's hoof and several inches of furry lower leg connected to a naked white bone, then fit it together like a puzzle with the meaty top and shoulder of a different leg, this one blackened by fire. "Someone brought in a car-killed deer last night and we ate some of it for dinner," he said matter-of-factly. He used a sharp knife to slice away the meat from the radius and ulna, the same bones we'd be working with. "That'll be lunch."

He was probably not yet forty, confident, warm, with a partially shaved head and a tree tattoo on his upper arm. "Find a bone that calls to you," he told us, and each of us took one from the pile.

Our first step was to separate the two bones by cutting through the connective tissue. I soon settled into what I realized would be a long, repetitive task. At their ends, the bones fit together so tightly it was hard even to find the seam. Along their length, the narrow gap between them was entirely filled with sinew. I made tiny strokes with a craft knife into those steely fibers: dozens of strokes, hundreds of strokes, and once in a while a fragment came loose and I picked or peeled it away.

The work wasn't tedious, though. It felt good; it was pleasure. As soon as I'd touched the bones I'd noticed that they felt slightly greasy, and while I worked my hands were picking up that oil, with its smell somewhere between leather and venison. The essential oil of what deer eat and are, a scent as unique as pine.

Josh told us these bones came from deer he'd picked up by the side of the road. He said he did this eight or ten times a year, providing food and materials for many kinds of projects. "Every year, I think, 'This is the year I'm going to hunt,'" he said. "But I haven't hunted yet because cars keep doing the killing for me."

We scraped and scraped. Eventually one woman got to the next step: bone-sawing through the thinnest part of the ulna and then levering half of it up and away from the radius, with a meaty ripping sound. Everyone applauded, like she'd pulled the sword from the stone. I thought of Emily Dickinson's line "And all our Sinew tore—" It's from a poem of grief, the dismemberment of the heart. No accident that as we sat, most of us still working to separate one bone from another, we began talking about death. How our culture denies it. How, as life's necessary partner, death is actually very sacred.

Here was the idea that was new to me, though: that shaping and using animal parts, making things that could support human life, might be a way to honor and accept death itself. Somewhere near Josh's home, a deer had died a bad death, and now I was getting to know, quite intimately, part of its body, dismantling this structure in what might have been a form of atonement.

Finally, suddenly, the ulna came free. It was time to take up sandpaper and begin to shape the awl. Fairly quickly I sanded a slender, tapered point onto the end of the bone. The sandpaper was just regular old 80-grit from a hardware store, and someone asked what you could use if you wanted to avoid this modern product. Josh replied that you could take a piece of buckskin, get it wet, and then dip it in sand. "Bone is shaped more by abrading than by cutting or chipping," he said.

He told us he'd been developing these skills since childhood, when he first got interested in edible wild plants, and attending gatherings since he was a teenager.

Listening to him describe a life that revolved around processing deer and making things from their parts, I asked myself what I used my own hands for, and the first thing that came to mind was "typing." It's not often that I actually make an object, and I didn't think I'd ever made a tool before.

Which is why it caught me off guard to look down, a while later, and find a finished awl in my hand.

I'd sharpened the point until it was pretty fearsome, and I'd spent a long time polishing the surfaces, removing all the sinew I could with knife, sandpaper, and thumbnail. But the best thing—the eerie thing—was how the handle end needed no shaping whatsoever. It was already a perfect fit for my hand. There was a flattish, wing-shaped butt end that rested in my palm, and the protrusions on the underside, where it had fused with the radius, made grips for each finger to wrap around. It was made by the deer—not for me, surely, though it was hard to ignore its precise correspondence to my own anatomy. To hold it was a bodily embrace.

◊

I spent another couple of days at the gathering, sinking out of my usual sense of time, enjoying the anachronisms, and how I sometimes forgot which way they went. I made a pouch from rawhide that still had some fur on it, and I watched some women scraping deerskins over PVC beams. A four-year-old child chewed dreamily on some jerky, then fell asleep on a piece of buckskin dyed by acorns. Down the hill, there were several camper vans parked in a semicircle with antlers on their dashboards. In the tent where crafts were for sale, I looked at antler fridge magnets, expensive luxurious rolls of buckskin, buckskin anklets decorated with deer hoof rattles.

I had discovered another borderland occupied by deer. In this gathering, we were hovering somewhere between nostalgia and preparation. The movement had a complicated relationship with the past, as well as with Indigenous people of the present. Certainly there were Native people here, to teach and learn. And like many other organizations, the gathering was actively trying to correct for its overall whiteness. But what did it mean for a person like me, whose European ancestors had probably stopped making things from bone several thousand years ago, to fashion that awl? And were we here for enjoyment, or was it something more serious?

"These are skills that humans need," my neighbor in the camping field told me in sober tones. "We don't know what's to come." One class was taught by a man who said he'd foraged or grown 100 percent of his food for an entire year. Certainly, I thought, knowing how to hunt and process deer would put that kind of self-reliance within much closer reach.

It was another aspect of life among the ruins. For those who peer into the future—with climate crisis, social instability, and pandemics bearing down—and conclude that survival will mean going back to the land, a gathering like this might serve as a kind of boot camp. In this corner of our culture, just as for so many people through history, reliance on deer means a way to stay alive.

I kept thinking of something Josh had said near the end of his session. There had been a little contented silence while all of us were absorbed in sanding our awls, the dust of deer bones drifting down into the soil. "I always feel like it's a such a human thing," he'd said suddenly, "to be sitting in a circle, working on something."

◑

I went out to look for my younger daughter in the yard the other day, and found her digging a hole with a deer antler. Under the green plastic slide, wearing an old hockey T-shirt, she was scraping away at the ground with the antler's biggest, sharpest point.

It was working very well to loosen the soil, though a little slower than a metal trowel would have been. She'd scrape for a while, then scoop out the dirt with a thick, broken clamshell we brought home from the beach this summer.

"Wow, you're really doing it the hunter-gatherer way," I said.

"Really?" she said. She hadn't thought of that. It had just seemed right.

Part II
Struggling

CHAPTER 6

Capacity

WHAT MAKES A FOREST? THIS ONE HAD TREES, CERTAINLY:
maples, hickories, oaks.

They covered a twenty-acre wedge of rolling ground. A creek
cut a ravine through the red shale earth, and there was plenty
of shade down under the canopy. This was a blank spot amid
the bustle and press of a dense New Jersey township—two highways, a strip mall, and a state police barracks.

I was wandering among the trees behind a tall man named Jay
Kelly, whose bushy ponytail reached nearly to his waist. It was
easy to move here, easy to see. We had no need for a trail. We'd
part ways briefly, taking different paths around a shagbark or a
red oak, then come back together. No brambles tugged at us; the
ground was a uniform brown, covered in desiccated leaves and
spent acorn shells.

Kelly waved a flannel-shirted arm at the open space around
us. "There's nothing in the understory," he said. Beneath the
trees, these woods were full of emptiness.

Under my feet, I could see places where recent rains had
carved through the leaf litter, exposing the earth.

A forest is made by multiple layers—tall trees, shorter shrubs,
and a diversity of ground-level plants. The world belowground,
too (mycorrhizal fungi, roots, cicada larvae, voles) is intimately
conversant with the layers of the air. It is a system of systems.
Kelly was here to show me what it looks like when entire parts
of the system go missing. In this drab little park forty-five miles

from Manhattan, he was explaining, dense concentrations of deer were wiping out all the vegetation they could reach.

"You shouldn't be able to see ten feet into this forest," he said. But we could see a long way in every direction: across the ravine, up and down the slopes to the soccer field beyond.

The place was hardly unique. This is a common condition throughout the more populous areas of the eastern U.S.

"Deer prefer some species over others—because of nutrition, habit, or whatever—so when deer populations grow, those are the first things that begin to decline," Kelly had said before we arrived here. He named trees, like hemlocks and dogwoods, and wildflowers: trilliums and lilies. "But when deer get to densities around twenty per square mile, you see impacts throughout the forest ecosystem. Vegetation as a whole begins to be consumed at excessive levels, and then everything that depends on that vegetation—which is everything in the forest—starts to show impacts as well."

As we walked, both of us spotted deer evidence. I saw their tracks all over the ground, among the flakes of shale and broken glass. Kelly, an ecologist and professor, was attuned to other kinds of signs.

He reached for a low shrub, a native blackhaw viburnum. Its bushy shape was the result of repeated pruning by deer incisors. "It's being kept at knee height," he said. A few feet away, he found its parent plant—this one taller than Kelly himself, but with all its branches held high, like someone wading through a flood with a bundle on their head. "All the lower branches have been browsed," Kelly explained. "And the seedlings get mowed down every year. The next generation won't get tall enough to reproduce."

A forest is also made by multiple layers in time: the mature shrub forming its seeds, counting on some of them to grow, reach maturity themselves, and carry on the cycle. Because of high deer densities—more than a hundred per square mile in this part of New Jersey, five times what Kelly had said was the threshold for ecosystem damage—this forest was losing its ability to extend itself into the future. Oaks were at risk too. So were birds.

"Caterpillars of moths or butterflies are highly specialized," Kelly explained, "so if plants begin to decline, then caterpillars decline. And then birds that eat the caterpillars decline." Ground-level insects and arthropods suffer, too. Soil-level microclimates change. Water runs off differently. Temperatures fluctuate more sharply. Seeds have trouble germinating. In high numbers, deer—just by living and eating—can transform, in every facet, the character of the woods.

They can also make forests less resilient against pests and climate events. A thinner forest stores less carbon, too, potentially speeding up climate change.

After our walk, I would stand next to my parked car and notice how, from the outside, these woods seemed to sink away from the eye. What came forward was the divided highway and everything bellied up to it—a tire store, a dance studio—while the trees receded into a kind of nothingness.

But for now, we were still inside the forest. It had an addled, uneasy feeling. Traffic noise soaked in from the edges. At the lip of the ravine, a rusty upturned shopping cart leaned against a sapling.

Kelly grew up in this part of New Jersey, at a time when deer were scarce. "I distinctly remember the first time I saw a deer," he said. "I was nineteen years old." These days, the kids turning up in his classroom have been raised in a different reality: New Jersey's deer have been overabundant for thirty years, and hard-bitten forests like this one seem normal to many people living here. For a professor to bring students into a forest like this and talk about deer impacts is to trouble the young people's basic sense of *what nature is like*. It makes strange the woods that form the daily backdrop to their human world. "You have to explain the absence of things," he said.

Also the unwelcome presence. Where the native flowers and tree seedlings were missing, invasive plants like stiltgrass had moved in. He showed me a place where an old tree had fallen. "This is a light gap"—a break in the canopy where sun flooded the ground. "It should be a dense growth of young trees, but instead it's a dense growth of invasives. More of our forests are turning into messes of invasive plants," he said. "It's hard not to despair."

Despite a ready smile, and that extravagant plume of hair, Kelly struck me as a sober-minded person. He answered all my questions with great care; his language was precise. But later, when I looked back at my notes, I kept finding words like that— "despair." "Depressing." "Alarming." "Devastating." He'd gotten interested in deer populations years earlier when he was doing rare plant surveys and realized that many species were at risk from deer and a host of other pressures—climate change, invasives, human influence of all kinds. Now, after years of research, he had arrived at the conclusion that forests, at least in this part of the world, were in grave trouble.

We stood next to the creek, with its eroded red banks, and he said, "It's like a ghost forest."

That didn't seem quite right to me. A forest is made of layers of life and death, a churn of force and energy that forms a complex equation, always changing and exchanging. A ghost is simpler—a remnant of something that has died. And there was still a lot of life here.

Much of that was in the form of deer. Because of them, the forest was evolving in a direction that none of us would recognize as normal.

◖◗

It's not hard to find scientists like Kelly who will talk passionately, and convincingly, about overabundant deer. In the last century, a steady torrent of research has tried to pin down exactly how deer affect their habitat; they are one of the most heavily studied animals in the world. Yet a fog of uncertainty continues to hang over these animals. Even when they are right there behind the screened porch, eating the hydrangeas, they still confound us.

There's a general ecological law that says prey animals are more numerous than predators. It's also prey animals that tend to be capable of *irruption*: that is, rapid and unchecked growth in numbers. Absent some sort of external control on their population, deer are one of the animals that can breed themselves into a very crowded situation within a very short time.

At the fenced 1,146-acre George Reserve in Michigan, a seed population of 6 deer ballooned to about 220 only seven years later. It's a little harder to observe, but no less real, when an unfenced deer population irrupts. A deer herd may grow dramatically inside the safe zone of a national park, where hunting is prohibited. Similarly, if a suburban community outlaws hunting or makes it very impractical, its deer numbers are likely to jump.

Deer brim with life that is destined to transmute itself into life for other, fiercer animals. To subtract predators from this equation is as seismic as to buckle the crust of the earth. Those twentieth-century deer were actors in the wrong play. The scenery had blinked out around them, then reemerged in alien form. Clear-cut forests were growing back, creating a temporary bounty of food. The engines of their bodies kept going, running on biological genius. They ate, digested, bore young, and nursed. All around them was a shifting world, sometimes helpful, sometimes hostile.

In the world of deer science, people have been preoccupied with population numbers for decades. Even as early as 1928, when restocking was just getting underway, some observers were already predicting trouble. Even as deer numbers burgeoned, human worlds extended, one cul-de-sac at a time, into their habitats.

Among the general public, perceptions of deer changed quickly from one generation to the next—sort of like the way photos of a small-town Main Street, then and now, seem like totally different places. My grandparents likely imagined deer as rare, maybe even something to be longed for. By the time I was born in the '70s, they were common. By my high school years, people thought of them almost as vermin. The term *overpopulated* began to reliably appear in the conversation. They had increased at a speed that seemed unsettling when measured on the scale of a human lifetime.

In places like the park I walked through with Jay Kelly, *overabundance* is a label that seems clearly to fit. More broadly, when I began researching this book, I more or less assumed that that were too many deer in general in the U.S. I'd heard people say that so many times.

My own perception shifted early on when a wildlife manager explained the difference between biological carrying capacity—the number of deer the land can sustain—and cultural carrying capacity, the human tolerance for deer. The second number, he noted, tends to be much lower than the first.

That intrigued me. But still, I naively assumed that biological carrying capacity would be a fairly straightforward measurement—a known quantity I could find in a textbook, a tool as simple as a hammer. I was soon to realize that despite a vast literature on the subject, the question of deer in ecosystems is anything but settled.

How many deer are too many? Everyone agrees that areas with three hundred deer per square mile—a density that has occurred in certain places, and still does—are radically overpopulated. But even numbers over ten or twenty per square mile have been called overabundant. Biological carrying capacity isn't a tool like a hammer. It's more like a Swiss Army knife: a complex thing with many moving parts.

᪥

I spent months combing through deer studies, reading about the animals' destructive effects around the U.S. and the globe. Deer preventing the world's most massive organism, a millennia-old stand of quaking aspen clones in Utah, from regenerating. Deer shrinking and thinning shrub cover in the U.K., or being named Australia's worst emerging pest problem. Yet I found other studies suggesting that the presence of deer might actually be helpful to trees, to salamanders, to birds.

Disagreement on the particulars is one thing, but then there are deeper questions.

The idea of natural balance is enough of a cultural given that it shows up on cereal boxes as easily as it undergirds scientific research. It's that myth of Eden again: Things are supposed to work out neatly, stably, with elements interlocking like the cells in a well-tuned spreadsheet. But they don't. Ecological balance is far more layered than a simple idea of prey animals being evenly weighted with predators, or a place having "enough" plants to support the "right" number of deer. For any given species, there's a panoply of factors at play, an exquisitely tangled web of relationships within the flow of time. Across a world of change, rapid or slow, no baseline is truly stable.

In the late twentieth century—after decades of research detailing how deer injure habitats on multiple levels—some ecologists started to map this vast complexity, often using the new tool of computer modeling. No one argued that deer couldn't affect vegetation. The questions dealt more with what those effects really meant. "Natural systems are more complex than we would like to admit," read one study, explaining that human disturbance had shifted the entire system to a different state, governed by novel dynamics we couldn't yet understand. Change bred change. There was something almost Buddhist about these ideas. Or maybe a better analogy would be quantum physics, with its revelation of profound uncertainty.

These days, the leading edge of environmental thought asks not how to restore what's been lost, but how we can move forward given what seems to be the law of indeterminacy. Yet much of the research on deer still retains an air of clear-cut judgment.

What's more, it summons sorrow, distress, and rage. The language is tender with association. A *depauperate* forest: sadness. A future *monoculture* of black cherry trees, in a forest that once held oaks and maples and dozens of other species: deprivation. *Songbirds* in trouble: the urge to rescue music.

At a conference, I listened to one well-known researcher label certain habitats in Pennsylvania "crap," laying bare his desires, fears, and nostalgia. Wild berries could no longer flower and fruit, he warned, adding that soon there will be "no children picking blueberries for their mothers' muffins."

This kind of loss is real, and it's right for us to grieve it. Our old human longing for something eternal is always at play, even for scientists. We want to belong on the Earth, we want the Earth to take care of us, and when we confront what's broken, we start looking for a fix.

If our task is adaptation—figuring out how to live with the scars—we might have a lot to learn from deer.

Adaptation is fundamental to life on earth, but some species are better at it than others. Many deer species happen to be *very* good at it. In the U.S., whitetails especially are absolute masters of adaptation. They'll put up with noise and roads, and they produce even more fawns in town than in the country. Like their predator counterpart, the coyote, they have proven brilliantly able to remake their way of life—to reinvent what it means to be a deer. As long as there is about a one-mile radius of land through which a whitetail can roam, with something to eat and somewhere to sleep, that deer has a great chance of survival. The territory can include dangers (cars, fences, rifle fire in November), but most deer will still live long enough to reproduce.

They have a practical intelligence. The noise of chainsaws is said to be a dinner bell for deer, drawing them to the fresh browse they'll find when loggers have finished their work. They eat a wider range of foods than most people realize: not only plants but also mushrooms, insects, bird eggs. They may even be able to turn climate change to their advantage—giving birth later in the year, surviving winters more easily.

Urban ecologists, especially, seem to describe things observationally rather than negatively. Deer are generalists. They are "cosmopolitan" inhabitants of "novel ecosystems." Deer are "synanthropes" (animals, like raccoons and rats, that are well-suited to life near humans; the word comes from *syn-*, with, and *anthropos*, person). They are "protean"—an unfinished, improvisatory species, not consigned to a fixed place in the world but endlessly able to change their costumes and play a new role.

Thoreau's "maimed and imperfect nature" still surrounds us, and nature can heal, but that doesn't mean the old nature will come back. Something else will develop instead: life among the ruins.

We might try on this view: Deer are Anthropocene heroes. They are mashup-makers, remixers, shape-shifters, contemporary masters of disguise.

What animal could be a more perfect emblem for our own selves? Our precarious, fluctuating state?

CHAPTER 7

Decline

IT WAS ALREADY DARK WHEN MY FAMILY AND I CLIMBED into the big white pickup truck with Marcelo Jorge. A drizzly May night in the Ozarks; everything seemed soggy and muted. Jorge was upbeat, though. His work was going well. It was the peak of fawning season, and so far this year his team had captured and collared a dozen fawns.

Jorge had invited us to observe an evening of fawn work in a wildlife management area here in northwest Arkansas—part of a multiyear study he was leading for his PhD research through the University of Georgia. The study's focus was chronic wasting disease, a neurological illness that kills every deer it infects.

From its first appearance in Colorado in the late 1960s, CWD has crawled steadily across the country, and it is now found in more than twenty-five states and two Canadian provinces, as well as Scandinavia and South Korea. This study—a big one, pulling in state, federal, and academic partners—would try to answer a whole slate of questions about how CWD spreads, how it changes deer populations, and whether there is anything people can do about it. Heroes of adaptation they may be, but in CWD, deer face a serious threat.

We went bumping along dark gravel roads that threaded the forest; upslope, downhill, near rushing creeks and along the flanks of steep dolomite hills. Forest crowded the roads on both sides. Prescribed burns by the state's wildlife agency, Jorge told us, helped support the local deer. But CWD was likely pulling the numbers the other way. In this part of Arkansas, CWD wasn't detected until 2016, but the state soon learned it had likely been in the area for decades and was infecting more than one in five deer.

This area was, he said, Arkansas's "epicenter" for CWD, and the state wanted to know what that would mean for the future of both deer and hunting. The disease is caused not by a virus or bacteria but by a misfolded protein called a prion, which deer transmit through direct contact or by shedding prions into the environment. Ingested or inhaled, the prions cause no mischief at first but eventually eat away at the animal's brain and spinal cord, leaving it confused, weak, and physically wasting away. Eventually it dies. There is no treatment, and most ominously of all, the prions can bind with soil, where they remain viable for more than a decade and can even be taken up by plants, waiting in the leaves to infect more animals. Any member of the cervid family, including elk and moose, can be infected.

It's the deer equivalent of mad cow disease, and though it's never been known to jump to a human, the possibility lurks like a black cloud at the edge of the conversation.

"It seems like a juggernaut of a disease," Jorge told me. "It's a very insidious and scary thing."

It had taken Jorge a while to explain the scope of this intensely complex study. His team was in year two of a four-year process of capturing and collaring adult deer and fawns. They had also installed more than two hundred game cameras at three different sites. All of this would help them monitor the movements and health of individual deer, building a high-resolution picture of how fast the disease spreads. Just in year one, his cameras had captured over a million photos, every one of which would be examined individually. Then there were blood and tissue samples, genetic information, the weights of individual deer, cross-references between photos and GPS collars. It was big data for deer.

As we drove, we followed another truck in which Jorge's wife and senior research associate, Lisa Jorge, rode with two young biology grads working as field techs. Actually, all these scientists were on the young side; Jorge was the oldest at thirty-three. This was not work for people who prize an early bedtime.

Every so often, we'd see the other truck's brake lights come on, and its three occupants would emerge to stand on the running boards and peer into the woods through what looked like telescopes. In fact, they were thermal scopes that pick up heat; behind me, my kids and husband were passing around another scope, seeing occasional white silhouettes against the black of the woods. The researchers wanted to find does, because does could lead them to fawns. Sometimes they'd catch a promising glimpse and one of them, a tech named Parker, would trek off on foot, his flashlight beam sliding between the trees, then come back shaking his head. And off we'd go again.

"It's a lot of stopping and getting out," said Jorge. "And then sometimes you get lucky."

So far tonight, we were striking out. But he felt the team was on track to capture about fifty fawns this year, and they already had collars on about sixty other deer of different ages. Adult deer are hard to capture; it takes tranquilizer darts, nets, and traps. For fawns, the team had another trick: when capturing adult does, they'd inserted vaginal implant transmitters (VITs) that would alert them when each doe gave birth. These are about six inches long and T-shaped, with wings that fold out when inserted, and they contain a battery, a microchip, and a little antenna. During birth, the VIT pops out, registers the change in light and temperature, and sends an email to the researchers, urgent-looking text on a red background: IMPLANT EXPELLED! Then, using the doe's GPS collar, the team can go to her location and look around for her fawn.

Bearded and chatty, Jorge had a lot to say about this work—every aspect from data sets to public relations, enough to easily fill more than an hour of crunching slowly along the gravel. But after a lot of false alarms, the team figured we'd want to get some sleep. It was after ten. We were nearly back to our campsite when they stopped once more. Again the careful peering; again

Parker's light, bobbing through the woods. And this time a quiet call: "Fawn!"

That single word dispersed the tedium in an instant. Lisa and the other tech, Eva, were already scrambling out of their truck and grabbing backpacks, moving fast like firefighters. We hurried to follow, mounting a steep, slick bank before we saw Lisa and the techs kneeling on the ground over a small, gray fabric bag. Lying on it was a fawn, perfect and fine-boned, curled in a crescent.

Instinctively, my family and I stood back a little. Six hands in latex gloves were all working at once. There was an efficiency to the researchers' movements—like medics in an emergency— that we didn't want to interrupt. I could see they'd done all this before. The fawn already had a soft black hood over her eyes to keep her calm; deft hands slipped an expandable collar around her neck, its black antenna absurdly sticking up.

In a pool of light, blue fingers probed the hooves, and Jorge explained, "They can get a rough estimate of when it was born, because the hooves harden with time." These were soft, and the stump at the navel was still fresh and pink, so Eva wrote on a clipboard that this female fawn was just a few hours old. Somewhere nearby, her mother must have been watching us, unable to see her baby through this human thicket.

"We wear gloves to make sure we don't leave our scent on them," Jorge told us. For the same reason, Parker had moved the fawn twenty or so feet away from where he'd found her. Tools came out of a full pack tossed on the ground. A pair of pliers; plastic bags; a tag with the number 843. Everyone's voices were hushed. The fawn's DNA was sampled, she was checked for ticks, she was weighed and photographed, her spine and neck girth and legs were measured. The whole thing was over in less than five minutes.

"She's a little scrawny," Jorge observed.

"But still big," Lisa answered, referring to the fawn's body length.

As long as the fawn kept her white spots, they'd function as a full-body-size fingerprint, allowing the researchers to identify her on camera. "There's a little swish at the top there," Jorge said, pointing to where a few spots ran together on her shoulder.

This whole time—deploying the only possible defense strategy available to her at such a tender age—the fawn hadn't moved an inch. She was totally quiet, limp, an inert little lump of life. When the hood came off, her eyes were open, but she never made a sound. For a few suspended moments, we were all silent, like her. I heard an airplane drone through the dark sky overhead. Then Lisa cradled the fawn in both hands and carefully walked her back to where Parker had found her.

⚜

The fawn had somewhere around a one-in-two chance of surviving until fall. Two of this year's twelve fawn captures had already died; one of them was eaten by a bobcat within a couple of hours of birth. (Predators and scavengers are another means by which CWD can be spread; if a CWD-positive deer carcass is eaten by a migrating eagle, say, it's possible that the prions could even move across international lines.) One of the team's major goals was to understand how fawns would fare if they were born to diseased mothers. "Do the mothers choose poor sites to give birth?" Jorge asked. "And if their fat content is wasting away, do they have the nutritional capacity to maintain those fawns? Long term, is the population going to start slowly decreasing over time, because mothers can't get their young into adulthood?"

As CWD has moved around the U.S., it's brought human concern and confusion in its wake. Jorge and others have compared the situation to the COVID pandemic: Each state creates its own regulations, with no coherent national policy, and the public is often skeptical. There are deniers. "There's controversy, misinformation, public trust and distrust," Jorge told me. "It's mirrored in many ways."

A major vector for CWD is thought to be the transport of captive deer by the deer farm industry. State wildlife agencies find themselves trying to contain the disease in areas where captive deer have tested positive, but it's no simple task. Jeannine Fleegle, a wildlife official in Pennsylvania, told me that all but one of her state's disease management areas were established because of a positive CWD test on a deer farm. "If you want to back-calculate, think of all the resources that have to be put into a management area if one of those facilities goes positive," she said. "It's not like they don't escape. There are a lot of trees, and they fall on fences. There's no way you can say 'That facility tested positive, but it's [only] inside the fence.' It's just so frustrating."

The industry denies that farms are a problem, saying that because deer farmers are required to test all their animals regularly, it shouldn't be a surprise that CWD turns up on farms more often than in the wild. Farmers complain that quarantine requirements are overly harsh and threaten their businesses. Yet when captive deer are sold, they may get driven long distances, possibly carrying prions with them. One Wisconsin deer farm discovered an outbreak of CWD among its animals in 2021; officials soon realized that over the previous half decade, the farm had shipped nearly four hundred potentially infected deer around Wisconsin and to six other states.

There's a fundamental disagreement here about whether it's acceptable to put a native wildlife species behind fences, making the animals private property. Most wildlife officials find the idea repellent.

Because the disease can be transmitted by a positive animal long before it causes symptoms, it's especially hard for wildlife agencies to get a handle on what's happening with deer in a given area. Like Arkansas, many states have found themselves waking up to the problem long after CWD had already arrived. Fleegle told me, "We can't see them until it's too late. Once you have it, it's very difficult to keep up with it. You're often behind the eight ball." She added, "I wish the disease would evolve to make them sicker faster."

A mostly invisible, universally fatal disease that persists in the environment for years: This sounds like a recipe for disaster. I'd been thinking of deer as one of evolution's best survivors, and I'd taken it for granted, even knowing about their former declines, that now they were safe. That they weren't going anywhere. But now I found myself asking Jorge a question that had never even crossed my mind before: Could CWD actually cause the extinction of deer?

"I think it's a possibility that is on the table," he said. But he emphasized that extinction is only one of a spectrum of outcomes, and no one really knows what will happen. Some research suggests that certain deer are genetically less susceptible to the disease. Or the species could limp along in a diminished fashion. "This disease takes about two years to run its course, from first contracting it to perishing," he said. "And in that time, they can have fawns and some do survive, so another possibility is that we will have a deer population, but they'll all have CWD and they'll essentially only go up to a two- or three-year-old. It would be a much more stunted population."

It's thought that mothers can't pass CWD to fawns in the womb, but the disease might be transmitted through saliva within the first couple of hours after birth, as the mother uses her tongue to groom her baby. That's the same amount of time that Jorge and his team try to give newborn fawns to adjust to life on earth before they descend on them with collars. So like others in the study, by the time we reached her, this fawn might already have been carrying the very first few CWD prions that would kill her—if nothing else got her first—by about the age of two.

How to prevent disaster? States have tried culls to reduce populations and slow the spread, but hunters often oppose these actions. They also show spotty compliance with rules about transporting their kills and getting them tested. And deer farmers can be counted on to kick and scream about any new regulation on their industry.

Jorge's study would try to model the effects of different

management actions, but there aren't a lot of great options. The nature of the disease is to spread in stealth, and it seems that all officials can do is try to slow it down. In some areas, more than half of deer are already infected. States declare containment zones where they find infections, but without a clear picture of where the prions actually exist, these aren't very effective. As for more drastic actions, with so much skepticism at play, they're basically impossible to sell to the public.

Jorge said that because CWD is so hard to see, with animals looking normal until the end stages of illness, the disease is difficult for people to believe in. "We"—meaning humans in general—"are really bad at looking into the future. You see the deer now, and most of them look healthy. If we say 'They could go extinct,' it's hard to grasp. It's like climate change."

But in this part of Arkansas, Jorge told me, you could sometimes see CWD plainly. Near death, deer look and act weird. Their front legs splay out; they lose the alertness and wariness that is their very essence. "They're very obvious," he said. "We just drove by one last week—a deer hanging out on the side of the road." He pulled off the highway. "I started walking toward it and it just kind of stared. It was very skinny. Cars were driving a foot away from it and it wasn't even flinching." Locals have told him similar stories.

Back at the truck, we all felt bubbly after our last-minute success finding a fawn, but quite apart from our human projects, the picture for these deer seemed bleak to me. Jorge would later tell me that one of the central challenges of his work is walking "an impossibly thin line" between raising the alarm and causing despair. "I always worry about how others might perceive it," he said. "Do they just stop caring? Do they question why even study this, if everything looks so grim? Things could change with new information, and the only way to do that is through research."

The team dropped us off at our tent, and a whippoorwill sang us to sleep. The researchers wouldn't rest anytime soon, though; most of them would keep looking for fawns into the wee hours, while Jorge himself sat at a computer and plowed through images of scavengers eating deer carcasses.

The next morning, early, I went walking through the lush woods along the river. It was a place that felt remote and mysterious, a place to encounter small secrets, like the single-lobed prickly pear cactus I found growing on a ledge of rock, or the fossils pressed into a lump of limestone I picked up on the shore. There were other secrets here too, inside the brains of deer, clutched within particles of soil, slipping upward through the roots of plants and into their leaves, moving around through predator and prey, scavenger and migrator, water and stem.

It's counterintuitive for those who feel besieged by them, but deer in the U.S. are likely on the decline. Our best estimates show that their total population peaked around the turn of the millennium, at 38.1 million; we're now down to perhaps 30 million. Mule deer have been declining even longer; they're now at around 4 million, less than half their peak number in 1960, and certainly below their historic levels. The western deer are suffering from habitat loss in a way that whitetails usually don't. Whereas whitetails stay mostly within a small area throughout their lives, mule deer must migrate seasonally, which makes them more vulnerable to fences, gas wells, roads, and other human disturbance. Even the U.S.–Mexico border wall gets in their way.

Meanwhile, climate change is parching the land and causing hotter and more frequent wildfires. Compared with whitetails, mule deer suffer more when living among humans. Toby Boudreau, an Idaho wildlife manager, told me about a study that found populations would go down in areas that held more than six houses per square mile. "More people are moving to Idaho and they want a view," he said. "They're moving into mule deer wintering habitat in the higher elevations." Around their vacation homes, some folks plant ornamental Chinese and Japanese yew— attractive to deer, and fatally poisonous. "The deer actually have a heart attack," he said. "It's like putting a gun to their head."

❦

The whole conversation around overpopulation takes on a different cast when we consider factors like CWD and mule deer declines. Some places may indeed have an overabundance of deer. Others, going by historical or recent time scales, are losing deer rather quickly.

Deer populations are down in many parts of the Appalachians—northern Georgia, upstate New York, northwestern Virginia. What these mountainous places have in common is lots of relatively old forest. The fewer human disturbances are around (farmland, roads, neighborhoods, logging cuts), the less food deer will find. The mountains also harbor more predators these days: black bears and coyotes. That means fewer fawns survive their first summer.

Yet deer are strolling hospital grounds, leaving tracks on baseball infields, nibbling plants on the side of interstate highways. I saw one last night in a small-town backyard, just behind a coffee shop parking lot, browsing calmly beside a plastic playhouse. They're doing well in places where hunting is on the decline: dense neighborhoods in town, newly built exurbs, farmland interspersed with small patches of forest.

Our old attachment to deer as icons of unspoiled nature is precisely contradicted by what's happening to them now: the bulk of their population in North America is shifting away from wilderness—the protected places, the public lands—and toward private property and human settlement. They're becoming, on balance, a more urban species. That's another thing we have in common with them. As people, we may continue to leave cities and journey outward when we want to perform the ritual we call connecting with nature. Meanwhile, on the whole, deer—these large, wild survivalists—are moving inward, toward the heart of our human-made, carved-up world.

I wonder if, among the general public, the rather passionate use of the term *overabundant* for deer is in part, despite sounding like a complaint, a way to reassure ourselves of nature's ability to persist under the major stress we ourselves cause it. Even if we're losing countless species to the sixth wave of extinction, and we routinely see forests bulldozed for housing, and the news about climate change keeps getting more awful, we believe in the abundance of deer as an example of something natural that's doing very well.

🦌

Every question I'd asked about deer had humans lurking in the answers. For me, the takeaway from my research on deer populations was about uncertainty. Despite all the work that science has done and will continue to do, there's still so much we don't know.

Are there too many deer? It depends on whom you ask and where they're standing at the time. There are even a few scientists who argue that a deer population three times as large would be a good thing. Across the eastern U.S., they say, forests were historically much more open than the dense, dark woods we're familiar with today—more like an African savanna than a jungle. These forests, being sunnier, supported more ground-level plants, and in turn, they were awash with pollinators and birds. And they hosted large herbivores that no longer exist in the U.S., like camels and sloths, who ate young trees and kept most from growing tall. Deer are the last large mammal standing, and even they can't eat enough, in their current numbers, to restore those open forests.

This is a seriously maverick view, anathema to mainstream ecologists, who point to large-scale studies showing that deer are indeed affecting forest regeneration. One researcher I talked to compared the outsider theory to climate change denial.

But what intrigues me about this debate is the way it disrupts the generic picture of nature I've carried with me my whole life, just as Jay Kelly does for his students. The conversation demands that we reach our imaginations back into time, repainting a cherished backdrop. The shady forest beyond my back door, the place of trees I love—is it actually some kind of anomaly, much denser than it was centuries ago? Why do we think certain conditions are normal and others are a problem? Deer are a lever for shifting those foundations.

The argument demands, too, that we ask another question. What should we do next?

CHAPTER 8

Management

IT WAS DECEMBER 1887, AND TEDDY ROOSEVELT WOULDN'T be elected president for another fourteen years. But at age twenty-nine, he was already a big deal. When he hosted a dinner party on Madison Avenue, a cadre of powerful Progressive men showed up.

That evening would see Roosevelt—New York assemblyman and passionate hunter—propose the founding of a club. Its first stated goal: "to promote manly sport with the rifle." But this was about more than hobbies: The Boone and Crockett Club would marry hunting to the nascent conservation movement. In that Manhattan dining room, the fate of rural land across America was being steered, and an era in outdoor culture was beginning.

♦♦

A hundred and thirty-four years later, a scientist was waiting around to give his presentation.

"I gotta get me a muley," he said. He was bantering about mule deer with the moderator. "A friend of mine was able to kill these huge, 190-something muleys in Kansas. I'm like, 'Are you kidding me?'"

"That's great," the moderator said. "Everybody wants what they can't have."

I was watching a deer conference online. Scientists had come to present their thesis research and ecology projects: graphs, maps, scatterplots: more data added to the ocean of data on deer. This was day two, and I was beginning to notice a pattern.

One of the plenary speakers, in his headshot, was wearing a camo jacket.

Another had a rifle over his shoulder. Several speakers had set antlers prominently on the bookshelves behind them.

A different session focused on planting food plots for deer, and mentioned that the plots could be helpful to pollinators. But that was an aside to the primary goal of growing big deer for hunters. As the presenter pointed out in his Tennessee drawl, "A butterfly doesn't have a backstrap."

◖◗

Before I began researching this book, I doubt I'd ever heard the term *deer management*, but it came up a lot at the conference. Dull though it sounds, it's a big deal—a whole profession and the research that supports it.

Deer management boils down to controlling populations, a project shouldered by state wildlife agencies, who use recreational hunters as their most essential tool. This paradigm dates to Teddy Roosevelt's era. Every year, agencies fiddle with a dauntingly complex system of hunting seasons and permits, often fine-tuning their strategy one county at a time, hoping to encourage hunters to kill the right number of deer for the needs of each locale. In theory, their decisions are based on scientific data. Three groups—scientists, managers, and hunters—play different roles in this system. But, as I had learned, many scientists and managers are also hunters themselves.

"I still get goosebumps one-on-one with a deer in the field," one manager told me. "I love everything there is to love about deer." That connection dates back to childhood hunting in upstate New York, and it forms the bedrock of his professional interest in managing deer numbers.

In his position, management largely means killing. Yet it all stems, he says, from a "personal, maybe spiritual relationship" to the animals. Long before their academic training, many deer researchers and wildlife managers absorbed other lessons, through rites of passage in the field. Bundled in special clothes, under the wing of a father or an uncle, spotting and taking down a large, warm, wild animal, coming home with meat, a tale, maybe a trophy rack: These couldn't help but be formative moments. For young hunters who grow up to be wildlife managers, it all fits together—affection and death in one complicated whole; the idea that something we love is something to control.

To an outsider, though, it tends to seem very paradoxical. And the mechanics of how the decisions get made are extremely muddy, because the recommendations deer managers make (offering a certain number of hunting tags, for example), though they're science-driven, often run up against hotly emotional resistance from hunters. Managers know to brace themselves for an earful of blame, suspicion, and derision. Some have even feared for their physical safety; one Pennsylvania manager who was shaking up deer policy in the early 2000s started wearing a bulletproof vest to public meetings. Inevitably, all this pressure colors policy.

Yet hunters and managers are not really separate groups. And although ecologists might insist that deer populations should be cut, it's hunters who pay managers' salaries. The agencies were— and mostly still are—funded through the sale of hunting licenses.

Deer hunters, then, become very important patrons. And they often seem to expect that buying a chance to hunt will guarantee fairly good odds out in the field. If they see fewer deer than they did ten years ago, or younger bucks with puny antlers, they respond as though they've been cheated. All the administrative arcana of management has a real effect on the environment, but most hunters aren't in it for the health of the forest. They want bigger herds, and many of the traditions they fiercely cherish—a reluctance to shoot does, for example—are in direct conflict with what scientific deer management demands. It's a way of looking at an entire landscape, an entire ecosystem, as though it were created for a specific type of human use.

Bernd Blossey is a conservation biologist at Cornell University, and like many scientists, he sees the forest not as a backdrop for hunting but instead as a system in crisis. Deer damage worries him greatly. "I actually say that climate change is a far more minor problem, compared to deer, for conservation in the eastern part of the U.S.," he told me. "It's enormous. It's enormous." In 2019, he headed a widely cited study that asked a key question for the first time: Could recreational hunting actually help forests recover from deer damage?

In short, no. Blossey's study found that normal hunting—through which most hunters take zero to two deer per year—made no difference in the rate at which deer damaged oak tree seedlings.

"There's still this mantra [among managers] that says we can control populations and damage through recreational hunting," he said. "That is their bible, and yet we know that that doesn't work." His religious metaphors were pointed. The story driving management—the one that says hunters can kill enough deer to protect ecosystems—was a myth, he was suggesting, and the coziness between managers and hunters would never allow populations to be adequately reduced.

Blossey and others have begun to suggest a whole different model. Recreational hunting could have its place as a hobby. Real deer management would be accomplished by professionals. The new idea is actually an old idea: allowing people to kill deer and then sell the meat.

The 1900 Lacey Act, a pillar of the conservation movement, outlawed this model for deer's protection, but many observers now believe Lacey is outdated. State-certified market hunting already happens in parts of Europe, where wild venison is hunted and sold, ultimately ending up on restaurant menus or in supermarkets. "We need to incentivize, one way or the other, having deer taken off the landscape," Blossey told me.

It all points to the fact that as a society, we are making

choices. States are beginning to search for ways to fund conservation without selling hunting licenses. And they're also trying to confront the fact that more than a century after conservation saved the deer, it's now the hunters who are endangered.

🦌

For many reasons, recreational hunting is in decline. Folks are too busy working and commuting and being glued to screens. Development on what used to be good hunting land makes access harder. The Baby Boomers are aging out of the sport.

At this point, the number of Americans who hunt is a little less than 5 percent of the population. There are still about fifteen million American hunters, but it's striking that such a small slice of the population is being asked to manage the deer herd that everyone lives with. What's more, some of the states where deer densities are highest are those with the smallest percentage of hunters—in New Jersey, for example, fewer than one in a hundred people hunts.

Everyone in deer management is worried about this problem. Managers are looking with alarm at numbers that suggest their jobs may eventually become impossible. But if hunters are no longer keeping up with the work agencies rely on them to do, that's partly due to the demographics of who's been encouraged to hunt, all the way back to Roosevelt's time.

🦌

LéChan Christian is not the type of hunter the Boone and Crockett founders had in mind.

"There's no one in my immediate family who hunts," she told me. "They're not very outdoorsy in general; I'm the odd one out."

For wildlife agencies, cultivating new kinds of hunters is an urgent priority. Despite the chauvinism of Boone and Crockett's number one goal—"to promote manly sport with the rifle"—women are the one bright spot in the picture today. In 2003, 12 percent of hunters were female. By 2020, the percentage was 22.

I knew states were actively recruiting women hunters, so I'd gone to a women's deer-hunting workshop in rural North

Carolina. There were about fifteen women in the group, including Christian. I listened as they discussed the methods and gear. I watched their male instructor demonstrate the use of a tree stand before the students followed a fake blood track, made of Karo syrup, to a plastic deer hidden behind a log. I'd heard another instructor—a woman in her sixties—assure them they could drag a dead deer without help. "I've done it!" she exclaimed. "We're women—we can do it!" She pretended, with dramatic grunts, to drag the decoy by its front legs. "Use those big thighs!"

The class lasted all afternoon, but the teachers admitted it only scratched the surface. It couldn't replace the traditional father-to-son teachings. Their parting advice: "Find yourself a mentor."

For Christian, that was an obstacle. A twenty-five-year-old Black woman from Raleigh, serious and composed, she'd dreamed of hunting since she read *Where the Red Fern Grows* in childhood. Her family story was archetypal: Her grandmother had moved from a North Carolina farm to New York during the Great Migration, severing the family's rural roots in exchange for the hope of better jobs. "My mother's generation were city kids, born and raised in New York City," she said.

Christian herself had been born in Queens but moved back to the South when she was nine. Ever since, it seemed, she'd been working toward becoming a hunter. But her family couldn't help much; her resources were mostly books and YouTube videos. When I met her, although she'd been licensed to hunt for three years, she'd still never actually hunted.

This was no accident. American hunting has been conceived as a white pastime by design. When Roosevelt and his allies combined conservation and hunting, they also threw some elements into the stew that, to our modern eyes, mix very badly: racism and eugenics. But to those in Roosevelt's circle, these things all fit together.

Madison Grant's résumé, for example, included organizing the Save the Redwoods League, helping to establish Glacier Na-

Roosevelt in 1885

tional Park and the Bronx Zoo—and publishing a book called *The Passing of the Great Race*, in which he argued that Slovaks, Italians, Syrians, and Jews were displacing America's Anglo-Saxon stock and should be kept out. (Roosevelt called it "a capital book.")

Relating to the outdoors in specific ways framed how these elite men understood who they were. In naming the Boone and Crockett Club after two buckskin-clad frontiersmen, the founders claimed as their own a particular version of American history. Roosevelt himself had recently posed for portraits wearing buckskins, cementing the connection. For this crowd, contact with nature was a marker of "real" Americans, descendants of pioneers, as opposed to the immigrant newcomers who had begun to populate American cities. Fair-chase, recreational hunting was a way to perform ethnic identity, demonstrate manliness, commune with wilderness, and engage scientific knowledge all at once.

Before Roosevelt, around the time of the Civil War, sport hunting had tended toward the patrician—a way for Americans to imitate Europeans. It's very odd that Roosevelt, a New Yorker who was wealthy from birth, founded a movement that ended up catering to rural guys from the working and middle classes.

But the key trait that links these different groups is whiteness. In a way, the conservationists made hunting egalitarian—"a badge of ethnic identity for white Americans," as the historian Daniel Justin Herman puts it.

How did they perform this trick? First of all, they folded anti-Indigenous racism into the movement. The continent's original human hunters found themselves branded as dangerous, illegal, and cruel, and their hunting rights were systematically eroded. If they dwelled in the new national parks the conservationists helped establish, they were removed, and in a sense, deer and other large animals replaced them as the "natural" inhabitants. This was all a tragic irony, given that the figure of the buckskin-clad frontiersman—by then, a paragon of white individualism—was in part an appropriation of Native American culture.

In the South, conservationists mixed protection of wildlife with oppression of emancipated Black people. Black hunters had been a fixture there since long before the Civil War, but after emancipation, white people got increasingly nervous about Black communities having access to weapons and the ability to provide their own food. Meanwhile, poor white hunters had often looked suspiciously on any government restrictions of their own hunting activities. By appealing to anti-Black sentiment, conservationists were able to convince these white holdouts to go along with new game protections that, in effect, prevented Black hunting.

Conservation eventually collapsed many of the old binaries—rich hunters vs. poor hunters, trophy hunters vs. meat hunters—into a new monolith that aligned under a banner of American sportsmanship. And because white supremacy was baked into the movement, hunting came to be firmly associated with white hunters.

Today, after more than a century of white-male-identified hunting culture, the project of recruiting hunters rests not just on education but on justice. Black Americans—13 percent of the population—own less than 1 percent of rural land. Though public land is supposed to offer places for anybody to hunt, in reality, there are barriers. For LéChan Christian, access is a problem. "There's a historical reason why you don't usually see Black people in the woods," she told me. "It's not safe for us there." Even if she could get access to private land, the journey there could be fraught. "Even driving down to the [workshop], I thought, 'I have to be careful. I'll just take the highway and go straight down there, and try to avoid interacting with cops.' It's a worry for me, traveling in a rural area."

I remembered how much I'd enjoyed the drive to that same destination—feeling free and easy, in road-trip mode.

Like many of us, the hunting world was talking about diversity more in 2020 after George Floyd's murder. That summer, the hunting website *Outdoor Life* ran a piece about recruiting Black hunters. When I called its author, Eric Morris, he echoed Christian: "Black people in the South have a long untold history of being hunters and guides," he said. "The mainstream media has traditionally omitted us from the outdoors." Yet he challenged a U.S. Fish & Wildlife statistic that said only 3 percent of America's hunters were Black.

"I know for a fact that's not true," said Morris, who teaches workshops and hosts a TV show on which he mentors a diverse group of hunters. "I can fill an auditorium with Black hunters and outdoorsmen. You have to question the statistics—did they get the survey?"

As for women, the students at the workshop I observed had seemed determined, despite long traditions that mostly excluded them from the hunt. If it's hard to get started, apparently it's even harder to keep going: here in the Southeast, almost half of the women who buy hunting licenses opt not to renew them.

But when I go to the website of the wildlife agency for my state, Virginia, and click on "Hunting," the first three people I see are women. They're of various races, and they're all holding rifles.

◉◉

A year had passed. Again the deer conference had come around, and the scientists had arrived with their latest research, meant to help steer this big unwieldy ship called deer management. Again I was watching online. And here was Philomena Kebec—a member of the Bad River Band of Lake Superior Chippewa, and an attorney for the Wisconsin-based tribe—saying a startling thing: "Humans are the most vulnerable aspect of life."

I sat up a little straighter.

"We don't have hair on our skin, big claws or teeth to hunt," she continued. "We don't have very keen eyesight or a good sense of smell." We're latecomers compared to the four-legged beings, who are so much better equipped for survival. When humans came along, she said, "the animals had a council and they talked about the pros and cons of allowing us to live. The deer said, 'They can have part of our bodies in order to live.' The birds talked about how they would entertain us and provide us with song. And so the way that we understand our relationships is that we have a *dependence* on these animals. It's not that we have dominion over them, but that they have kindly given us life and life force to continue."

This was a very different model from the biblical, humans-at-the-apex mindset that underlay everything else I'd observed in the deer management world. That had all stemmed from the basic notion that humans had to keep deer under control. But Kebec was suggesting that whole paradigm was flawed. That perhaps love does not have to translate to domination.

She saw deer as actors, not automatons. "Our conception of deer nation is that they have collective and individual agency, rights, and responsibilities. I'm going to throw this out there," she said to the group. "Perhaps the only real management we can do is managing other human beings through laws and regulations."

Kebec's message felt like a shot in the arm—a relief from what I realized was a species of loneliness. To be king is inherently solitary. But if humans weren't the only possible actors, if we weren't just puppeteers hovering above the ecosystem, then there was the possibility of collaboration. Of co-creation.

Kebec made another connection. She linked deer management

to the Euro-American persecution of wolves, which had been justified in part by a notion of "saving" deer for human hunters. "This whole idea that we wipe out predators in order to make sure we have enough deer is stupid and asinine," she said. "This idea that we have to manage wolves is antithetical to our cultural teachings because we know wolves as our brothers and sisters."

Wolves often come up in these conversations. But I'd so often heard the topic couched in the absurd. *We'll have to keep struggling with this, unless we bring back the wolves, ha ha!* For Kebec, though, it was perfectly serious, because predators were just as integral to the system as deer, people, and plants.

Substituting human hunters for predators is, in fact, a profound intervention into herd demographics. Even if the *number* of deer taken were equal, they wouldn't be the *same* deer. Animal predators are more likely to take young, old, or sick prey, whereas human recreational hunters focus on deer in their prime. And, of course, many hunters favor male deer.

Some people argue that humans' very nature compels us to manage and control—that to refuse to do so would be to deny our humanness. We've already altered so much about the world; it's hardly possible to now take our hands off the wheel. Certainly, there are very few, if any, deer in the U.S. that could be called unmanaged.

Perhaps the era that started at Roosevelt's dinner table is due to conclude. Others in the scientific world are beginning to echo, in a way, what Kebec is saying: that animals have enough agency to participate in their own conservation and management. It's a less hierarchical approach, maybe—not so much a ward-and-warden relationship, more like a partnership. Maybe with both deer and wolves as our partners.

None of our management decisions were inevitable, I'd already decided. What seems like rational decision-making in one era often seems deeply biased in another. The control of wildlife had clearly gone hand-in-hand with control of certain groups of people. Maybe management *itself* wasn't inevitable either.

When Kebec talked about humans and deer, it felt less like absorbing data and more like hearing about characters in a story.

"Humans are the silliest parts of creation," she said. "We're pretty young compared to many of the other different animals that we share the world with. And oftentimes we are led astray and we make decisions that are comical or unfortunate, or based in our own selfishness."

For her, deer have quite a different nature than the mindless eaters and breeders that deer management often imagines. How would we respond if we pictured them as a nation, one that shares and provides? "You know how kind and gentle their souls are, how big their eyes are. We understand that as embodying generosity."

CHAPTER 9

Should Not Be

"IT WAS KIND OF A SLOW DAY FOR COURT," ANTHONY Worley told me when I asked about that strange day in December 2021. He's a security officer at the Transylvania County courthouse in Brevard, North Carolina; he mans the X-ray machine that scans people's bags when they enter the building. The incident happened during the sleepy afternoon dip that follows lunch.

"I was sitting at the security desk down here, and I had all the cameras pulled up," he said. "I just happened to glance over and in a split second I saw something moving very fast toward the glass. There was just long enough for me to kick the chair out from underneath me and grab my gun."

Worley is also an ex-Marine, and when he saw a mysterious object hurtling toward the door, his instinct was to protect everybody inside. Another officer behind him, thinking someone was ramming a car into the building, dove behind Worley's chair. "But when I saw it was a deer, it was like 'Oh, OK, let go of the gun.'"

A yearling buck crashed through the glass with a sound like dishes breaking. "I guess it had its front legs all the way out, in full stride, so it went through the door like it was nothing," Worley said. It landed and started to scramble. "The floor is a smooth tile surface and it couldn't get traction on the floor, like a dog trying not to slide in the kitchen. And that's how we were able to get control of it." He and the other officer tackled the deer and had it immobilized within seconds. Then came the hard part.

"The other guy, he's like 'Keep its head down, I don't want it biting,'" said Worley. "I'm like 'It's an herbivore.' I knew the hooves were the dangerous part. So I maintained control of the legs, which was exhausting." Blood smeared on the floor; the deer had been cut by broken glass. "One of the clerks of court, she was kind of petting it on its head, saying 'Poor baby, it's okay, it's okay.'" The officers felt they needed to wait for more trained help before moving the deer outside, which left the two men and the buck trapped in a stalemate there behind the X-ray machine. They'd radioed the fire department, animal control, and a government wildlife biologist, but it was fifteen minutes before anyone could get there.

Meanwhile, Worley said, "it kicked the ever-living fool out of me." It was two months after the incident when I interviewed him, and he claimed he still had deer-inflicted bruises on his arms and legs. He was also bleeding—his blood mingling with the deer's blood on the floor and on his uniform pants—but in the heat of the moment, he felt no pain. "I didn't realize it was working me out." He tried handcuffing the deer's back legs to subdue it, but it whipped the empty cuff around like a nunchuck, battering his hands.

Finally a firefighter showed up with a rope bag, "like you'd use on a whitewater rescue," Worley explained. They tied up the animal and carried it outside through the shattered door. Other than cuts, it was unhurt. They let it run off.

The incident made the rounds on the news and on Facebook; Worley changed his profile picture to an image of himself holding down the deer. Nobody knew what became of the buck, but they did use video footage to piece together what had happened right before it burst into the courthouse. For some reason, it had been running wildly among parked cars and had charged head-first into the brick wall of a veterans' history museum next door.

⚜

As human space unfurls its fingers further into the landscape, and as deer populations swell in suburban zones, animals inevitably wind up in the places we think of us as belonging to us. Deer should not be in schools, offices, grocery stores, flower shops, sandwich joints, hospitals, drugstores, shopping malls, nursing homes, museums, banks, hair salons, dormitories, convenience stores, furniture showrooms, laser labs housing million-dollar equipment, Tescos, or Walmarts. Deer shouldn't be dashing through crowds of 5K runners or joining in Black Lives Matter protests. They shouldn't be knocking down a guy as he's walking through a McDonald's parking lot. They shouldn't be photobombing a couple's engagement portraits on the beach, or shutting down traffic on the George Washington Bridge. They shouldn't be cantering through a car park in Scotland. They shouldn't be jumping into school buses and landing on students.

But they are. And in lots of houses, too. "Come on!" barks a man in a video of a buck trapped in a midwestern bedroom. The deer doesn't seem to know what that means; it just clatters back and forth between the bed and the armoire. This deer, like others that have entered homes, will wind up dead.

Something about these events needles the modern mind. The very idea of "order" rests on an opposing idea of "disorder"; once you draw lines through the world, designating separate human spaces, you've opened the possibility of animals violating those borders. Then those animals become vermin: a kind of living pollution.

Scholars use words like "wrenching" and "uncanny" to describe such accidental dislocations. But the accidents are in our minds as much as in space. Although we conceive of cities as being animal-free, they are in fact teeming with animal life. We also can't tolerate the incursion for any length of time. Of course we classify groups of people in the same ways we do animals. If we're in a position of power, we are often quite willing to look at the marginalized as a form of pollution. This is no less true when those people—or animals—are displaced from their own homes, the places and ways of life they themselves would prefer. Animals, too, can be refugees.

We may try to corral the unsettling reality by getting cutesy. "This guy *really* wanted to learn!" commented the head of a South Carolina school entered by a buck. After letting a deer out of a school in New Hampshire, police made a suspect sketch of the animal and put it on Facebook. Deer are said to "tour museums," to be "surprise guests," to "do some shopping."

More often, we use language that blames. Deer are "sneaky" or "nosy." We say that deer "break in," "barge in," "run loose," "run riot." They go the wrong way through emergency exits; they "leave a bloody trail" and "trash the room" and "send customers running for cover."

These terms tend to emphasize the human perspective, but the deer must be as anxious as any person, lost and alone in the wilderness, would be. Sometimes we do glimpse a playful aspect of their behavior—they've been said to score soccer goals in backyard nets, then do a victory dance; to frolic with poodles; to nose experimentally at wind chimes. But humans hold the title for most elaborate amusements. One business in Syracuse, New York, called iSmash, offered "rage rooms" where customers could pay to smash electronics and glass. Two groups of customers were there one Sunday when a whitetail crashed through the front window. The manager and the police chased it out. "Our priority was to protect customers," the manager told a reporter, adding that no one was injured by the flying glass. From the window, that is. Presumably the customers then returned to smashing glass.

❦

Two thousand years ago, Ovid imagined a golden-antlered stag, bedecked with jewelry, both beautiful and tame. He "approached / the homes of men; he let his neck be stroked / by all." But Cyparissus, a handsome youth, is his special human friend. The boy weaves garlands for his antlers and rides him like a horse—"joyfully / with purple reins that guide his tender mouth."

All the more crushing, then, when a javelin thrown by Cyparissus accidentally kills the stag as it snoozes in the shade.

Torn by remorse, Cyparissus begs the gods to let him grieve forever. He cries until he transforms into a cypress. "The boy was now a rigid tree / with frail and spiring crown."

Deer in close proximity to human spaces inspire both anxiety and desire, and humanity has a long history of fantasizing about their taming. Mythical deer riders include the sixth-century Welsh saint Edeyrn (the deer carries him to a new place where he builds a monastery), the Hindu god Chandra, and the Slavic figures called *vile*, female hunters who bewitch men with their beauty. Deer riders gallop through pop culture in the video game *Zelda* and the anime movie *The Deer King*.

Other works imagine deer as milk givers, like cows.

This image comes from a fresco recovered from the ruins of Herculaneum, a town that, like nearby Pompeii, was destroyed by the eruption of Mount Vesuvius. The baby's name is Telephus, and he is suckling the doe because he's been abandoned by his mother, Auge.

There are six other living beings in the two-thousand-year-old painting, including Telephus's father, Herakles. But only Telephus and the doe, down in the corner, engage in an interaction, and it is a fervent one. The baby gulps milk; the doe, her ears laid back with effort, licks the child's thigh. They form a closed system, a circular emblem of give-and-take.

The doe's completion of the circle suffuses the image with questions. If she were chewing her cud and looking bored while Telephus fed, it would be far less potent. She is giving on both ends, but what does she receive in return? And why is she so tender about it—more like a mother than a dairy cow? It's a welter of broken taboos—troubling, almost queasy.

The nursing-doe image recurs around the world, including in China, where a popular story recounts how a devoted son, Zhou Yanzi, disguised himself as a deer in order to obtain doe's milk to cure his sick father.

Healing power, life and light: in sources from German myths to Italian legends, does' milk brings all these, and wisdom, too. The Irish High King Nia Segamain was said to have inherited from his mother the magical power of making deer give milk; during his reign, the does of Ireland behaved like domesticated cows. Other Irish and Scottish tales tell of goddesses or otherworldly women who herded and milked does, delightfully called "fairy cattle."

At times, these herders shapeshift, becoming deer themselves. Warm doe bodies, big enough to encircle us, seem to touch the corners of our collective psyche that need to be mothered.

It goes both ways. At least one anthropologist recorded native women of Guyana suckling fawns.

ꙫ

A deer bursting through a storefront window might seem like a mistake. But in fact, there is a long cultural history of mutually crossing the borders that separate us from deer. And these events aren't random at all; they're an emblematic issue of our time. Each collision of deer and human reality is an accident of our own deliberate making. We built the store, and in a real sense, we put the deer—complete with instincts honed over millennia of evolution—in front of the glass. One could argue that in many ways, our support of deer's existence in dense human spaces is passive. But people all over the country also actively support deer by feeding them. Examine their motives and you find more accidents, more fuzzy ethics, more fantasies.

Not so long ago, feeding wildlife was sanctioned. Some states fed deer to support herds for hunters' sakes, and Yellowstone National Park rangers in the early twentieth century would feed bears as entertainment for visitors. Encouraging a carnival-type atmosphere, Yosemite kept deer behind fences in a park zoo until 1932. A 1929 photo shows a Yosemite ranger helping a deer smoke a pipe.

But these days, like their counterparts in other countries, wildlife experts in the U.S. discourage feeding wild deer, and many locations ban it outright; Minnesota, for example, forbids the practice in about half the state. The Minnesota wildlife agency's website shows stark photos of the problems feeding can cause: vehicle accidents, herds of dozens of animals clustered at feeding stations (which helps to spread diseases like CWD), and—oddly—deer that die of overeating. Though corn is a popular supplemental feed, it can be dangerous for deer in the winter, when their systems are geared up to digest woody browse, not starchy carbohydrates. A deer can die within twenty-four hours, very unpleasantly, after a big meal of corn.

Supplemental feeding blends at least two of deer's cultural roles—as victims and as pests—and it troubles our assumptions about where they should be found. Should a deer be in a backyard, eating purchased corn? Is it a pest if it then wanders next door and browses a neighbor's apple tree, or is the real pest the human who provided the corn? Isn't a deer a victim if it suffers convulsions, tremors, frothing at the mouth after we feed it inappropriate food? Is it where it shouldn't be if it runs across a road on its way to and from the feeding site?

But deer food is a big business and, more important, it's a big part of how many people understand themselves to experience, and "help," wildlife. It feels good to be benevolent. Whatever is natural—whatever natural once meant—is pretty far beyond the equation.

⚶

From the deer point of view, humans must seem a strange and unpredictable nation. Only sometimes do we offer nourishment. Other times we actively drive them away from what they perceive as food sources. When we do invite them to eat, it's with unknown motives. To take food provided by humans is to risk one's life, in various ways. The food could turn out to be a simple gift. Or it might be unintentional poison, or very intentional bait.

McCall, Idaho, a ski town of three thousand people, has "a long history of residents feeding deer in town," state wildlife biologist Regan Berkley told me. That includes part-timers who enjoy feeding deer for the week or two they're in town for their ski vacation. When they pack up and go home, the deer are left to wander the streets in search of a different pile of corn.

As a result of all the free food, the McCall herd—they're mule deer, a species that normally migrates between winter and summer ranges—have given up migrating and simply hang around town all winter. "The deer herd grows every year," Berkley said. "Generations of them haven't had to migrate." Predictable problems have followed, from car collisions to the presence of cougars attracted to the deer. Officials are talking about a feeding ban, and they've even considered trapping and relocating the town deer to winter range where they could learn to migrate from their wilder cousins.

Tame or semi-tame deer can end up where they shouldn't be in a very different sense. They cross the boundary that designates them as innocent, gentle animals and enter the territory of aggression. It happens if deer feel cornered—urban does, for example, will defend their fawns in spring from dogs and the people who walk them—but it can also stem from frequent feeding. In Teller County, Colorado, a seventy-seven-year-old woman was attacked in her kitchen by a deer that had come to expect hand-outs from some of her neighbors. She'd propped her door open to bring in groceries, and the doe followed her inside, then kicked her and headbutted her when she tried to shoo it out. A wildlife manager was there to euthanize the deer when, as the woman predicted, it showed up again the next day.

Even worse was the experience of Patty Jean Willis, in Au Gres, Michigan, who was attacked in her backyard by a buck wearing an orange collar. "That deer was coming right at me with his antlers," she told a reporter. The buck knocked her onto her back, but she grabbed his antlers and drew up her knees to protect her organs. "I thought I was going to die. I just screamed and screamed." Her strength had nearly given out when her son appeared and chased the deer away. Willis spent three days in the hospital with severe puncture wounds. The deer could not immediately be found.

Worse still: A forty-six-year-old Australian man was gored to death by a pet deer he was keeping on his property. He'd been attacked when he entered the deer's enclosure; his wife tried to help him but was critically injured as their son ran to get a gun. Police shot the stag before a helicopter whisked the woman to the hospital, but it was too late to save her husband.

Deer are not native to Australia; they were introduced by European settlers. This particular animal had lived inside a pen, in rural Victoria state, for two years. It was a cross between species, red deer and elk, from faraway continents on the other side of the equator. Lonely dislocation; lonely, monstrous genetics.

🐾

In the U.S., it's an illegal but common situation when a private citizen tries to tame a fawn for a pet. But there are other, more bizarre scenarios into which deer get drafted.

In 2016, Kelvin Peña, a seventeen-year-old living in the Poconos, found viral internet fame thanks to some videos he posted of himself feeding deer in his backyard. His first deer friend was a large-antlered buck he named Money; an early video shows

Money eating some crackers off the ground before Peña appears in the frame, sounding slightly defiant. "Y'all see it, man. This shit ain't regular, man. Who got a pet deer? Let me know."

He would later explain to a trio of Philadelphia-based filmmakers, whose short documentary about Peña screened at Sundance, "I called him Money just straight off the dome, it was the first thing that came to my mind, cause I love money and I felt like I love the deer." After Money, Peña soon named and befriended others: Tequila, Lola, Lil Baby Carmen, and a prized doe he called Canela. He tried out some new names for himself too. "Some call me the Deer Whisperer. Others call me the Dominican Snow White." Before long he settled on "Brother Nature." And then Brother Nature became a brand.

There was merch; there were very bad rap videos; there were fashion collabs, like when the Sandalboyz company issued shoes printed with deer and marketed them with the name Canela the Savage. Something about Peña struck a chord that the usual (read: white and middle-aged) exemplars of the wildlife watcher had never been able to touch. On Instagram, he collected 2.7 million followers.

In one early video, Peña roams a cul-de-sac along with a five-year-old cousin, who opens a package of crackers and shakes them out into a plastic tray. "Y'all see it, we bout to feed the squad." Peña takes the tray, turns the camera back on himself, and holds out a handful of crackers to Canela. "Ready one two three?" She starts eating, and he chants, "Chug chug chug chug chug chug chug . . . come on Canela! Stuff your face, come on, chug chug! Yeah, you did it, girl!" The word "FEARLESS" appears on the screen. "Mm-hm, mm-hm. Proud of you, girl." The same video later segues to a sequence where Peña spends minutes on end trying to feed a crumpled dollar bill into one of those arcade games where you grab a stuffed animal with a claw.

Peña's persona matured as his fame increased; he traveled the world, started a foundation called Everybody Eats, and marched for climate justice. Born in 1998 to parents who split up when he was four, he'd bounced around between Puerto Rico, Texas, and New York before landing in Pennsylvania, and he'd obviously done a lot of his real growing up online. (In 2018, he got called out for some racist tweets he'd posted way back at the age of twelve.) Nothing in his videos suggested a true familiarity with the outdoors. But then, it seemed that like many people his age, he hadn't had much of an opportunity to spend meaningful time there. His videos take places and animals as content, nothing more, with the uncanny safely wrapped in the ironic. Once he put a gold chain around Canela's neck, invited her to "flex for the 'gram," and then feigned outrage when she ran off still wearing the jewelry, a modern-day stag of Cyparissus.

♊

Human whims can be dangerous to deer. Officials in Utah asked residents not to feed or interact with an orphaned mule deer that frequently wandered through the town of Herriman. But they just couldn't resist. "Everybody loves that picture for Facebook or Instagram," said Scott Root of the state wildlife agency, "but you're really doing that animal a disservice and maybe giving it a death sentence if it becomes too domesticated." That, in the end, is exactly what happened: someone complained, and Root's agency showed up to euthanize the deer. Locals had named it Cooper, but the state called it a public safety concern.

In 2012, an Oklahoma ranch family noticed there was a white fawn hanging out with their livestock—even nursing from their cows. They called her Christmas, and she stuck around their fields for years, earning the affection of many locals, who'd pull off the road to watch her through binoculars. But Christmas met her end on Christmas Day, 2021, when she was shot by a hunter. The rancher, Paula House Silzer, called the death "heartbreaking," though she acknowledged nothing illegal had happened. "We [ourselves] are deer hunters," she said. Christmas had morphed from anonymous wildlife to named object of affection, and her death was a violation. It impinged, that is, on human feelings.

Culture trains us to look at animals in all kinds of different ways. A white fawn who mingles with farm animals triggers re-actions in us that say more about our fantasies than anything real in the world. When we say that deer "make friends" with our puppies or toddlers or even the snowmen we've built in our yards, we're expressing a wish that nature could get on board with our presence, our program, our power. These peaceful en-counters seem like a reprieve from the gnawing dread about our own tendency to destroy, and the menace of that destruction in-evitably folding back on ourselves. We can be soothed by our Sierra Club calendars, but maybe the trusting presence of a deer, nosing our palms for treats, works even better.

Personally, I'd never considered feeding deer. It always seemed to me an obvious violation of what one "should" do. My assump-tions were nice and comfortable until I went to Fripp Island, South Carolina.

If you're a human guest on Fripp, things are pretty pleasant. It's a gated, three-thousand-acre private resort, all broad shady porches and breezes through sea oats. The beach is wide, stud-ded with big, beautiful shells. The streets are leafy, graceful, oc-casionally crossing dark creeks overhung by palmettos and live oaks, sometimes opening onto vast glimpses of marshland. Peo-ple tool past on golf carts, trailing that delicate atmosphere of leisure which prevails in places like this.

I hadn't come to relax, though. I'd come to see the deer. With my family, I stepped out of our rented townhouse and there they were: three small whitetail does and a six-point buck, nibbling at the very short grass in someone's front yard. Weirdly, one of them also seemed to be eating mulch. A block farther on, as the road gave way to a beach path, more deer emerged from the sea oats. Six of them. They approached my daughters. Rosa held out a hand and one of the deer nudged her fingers. She turned to look at me, wide-eyed. Finding no food, the deer turned away.

We continued toward the beach and I kept an eye on the little herd. They were browsing the slight hints of green among the brown dune grasses, slowly making their way toward a riprap bank near a row of condos, where there was a shallow strip of grass. One of them arched her back and lifted her tail, dropping pellets.

It was late afternoon and we'd just arrived on the island. I'd wanted to come here for a while, ever since hearing that it was a seriously overpopulated place, where if a person rolled down her car window and crinkled a chip bag, the deer would walk right over for a handout. I also knew it was a place where researchers had spent several years injecting does with sterilization drugs.

My family went back to the house while I kept walking around with my notebook. The most recent count of the total deer population on Fripp, one of the island's naturalists had told me, put the deer density at more than 175 per square mile. I wasn't here to do a scientific count, but just to test what it felt like to move through such a saturated habitat.

Disorienting, it turned out. I saw a buck under a palm tree. A doe in a side yard. A buck crossing the road in front of a truck. A buck lying under a porch. A doe and a fawn behind some palmettos. I was trying to write down every sighting—"1 buck near a mailbox / 1 doe with splayed rear legs / big buck crossing road / second doe behind / 2 fawns following"—but at times, I couldn't write fast enough. I'd lift my eyes and see four, no five—six!—deer, staring back at me. I turned and glimpsed a buck bending over a stream. I peered down the road and saw does in the fire station parking lot.

On my walks that day, I counted fifty deer. This place distorted my usual sense of what the landscape is made of, how densely life can exist within it. Deer moved and receded, drank from hoses in construction sites, watched me from behind rustling palms. Bucks with trophy-sized racks quickly stopped seeming remarkable. I started to see deer even where they weren't, imagining a profile in the arch of a frond, or legs in the shapes of dangling leaves. I almost expected to find them perching in the trees.

It was early January, and the island was very quiet, its beaches lonely. What would happen when summer came and it filled with vacationers? I'd seen videos of people feeding the deer by holding pieces of bread in their mouths, "kissing" the deer when they took the food. And the first time I'd gone to the resort's website, I'd seen a photo of a lovely bride, crouched on the grass, reaching toward the outstretched nose of a buck.

It was obvious these animals inspired some mangled form of devotion, and obvious too, from their behavior and their small, ribby bodies, that they were malnourished. Fripp is thickly vegetated, but most of what grows there isn't good deer food. The deer I saw seemed to be living on grass—though they are not grazers by nature—and the occasional snack of Spanish moss. For them, there was no leisure; they were on a full-time quest, scouring the island for food, trying not to starve.

The people of Fripp have elected not to practice culling, though at one time, before it was a resort, the island served as a hunting preserve. The sterilization study was conducted between 2005 and 2011, and while the drug—derived from a protein found in pig ovaries—did temporarily slash the birth rate, it was never intended as a permanent fix. Ten years after it ended, fertility control is still an experimental, niche technique for controlling deer. Meanwhile, on Fripp, the effects of the drug had long since worn off. By the time I visited, the only constraint on the island's deer was the most old-fashioned force: the effects of scarce food on living bodies.

Early the next day, I took my girls on another walk and supplied them with apple slices in a chip bag. Does slowly approached, stretched their long necks, and took the fruit right from our hands. One group of does and fawns took a break from rooting through a pile of yard trimmings to accept our offering. Quickly, the girls started seeing the deer as individuals. We compared coat colors and body shapes and the girls bestowed names, Round Chest and Zebra and Spanish Inquisition. A buck with missing antlers sidled up, warily took an apple slice, then fled across the road.

"They wanted to live. That's why I fed them," writes the naturalist Elizabeth Marshall Thomas about a group of deer she began feeding on her New Hampshire property during an especially harsh winter. Animal-rights proponents often argue from the same foundation: Each individual animal, they say, has the right to live and not suffer. That's why, for them, hunting is always wrong and feeding is a simple good deed.

Biologists universally condemn feeding, though, for the sake of both deer and people. After that walk with my kids, I saw a big sign by the road with a cute picture of fawns and the legend PLEASE DON'T FEED US and felt a pang of guilt. But on this island, I found it hard to stay planted in the moral universe of herd management. What does it mean when, among carefree human beachgoers, hundreds of hungry animals roam? The deer are trapped by the island's geography, while we humans can hop in our cars and sail away over the bridge when we're ready to leave. Fripp's ethics were topsy-turvy. I'd been disoriented not only physically but also morally by the swollen population.

I couldn't say what it might mean to love these deer, which many island-goers profess to do. On my last walk, I passed a large house with a fancy double staircase leading to its front porch. Its railing was decorated with an iron panel embossed with the image of powerful, big-antlered bucks. I looked at it for a moment, then turned and spotted two scrawny does, scrounging what nourishment they could from a tiny patch of clipped grass under a basketball hoop.

CHAPTER 10

Bodies

ACROSS THE ROAD, VULTURES FESTOONED THE BIG SYCA-mores. They rose from the branches and settled back down, over and over, flapping noisily as though to send a message: Clear off.

Scavengers like to start with a body's obvious orifices. They'd already eaten his eyes, and his tongue. Though they wouldn't gather around this young buck again until I was out of the way, glossy green flies and a few small bees were undeterred by my presence, a constant buzz marching in and out of eye sockets, thickly dotting flanks. They spiraled and looped in the air just above the body.

The buck had antlers about three inches long—just spikes, no forks. He lay at the gravelly shoulder of the small back road, hooves pointed uphill. This was October, the season when deer go into rut. Before this young buck died, he was probably walking for hours every day through the landscape, looking for does, a bit crazed by hormones; reckless, maybe. A collision with a vehicle, perhaps one coming down this hill a little too fast, possibly at dusk or dawn, when visibility is worst. A scramble, a thump, a short flight through the air before he landed on this spot.

"He"? Or "it"? Was he now just a collection of parts?

He looked fairly intact. It was hard to tell which injuries had actually killed him—his torso looked mostly unhurt, but he had some raw abrasions on his face, blood spots inside his ears and under his front legs. His mouth was open and bloody. The most grisly sight was the way the hide was peeled away from the pelvis, exposing bone, gristle, and a pale gray-green organ.

Upwind, there a was smell, and his belly was swollen; he'd been dead for some hours, at least. Yet much of him was exactly as he was when he was full of life and sprinting across this road. His neck, his back, the outsides of his ears looked sleek and healthy. Long orange hairs stood out from brown and gray. Still a complete shape, just starting to come apart.

⚈

Three days later, he was gone. So were the vultures. The ground still had a rust-colored stain, and a smell lingered in the air. There was also a lot of fur, mixed with leaves and a beer can, forming a windrow that extended about six feet along the shoulder.

It takes much longer than three days for scavengers to make a deer disappear; the highway department must have scooped up the carcass. But there was little sign of anyone's work, animal or human: no scrape, no tracks, no prints. Except for the fur and the blood on the road, there was no signal that the buck had been here.

Suddenly my eyes picked out an outline of its body—a subtle impression of its weight—torso, legs, neck, and head stamped onto the rough texture of the leaves. And then I lost it again.

⚈

Of all the interactions between humans and deer, the times when we hit them with our cars might be the most violent—even more so than hunting, which at least people do intentionally. Every driver knows it could happen, and for more than a million people per year in the U.S., that fear comes true.

Deer interact badly with motorcycles, trains, and even planes. The FAA considers white-tailed deer more hazardous to U.S. civil aircraft than any other animal.

Unlike culling or hunting, deer–vehicle collisions were something I had personally experienced before I wrote this book. It was one of those dangers that, like the flu or falling trees, had intersected with the particularities of my life, leaving me with my personal stories. But I wanted to understand what those accidents meant in a larger sense, and so I found myself standing under the highway with Bridget Donaldson, looking at bear tracks in the mud.

We were in a concrete tunnel called a box culvert, ten feet high and twelve feet wide, running in a long straight line through the earth under I-64 outside Charlottesville. The tunnel's cool, muffled air belied the bright summer day outside. Donaldson is a scientist with the Virginia Transportation Research Council, and she might have been the reason a black bear had ambled through here within the last couple of days. She'd been trying to coax wildlife to use this culvert as a crossing since 2016.

For years, she'd studied how wildlife and cars interact on this highway. After the interstate skirts the outer edges of Charlottesville, it cuts through hundreds of acres of forest as it climbs a ridge west of town. Down the other side, the highway passes through the kind of patchwork landscape that's typical in rural America, the mix on which deer thrive: housing developments, fields, woods, and a network of smaller roads.

The stats for this area were rather grim, about nine deer-related crashes per mile per year. "That's high," Donaldson said. "That number can be decreased." Even though she gathered information from VDOT, the highway department, about how many deer carcasses they pick up, she still didn't have a complete picture, since deer often run off some distance from the crash site but later die from their injuries.

As a regular user of this highway, I'd spotted deer innumerable times within a stone's throw of the travel lanes. My experience bore out what Donaldson said: "Deer raised near highways become habituated." But evolution hasn't prepared them for the speed of motorized vehicles.

This explains what can look to drivers like very stupid behavior—the classic blank stare into oncoming headlights, or the fact that deer sometimes run directly into the sides of cars, or leap off embankments onto a vehicle's roof.

What deer *can* understand, as gardeners well know, are eight-foot-high fences.

Donaldson joined the VTRC in 2003, and brought with her a love of animals and an interest in wildlife ecology. She knew that especially in the West, some roads were constructed with underpasses specifically for animals. Those work well, but they're expensive, and very tough to retrofit. "I thought maybe we could make better use of existing underpasses," she said. Her idea was to study whether roadside fences could funnel animals toward safe crossings that were already there.

Donaldson identified two spots in her I-64 study area that could serve as wildlife passageways. One was ideal for deer: a tall, wide space under a bridge with a small river, the Mechums, running through it.

The other, the box culvert, was less inviting. Dark and nearly two hundred feet long, it had been built in the 1960s along with the interstate, to accommodate cattle on a farm bisected by the new highway. From one end, the other side was just a small square of sunlight framed by blackness. Studies have quantified what makes for a deer-friendly passage, and Donaldson knew the narrow tunnel would not be a preferred route. But would they use the culvert if fencing forced them to?

Donaldson and her colleagues started out the way hunters do these days, by spying on deer with game cameras. For two years, a string of cameras, ten per mile, collected images of deer at the roadside: feeding, attempting to cross, even mating and sparring. There were close to five thousand deer visits in the two miles of roadside she observed.

Donaldson found, as she expected, that deer were more willing to walk under the bridge than to enter the box culvert. Also unsurprisingly, they frequently crossed the road at both sites.

But then a mile of experimental fencing went in at the box culvert in 2016, and another mile at the Mechums bridge in 2017. The fence was pretty simple: eight feet high, made of woven wire attached to metal stakes, with occasional one-way "jumpouts" that let deer escape if they get trapped on the wrong side.

Donaldson gave me a tour of the fence in a big white VDOT

van, creeping along the shoulder with hazard lights on, then took me to see the box culvert. We put on safety vests before we opened the van doors and scrambled down a steep bank next to one end of the tunnel.

Walking near a big highway is always unnerving. Even down here, well below the road, the sound of trucks whipping past overhead awakened a touch of instinctual fear. Trash and invasive stiltgrass and wineberries were everywhere around the culvert entrance. The highway seemed to cut through the forest like a corridor of noise and garbage.

As Donaldson bent over to check on her game camera, its lens trained on this end of the culvert, I started examining the tunnel's flat earthen floor. I saw raccoon tracks, with their delicate digits, like tiny clawed handprints. Donaldson had told me that smaller animals, from foxes to bobcat kittens, were using the tunnel 50 percent more than they did before the fence. And, sure enough, I saw lots of deer tracks.

We walked the length of the tunnel, stepping over occasional wet spots. It seemed to go on for a long time. If I had to cross the highway, I'd probably brave the road too instead of entering this murky, damp space. At night it must have been pitch-dark. I could understand why it took a physical barrier to force deer to use this as a crossing.

Yet the fence had worked better than any scientist would have predicted. In the mile surrounding the box culvert, the number of crashes since VDOT added fencing had dropped by over 96 percent. The study at the Mechums bridge was just as promising.

"Now they realize they have to use it," said Donaldson. It was safe to assume that at the two sites, the fence had prevented more than thirty deer strikes. Images of does bringing their fawns through the culvert suggested that a new generation of deer would learn to use it as part of their normal movements.

"They're right to be nervous," Donaldson said about deer entering the tunnel. The language of the project—the language of force—embodies the inherent compromise of the situation. Deer don't like tunnels because they fear predators, but the animal predators are gone. At the same time, we've put a river of death into the landscape, traveled by mechanical predators that no creature has evolved to fathom. Now the best we can do to protect the animals is to interrupt their movements, and thwart their instincts, even further.

It was near the far end of the culvert where I spotted some large, ragged tracks, too big to be human. Most were unreadable. But one looked like bear to me. Bending over to squint at it, Donaldson agreed.

Later that day, back in her office, she'd discover proof when she reviewed footage from her cameras. Two days earlier, at six in the morning, a black bear had lumbered, pigeon-toed, out of this end of the culvert, its head swinging side to side, its shoulders rolling under its opulent fur. And sometime after that, a deer fawn had passed through, leaving its own tiny hoofprint in the center of the bear track.

⚹

It was from Donaldson that I learned the term DVC: deer–vehicle collision. Deer strikes are so common, and require so much prevention and management, that they have their own acronym. The insurance industry is involved. Highway departments are involved. The police are involved. Ecologists. Biologists. Body shops.

Then there are the people who do the dirty work: scraping the carcasses off the pavement, hauling them away. For state governments, removing carcasses is part of the charge to promote human safety. In my home state, the workload amounts to more than 55,000 carcasses, and costs VDOT more than $4 million, every year.

It's a tough and usually invisible job. I talked to a carcass-removal pro named Andy Albertson after spotting a local news segment from where he lives in Kent County, Michigan. A TV reporter had made much of Albertson's unofficial title, the Deer Sheriff. But the folksy nickname didn't really capture the day-to-day reality of this work.

"It's public service with a capital P," Albertson told me. As an employee of his county's road commission, he'd been cleaning up roadkill for eighteen years, and the news report had been prompted by a milestone: He'd scooped up his forty-thousandth deer. On the morning we talked, he was getting ready to add another couple of dozen to that total.

"I come in about six, and by seven or seven thirty I've got my list," he said, explaining that reports of roadkill come in from police, citizens, and township supervisors. On this day, he said, "I have a list of nine animals, but by the time I'm done today I will probably have twenty-five or more." Deer made up about 95 percent of his workload.

The worst were deer obstructing traffic lanes. "If I get a call on a blocker, I have to reroute," he said. "It can be hazardous. I had one Monday morning on the M-57, a busier road; it was dark, and you're in high traffic. I gotta worry about where I'm placing the truck and where I'm standing." He doesn't set up cones or flares: "I've got flashers on my truck. It's just duck and go."

Albertson's tools are minimal: rubber gloves and a "deer puller," a two-foot piece of pipe with a loop of wire on one end. "I put it on the deer's hoof. I use that when I don't want to touch it." Some animals are so mangled he needs a shovel or a pitchfork. But almost always, he just pulls on the gloves and drags the deer by hand.

"It keeps me in fairly decent shape," he told me. "I'm fifty-five, and it's managed to keep the weight off. So far the back's good, the knees are good. I have a little arthritis in the hands."

As for the smell, he said simply, "You never really get used to it. Summertime is brutal."

Kent County is home to more than 650,000 people and includes Grand Rapids, the second-largest city in Michigan. When Albertson started doing this job in 2005, he was able to collect all the day's deer before lunch and then join a road-patching crew in the afternoon. But over the years, urban sprawl and traffic had increased enough to make roadkill a full-time job. He was even pondering whether the work might become too much for one person. "Thirty-seven deer yesterday is a lot," he said. "It's getting to the point where we may have to have another truck for the south end of the county."

Once in a while, he has to call the police to euthanize an animal. I asked him whether his job ever got depressing. "The saddest thing I see is fetuses knocked out from the mother's womb," he said. "There's always two, never one, and that's sad." But generally he took it in stride. "People say it's a shame. I think it's just part of nature."

⚘

The destination for all of Albertson's deer is a landfill, just like most American roadkill that gets picked up. In the past, workers would just throw dead deer farther off the road, but that's illegal now. Some localities put dead deer into incinerators, rendering plants, or chemical digesters. Sometimes bird and animal sanctuaries take the carcasses to use as meat for the creatures they rehabilitate.

Putting bodies into landfills is becoming more expensive, because of the way landfill technology is changing. Newer systems are more finely calibrated and less able to handle decomposing animals, so some landfills charge high disposal fees when contractors show up with truckloads of deer.

In 2013, Bridget Donaldson and her colleague Jimmy White studied several different systems that VDOT could use to compost deer at its own facilities—enlisting microorganisms to eat up the carcasses. They tried composting in rotating drums, in windrows made of wood chips, and in forced-air compost bins. The forced-air bins worked best: they destroyed pathogens, broke carcasses down efficiently, and didn't take up much space. "We've taken a natural process and sped it up," said White. In one month, this system can take a fresh deer carcass and turn it into a pile of sawdust, mixed with perhaps a few fragments of bone and antler.

The half-dozen forced-air compost facilities installed during that pilot study are still in operation, said White, and are scattered around the state. Eventually he'd like to see more of them built. I drove down to a local VDOT headquarters outside Lynchburg so that White could show me a set of animal compost bins.

In White's air-conditioned car, we approached the compost area, situated at the outer skirt of the yard. It was unceremonious: a row of four concrete bins under one large shed roof. Each bin was about ten feet wide and eighteen feet deep, with a swinging metal door across the front. You could easily mistake them for bins meant to store mulch or topsoil, until you got close enough to read the sign attached to one of them: PLACE DEAD ANIMALS HERE.

In a backyard compost pile, you throw in food scraps like apple cores and coffee grounds (nitrogen), cover with leaves (carbon), and turn the pile now and then (oxygen). In this case, the carbon came from the sawdust, and the nitrogen from the deer. Along the floor, thin PVC pipes hissed with the forced air that delivered the oxygen. Microbes did the actual work of decomposition, and they created heat—the temperature inside the piles got up to 140 degrees Fahrenheit during the hottest part of the cycle—as well as a leachate that drained through channels to an underground tank.

To use the bins, workers would line the bottom with sawdust and lay deer over it, resting back to front like spoons in a drawer. They'd continue layering animals and sawdust as the pile built up. I was stunned when White told me that each of these bins can hold up to a hundred deer at once. I reckoned that was more than seven tons of meat, bone, and offal.

During the fall rutting seasons, when the number of DVCs reliably spikes, the bins did sometimes reach capacity. But White said that when all the ingredients are in balance, it's odorless.

"It might take a month to fill it," said White, "and then it sits for another month until it's finished. The guys that operate it can tell by the odor if it's out of whack."

We stepped out of the car. Today was a hot summer day, and

indeed, there was no particular smell as we walked around the bins—just the usual August scent of warm pavement, dust, and weeds. White first showed me an adjacent shed holding finished compost, which looked like dark sawdust studded with bones and antlers. It would be added into new piles as a starter, just like a yogurt culture, full of microbes to get the next batch humming. VDOT also used it as a fertilizer for grass on poor soil.

Those antlers half-buried in the compost drew my eye. Like geodes or butterfly wings, they're artifacts that always seem valuable when found in the wild.

Then White swung open the big door of a bin—the one with the sign on it. Our perky conversation suddenly hit a bump. Now we were looking at death. Here were three animals lying on their sides: two deer, and a medium-sized dog.

Both the deer were does—it was easy to tell because their teats stood out from their swollen bellies. One was bloated enough that her stiff front leg hovered off the ground. Some sort of bloody gunk oozed from her anus.

White seemed a little embarrassed by the dog. We hadn't discussed road-killed pets at all, and I imagined he worried that if I was a dog lover, seeing it here might turn me off the system he promotes. But what I found sobering about this wasn't the idea of compost.

What hit me was the ignominy of the deaths, and the fact that living beings are transformed into garbage—their bodies seen as a troublesome, unwanted sort of material. It was the difference between the technical way of treating these deaths and the reverential way we believe we should handle human bodies. And of course the presence of the dog pulled these questions in other directions: why we grant some animals human-like burials, how human love transforms a pet dog into an honorary person while a stray dog, unclaimed by people, has the lower status of wildlife.

I thought of how many dead deer I've driven past in my life— thousands? tens of thousands?—and how the sight of their bodies is both a regular part of the landscape and a problem for the government to solve. Humans have dealt death to so many other creatures, and we can't even let those creatures lie and melt back into the earth, because of how we value our own safety and our own sensibilities.

White and I shook off our discomfort and moved on. I felt, somehow, that I needed to demonstrate my toughness—that I was prepared to see death, that I was not shocked by it. We looked at the air pumps, we looked at the leachate tank, I nodded and wrote things down. He dropped me off back at my car.

On my way out, I passed a public school; then a day care center, an assisted-living facility, a bank of storage units. Containers for everything that's messy about life. I remembered something I'd noticed in an empty compost bin—a dark stain on the wall, topped by a pale, sloping line: a mark on the concrete left by all the rounds of deer death and bacterial life that have come, seethed, eaten, transfigured, and gone.

◊◊

Most people don't know or use the acronym DVC. They just say "I hit a deer." This is not really accurate; it's a shorthand so efficiently reductive of its truth that it ends up obscuring reality. As humans, we do sometimes hit each other, but what we do to deer is different—we pilot high-speed ton-and-a-half machines against and through and atop and within the space their unprotected bodies, rib and muscle and glistening innards, had fleetingly occupied.

Although one study found that 92 percent of DVCs caused death for the deer, that death doesn't always happen instantly, despite the wildly inequitable physics.

One night years ago, I was driving through rural Pennsylvania, away from my brother's wedding, in our Volvo station wagon. The wedding had been held at a farm; now our destination was a hotel near the interstate, maybe twenty minutes away.

It was late. My husband, our two exhausted daughters, and I were traveling, as humans so often do, in a state of blind indifference to the surroundings, and I as the driver was attuned only to a single sense: the narrow visual field of headlights and fringed roadside. Perhaps there was a yellow centerline. I don't remember that detail, nor the collision itself. I do know I was wearing a floor-length purple bridesmaid's gown, and that within five minutes of leaving the party, we had sentenced a deer to a painful, groaning death, a few feet into the woods off the road's edge.

I pulled over. We humans were fine. John heard the deer cry out as he walked back to collect a few nonessential pieces of our car from the pavement, a scatter of steel and plastic.

I have to assume there was also some kind of bio-mark on the road, blood or gore at the crash's ground zero. But I didn't have to get out and look, and I didn't feel bound by any code of honor like the one that obligates hunters to track and finish off a deer they've wounded. We were glad our car could still be driven—who wants to wait for a tow truck at midnight, in a party dress?—and so we drove.

Our most salient response to the dreadful situation was to remark that it was too bad we didn't have the tools or the know-how to—another wildly reductive phrase—put the animal out of its misery.

⚁

Several years later, I wound up talking to a man who did have the tools and the know-how, as well as the code of honor. I'll call him Henry; along with his wife, he runs an outdoor skills school and teaches people how to forage wild plants, build shelters, and so on. He told me a very different story about hitting a whitetail, on a spring evening, at a rural spot where a two-lane road dips down toward a stream.

"I've seen them cross there a ton," he said. "That deer bolted across the road and smacked the car."

Henry pulled over and sized up the situation. The car had minor damage. "The deer was pretty mangled," he said. "It had bones sticking out of its leg." He moved it off the road and sat next to it on the ground.

He is also a hunter of deer, one who gives a lot of thought to the ethics of the practice. "If you're going to take life, do it in the least painful way for the animal," he said. "It's not okay to let it suffer. This deer was way beyond repair." He thought about other deer he'd seen injured by cars. One was hit near his property and took a week and a half to die, a time during which he observed it being visited by other deer.

It was his responsibility this time, he thought, to finish what he'd inadvertently started.

"Because of the business I'm in, I always have a carving knife handy for carving wood," he said. He fetched it, returned to the deer, cut into its jugular. He talked to the deer and prayed over it while it bled. "Within thirty seconds the light faded from its eyes."

Now the deer was a body. He might have left it there; it would probably have been hauled away to a landfill. But Henry didn't see it as garbage. He field-dressed the animal and put it in his car. "I put the rest of the parts away from the road," he said. He wanted to prevent further damage to scavenging animals, which commonly happens when they feed too close to travel lanes.

He drove the deer home, skinned it, butchered it, ate the meat, and tanned the hide for buckskin. I can only imagine how different all of this felt compared to my own experience of meekly, guiltily driving away.

Many of the deer parts I'd seen and touched at the primitive skills gathering had also come from roadkill; in that world, people were making a regular practice of collecting and using those bodies on the shoulder, and were full of tips about judging the safety of the meat, or which parts tended to remain usable after a crash.

I'd noticed that the preferred term among those folks was *car-killed*. I'd asked Josh, the teacher of the bone awl workshop, about that. "Roads don't kill things," he'd answered simply.

🦌

Henry's actions, considered and skillful though they may have been, were "probably illegal," he acknowledged. He's right, since he was in Virginia at the time, but there are around thirty other states in which it's legal to harvest roadkill for meat. Some states require people to report the death or to get a harvest permit. Some mandate that the animal be inspected by a state official.

The fact that some Appalachian states, like West Virginia, legally designate roadkill as food has long been fodder for easy comedy. Tennessee endured scathing jibes in 1999 when its state legislature took up the issue. ("Grease the skillet, Ma!" read one headline.) But the practice is also legal in more urban, blue-leaning states: Massachusetts, California, New Jersey. Oregon joined the list in 2019.

Venison is good meat; it's lean, nutritious, organic, and free-range by definition. Some states have programs that organize the collection of roadkill meat for soup kitchens, church groups, food pantries.

These are all ways of acknowledging, as a culture, that farm-raised chicken and beef are not the only, nor even the best, sources of meat. Just outside the mainstream of the American diet, there are millions of pounds of food walking around on the hoof. Walking, running, and often trying to cross the road.

⚊

Not only do DVCs have an emotional cost, but they're also financially expensive. In the worst states for DVCs, about one in forty drivers files a deer-related auto insurance claim each year. "It doesn't take much to do a lot of damage," said George Bragg, a body shop owner in Virginia. "A good hit can render $2,500 worth of damage to an average car." State Farm reports an even higher figure: $4,341 per claim on average. If deer shatter windshields and set off airbags, a car can be totaled. "We've seen that happen at less than five hundred miles," Bragg said.

A 2008 federal report on wildlife collisions tallied a few other average costs of deer hits: $2,702 in medical costs, $125 in towing fees, and one other that's very curious: $2,000 for the monetary value of the deer itself. That represents a loss to the state and the economy, based on the cost of hunting licenses and the wider hunting and wildlife-watching economy.

Whatever their "value," it's the size of deer that make them so damaging to cars and so dangerous to the people inside them. The average whitetail weighs 150 pounds, and they're tall enough that the physics of collisions often send them flying upward rather than falling under the wheels.

From the human point of view, terrible things can ensue. In February 2020, a man was killed in Iowa when a deer—hit by a different driver—flew through his windshield and struck his body. Two days earlier, something very similar had happened in Florida, killing an eighty-one-year-old woman. In the same week, a driver in Texas hit a deer, ran off the road, and was impaled on a fence post.

The previous December, a sixteen-year-old boy hit a deer, pulled over, and tried to drag the deer out of the road. He himself was then hit by a car and died. It's heartbreaking to think of this boy, a new driver trying to do what he thought was the right thing, falling prey to the same overpowered technology that had, minutes before, cast him as the killer. And it's sad, too, that a more seasoned driver would have told him to ignore his urge to take responsibility.

Our collective experience with roads, machines, and repeated death feeds our prudence, not our hearts. One wildlife manager, explaining to me why drivers should never swerve to avoid deer, asked, "Would you rather hit a deer or an oak tree?" The answer is obvious, but only if the welfare of the deer is given no weight.

Several hundred people die in America annually because of deer–vehicle collisions. But deer get the worst of it: Both the U.S. and Europe likely see more than a million deer deaths, by car, every year.

🦌

In the fall, after bucks have shed the velvet on their antlers and dispersed from their chummy summertime "bachelor groups," they find themselves restless and driven, propelled by the highest testosterone levels they'll have all year. Does, meanwhile, have weaned the fawns they birthed in the spring and, as the days grow shorter, prepare to come into estrus, meaning they're ready to breed. Searching for mates, both sexes crisscross the landscape more frequently than at any other time of year.

For years, everyone whose jobs involve DVCs, and many members of the driving public, have known to expect a major spike in accidents during the fall rut. November is the worst month for collisions between deer and cars, closely followed by October and December. Of all the DVCs that Bridget Donaldson recorded during her study period, more than half occurred during October and November.

While bucks travel alone in autumn, does continue to move in social groups. Led by an alpha female—usually their mother or grandmother—younger does and fawns follow the alpha whether her decisions are good ones or not. She may take them across a road or a bridge; if she jumps to her death, her followers do, too. According to a 2022 report from Johnsonburg, Pennsylvania, one particularly hazardous overpass saw deadly leaps by no fewer than twenty-five deer in one season. In a TV news segment, disturbed residents pointed to a hillside strewn with bodies.

It doesn't help that deer are neither nocturnal nor diurnal but crepuscular: most active at dawn and dusk. Unfortunately, in the fall, those are often the same hours that people commute to and from work. While DVCs can happen at any time of day, the overlap of deer and human rush hours means more chances for fatal contact.

Of course, deer's predilection for edges comes into play too. As human development extends its fingers into the landscape, and deer move along the edges of those corridors, DVCs may become more of a year-round phenomenon. Bragg, the body shop owner, said that in the last few years, he'd seen more deer-damaged vehicles arrive in his shop in every season, not just fall. He attributes this to rapid development in his part of Virginia. A similar report recently emerged from a heavily populated part of Pennsylvania.

Crash mitigation methods fall into several main categories: changing animal behavior, changing driver behavior, and the design of the roads themselves. There are some relatively flashy solutions, like a "sky bridge" installed in 2018 near Salt Lake City, allowing animals to cross high above an interstate on a surface dotted with gravel, boulders, and logs. Such overpasses are more common in Europe, and Canada's Banff National Park is known for its wildlife bridges that cross the Trans-Canada Highway.

There's no shortage of strategies: special signage that comes alive with flashing lights when the system detects a large animal at the roadside; chirpy PSA campaigns, including a spate of media stories every fall warning drivers about the deer rut; cutting down vegetation; adding streetlights. As for the deer, people have tried to discourage them from crossing via mirrors, nasty smells, even "hazing"—as in training the animals to be terrified of roads—by firing cannons or setting off fireworks.

Regardless of our larger brains, deer behavior appears easier to modify than human behavior. Asking drivers to slow down and putting up warning signs are two of the least effective strategies to reduce DVCs, according to one study. Fencing and underpasses, the hallmarks of the Charlottesville project, are the two best bets.

Unless, that is, we consider solutions at a bigger scale—an ecosystem scale. In 2021, following Donaldson's success, Virginia lawmakers passed the second of two wildlife corridor laws, requiring state agencies to figure out where and how wild animals travel and account for that when planning new roads. Governments may be in the process of catching up to the science; in the same year, Congress set aside $350 million for improving corridors and preventing animal collisions.

One study suggested another surprising fix. Having wolves in an area might unexpectedly reduce DVCs—not simply because wolves kill deer, but because they create a "landscape of fear" that changes deer's habits. Wolves themselves like to travel along roads, so deer learn to stay away. The study came out of Wisconsin, where counties with growing wolf populations saw their DVC numbers drop by almost a quarter.

◊◊

Every deer–vehicle collision is a violent clash between flesh and machine, but more than that, DVCs are one place where natural laws collide with artificial power. The speed and toughness of any animal has its upper limits; certainly deer, those incredible athletes, easily outdo humans in those terms.

When we climb into our cars, though, we amplify our own bodies' powers exponentially. Fossil fuels have changed our experience of being embodied in many ways, from our ability to climate-control our houses to the changes in our sleep patterns caused by artificial light and the ubiquity of screens. The shift in our experience of movement—the sheer speed vehicles permit us—is as profound as any of these.

To be without a car in almost every part of America now is to be severely disadvantaged; our bodies alone are simply not enough to navigate society. We have created an infrastructure that all but requires every person to enhance their physical powers using fossil-fueled transportation. We hardly acknowledge that only the last handful of generations of Americans have known the experience of traveling over the surface of the earth at fifty, sixty, seventy miles an hour—much less doing this routinely, day after day.

Moving millions of people around this rapidly requires not only the enormously complicated infrastructure of roads and vehicles but also a deep revision of how we understand space. How do our bodies relate to our surroundings? How does a human fit into the scale of a city, a county, a state? How does distance translate to time? I routinely travel to Charlottesville; whenever someone asks me, I say that town is forty-five minutes from my house. But minutes are not a measure of distance, unless the rate of travel is highly standardized, highly predictable.

If we've been numbed to the truth of distance, we've also been anesthetized by the very common sight of roadkill. Death is part of the routine. We accept almost completely that those smears, clumps, mounds, and stains of once-living flesh are an inevitable part of the setting for our travels.

It echoes the deer's ancient role as psychopomp—the escort of recently departed souls—when they appear dead on the roadside. We may no longer bury our dead with deer antlers, but in a distinctly modern way, deer remain associated with the blunt end of life. That reminder both unsettles us, since it makes death present, and reassures us, since they are other—animals, not people. Some part of us knows how close death is every time we drive. But our lives demand that we push this fear away.

Given that, our annoyance at deer in the roads is a classic blame-the-victim reversal. Maybe the reality is that humans have no particular right to move through the landscape as quickly as we do. We're just very, very used to it.

🦌

Around the same time that I visited the deer compost bins, so did a young artist named Madison Creech. She was in the midst of a fellowship in Richmond, studying fiber arts, and had moved around the country a lot for residencies and teaching posts. In fact, by the time I caught up with her, she'd moved a couple more times and landed in Wilmington, North Carolina. Like many Americans, her life experience has been scattered over a collage of disconnected landscapes. When she was a kid, Madison's dad was a missile launch officer in the military and the family mostly lived in wide-open places. She remembers playing outdoors on a base in Wyoming, where antelope would routinely wander through the yard.

Sitting in her home studio, she told me that in her work, she tries to find motifs common to all these different places.

"You encounter roadkill when you're moving and every place you live," she said—the ubiquity of humped bodies with vehicles flashing past them, from ocean to mountains to plains. When she heard about the composting system, she thought, *I've got to see this for myself.*

At the bins, she climbed right up onto the compost in process. It was fall, and the bins were packed with bodies. A truck pulled in, bringing more. She took many photos, including a ghostly image of a fringe of fur threading through a mound of compost, like a geological stratum.

Back home, she made drawings based on the compost and on photos of road-killed animals she found on a citizen-science database. Ultimately these became part of a large fabric piece she called *Compost Toile*, a roiling composition in which the profiles of broken animals half-emerge from a background of tiny swirls and marks. They're almost but not quite readable as the creatures they once were; like the deer in the compost bins, they're in the midst of dissolving back into base material.

Moving often as a child, she didn't always have friends, but wildlife filled that role. When she got older and began driving, she hit a deer in the Nebraska night and cried. I told her I remembered the first animal I'd hit, too, and how guilty I felt. It was an American rite of passage.

Those connections to animals that feel "abrasive," as she put it, seemed to me like a perfect theme for an artist in our time. It's a problem we all live with, a problem that's not going anywhere. Creech told me, "I want to play with things that are there, but not there."

⚘

The other day, I was taking a run on the road where I live and saw, a few hundred yards away, the white tails of several deer bounding off through a big clearing. I assume it was I who'd spooked them; there were no cars, no other people around. By the time I got closer to where they'd been, there was just one still in view.

She was small and delicate. She stood near a red shed, staring back at me. I stopped in the middle of the road, with my hands folded, to watch her. We faced off for a long time.

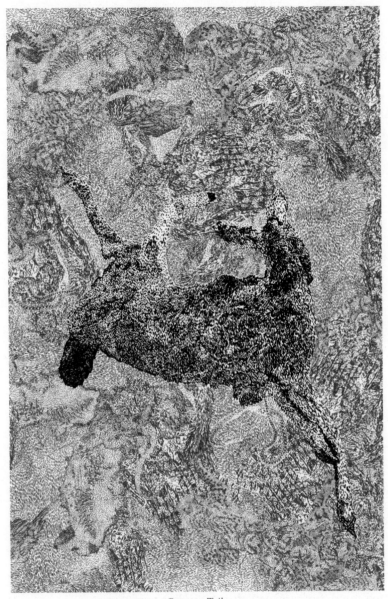

Compost Toile

I thought about how the gaze of a predator is in itself a kind of weapon. My eyes are different from the headlights of a car, which do have a human intelligence behind them, but one step removed. My eyes and the doe's eyes communicated directly, and neither of us moved, except for the way her ears continually swiveled in all directions.

Finally she seemed to decide that I intended no harm and risked lowering her head to the ground. I could hear her tearing off leaves and chewing, even at this distance, the way you can listen to cows or horses eating. She kept interrupting her feeding to raise her head, listen, gaze over her shoulder. Then she started to walk directly toward me.

There was a delicious feeling of encounter. How close would she dare to come? With every step she took I could sense her in greater detail: her shaggy, even matted neck; the click of her hooves as she stepped on a gravel driveway. Gradually, she turned. Each of her front feet pointed backward, balletically, with every step. I tried to understand, as I always do when I have the luxury of a long look at deer, the form of her body—finely boned head, broad flanks, wide-set eyes.

She came within thirty feet and then started circling me, as though I were the point of a compass and she were drawing an arc. Several times, she stopped to look at me, point the dishes of her ears toward me, and conspicuously sniff in my direction. I thought about how her sense-world must be so much richer than mine, with so many messages arriving through channels that are crude in my body, highly developed in hers.

Finally, she walked slowly across the road, snaked under a barbed-wire fence at the shoulder, and stepped into the woods. I watched her a little longer as she moved deeper among the trees. I still stood in the middle of the road—listening, in the back of my mind, for cars, as I always do. But none came.

CHAPTER 11

Pests

The first of March. IN THE WOODS AT THE REAR OF OUR property, an inch of snow is capped by hard ice, slow to melt. It records many turkey tracks, crossing the lane and up onto the hillside, and these intersect with lines of deer tracks, which climb and traverse the slope in their own manner.

We just planted our first round of seeds yesterday for this year's vegetable garden. Lettuce, chard, parsley, and the brassicas: kale, broccoli, cabbage, and all their cousins. The seed flats are safely indoors on shelves, waiting to sprout. Some of those seedlings will be facing "deer pressure," as the phrase has it, the minute they go outside to be transplanted in a month or so.

In that period hostas will sprout, too. They're a favorite of whitetails, and once they get eaten, they don't regrow; they just hang around for the rest of the season, looking maimed.

In Nordic mythology, no less than the world tree itself—the ash called Yggdrasil—is vulnerable to the appetites of deer.

There are four of them—stags named Dainn, Duneyrr, Durathror and Dvalinn—and they chew the leaves of Yggdrasil incessantly. This is no small matter, since the tree's branches support the very weight of the cosmos. Its roots reach into the underworld and eternally replenish its life force, nourishing the deer through their relentless feeding.

It's a story with no beginning or ending. The stags always eat and the tree always gives; they balance one another, yin and yang. And this dance includes humans, too.

"We are told," writes one mythologist, "that dew comes from the tree, and that when the hart feeds on its branches, her milk becomes shining mead which never gives out, and is used to provide drink for the warriors in Valhalla."

In contemporary America, deer still play many of the roles they've traditionally held around the world, from hunter's quarry to valued neighbors. But more and more, they grow into another costume. Now they are very often pests, and one of the prime ways they bother us is by eating the plants we call ours.

For us, the deer who eat of the world tree are no longer perceived as adding anything of value. They only subtract. It's become a zero-sum game.

◊

Late April. We've put all our cool-weather plants in the ground and are keeping the fences shut at night. There have been some animal tracks in the non-fenced beds—not clear whose. Nothing seems to have been damaged thus far. I keep meaning to protect my hydrangea, which surprisingly grew back after last year's damage, by rigging up some chicken wire around where it grows.

We gardened for years with no fences and vaguely knew that we were getting away with something. People would ask us about deer and we'd just say "No, they don't bother us." Then, suddenly, they discovered our place. Mothers with fawns added us to their daily routes, like postal workers keeping their rounds. The experience of having our plants destroyed changed our whole relationship to the garden. It became a citadel. We enclosed all the beds we could. I dream about how we could wall off our entire yard—like the fancy estate garden I once visited, where the whole expensive, perfect fantasy (the specimen trees, the sculpted yew) was made possible by a tall, mighty fence, just beyond sight.

◊

Mid-June. More deer sightings lately on the roadside, including roadkill. Some obviously deer-browsed weeds around the edge of the yard.

Early this morning I was alone in the quiet garden, barefoot, tending to comfrey under the pear tree, looking at the almost-open buds of the bee balm. Then I noticed my asters had been nibbled—*hey!* Immediately I thought of the green beans, outside the fence and unprotected. I ran to check on them, stepping on something painful in the grass. Sure enough, they'd been hit. Formerly lush and perfect, they were now reduced to dozens of naked green stems standing straight up. Hoofprints were everywhere in the loose dark soil. I limped inside and told John about this, and he had the same reaction I'd had: a string of curses.

What is this feeling? It's not the anger of a deep violation, like if a person broke into our house. But it's a severe species of irritation.

And it's eerie: These large animals were right outside our bedroom window, eating, destroying, and we slept right through it.

🐾

Deer have been bothering gardeners for centuries. As far back as the 1300s, William Langland had a speaker complain, in his Middle English poem *Piers Plowman*, about "bukkes that brekken down myne hegges" ("bucks that break down my hedges"). He goes on to implore a nobleman to control the deer by hunting.

The growing sense that deer threaten the human order bleeds into the literature of our own time. Rumaan Alam's 2020 novel about a family vacationing on Long Island, *Leave the World Behind*, makes deer into a harbinger of apocalypse: "Where the yard shrugged away from the house, the grass grew patchy and was then just dust and leaves and weeds at the hem of the woods or wilderness or whatever it was. In the space beyond that, Rose saw a deer . . . There were five deer, there were seven . . . There were dozens of deer. Had she been up higher, she'd have understood that there were hundreds, more than a thousand, more than that, even."

The poet Cassandra de Alba strikes a similar note in her book *habitats*, which starts by describing how deer "begin / to roam in gangs" and imagines that they leave "scorched hoofprints," live off the tears they lick from mourners' faces outside funeral homes, and behave like teenage punks, wearing camouflage and "crushing cans into the floor."

Later in the book, they start stealing children. But in one poem called "the deer are teething," de Alba only slightly exaggerates our reality: "chewing on fences, / the corners of houses . . . the whole town marked with their teeth."

⚸

Late June. Yesterday morning I was woken before dawn by the sound of chewing right outside the window. I knew it wasn't in the garden, but still it got me out of bed, turning on the deck light, listening to the sound of departing hooves. Later I found that some wild roses had been nibbled, and some baby walnut trees that I don't really care about.

But oh, do I care about the garden right now. It's peaking. Many things are blooming or just about to: catnip and Culver's root, borage and nasturtium, echinacea, rudbeckia, sedum, sunflower. And lots of food crops are on the way. So much pleasure in sitting and looking, especially as we're eating most of our meals out on the deck these days, among the beds. We are just bathing in the sight of our plants.

Today when I got up I immediately checked on the hostas and other things I could see from the back door. Everything looked good. It took me until lunch to notice Elsie's big sunflower, six feet tall, stripped of all but one of its leaves. It looks sad and ridiculous now, with its stumpy torn-off stems. Her voice got a little quavery when she saw it. And then I found an entire comfrey plant destroyed. A zucchini leaf nibbled, a squash vine slashed. Holes where there used to be plants.

I want restitution. Tonight we busied ourselves with deer-proofing. More chicken wire, more row cover. Elsie and I blended up a deer spray from a Bob Vila recipe: garlic, egg, milk, cayenne, and water, currently putrefying on the counter inside a repurposed spray bottle. I pulled out some hair from our hairbrushes and tried to spread it over the leaves of threatened plants.

Military metaphors come to mind. Siege. Fortification.

⚜

Three days later. We struggled to get our spray bottle working; the cayenne powder in that smelly concoction kept clogging it up. In the meantime one of our hostas had been eaten away to nothing. Finally, after dinner on the deck, I managed to spray enough to get coverage on all the remaining hostas, comfrey, sedum, squashes. I felt very manic and middle-aged, doing this; I announced to my family, not kidding at all, "I have a feeling of power and control!" Then we heard a deer crashing around in the nearby woods. We all made predator noises to scare it off.

It's about to rain, which will wash off the spray.

⚜

Mid-July. We got home last night from a week away. We'd hired a house sitter in part to keep a human presence here, since we know from experience that deer can sense when we're gone and make bolder incursions.

But it was all in vain. Examining our garden by flashlight after fifteen hours in the car, we found all kinds of damage. Jalapeños eaten. Cucumbers eaten. Sunflowers eaten. And they'd gotten *into* our eight-foot fence and stripped all the new beans and the chard! Incredible. Prints and scat where the crops used to be. The deer netting sagging from its posts.

We looked around at the carnage: brassicas decimated by cabbage worms, the tomato trellis collapsing, squash bugs riddling the cucumber leaves. And that deer damage: ugly and irreversible.

It was the humbling moment of the year. Every gardening season has at least one, when you feel your hopes dashed. In a good year, it only applies to one or two crops. In a bad year, you stand there feeling foolish for all the time and money you spent, raising what turned out to be a ruin.

⚜

Why does it matter that my little veggie patch, or my pretty flowers, get rudely eaten by passing wildlife? Categorically, it doesn't. It's a struggle I've conjured from thin air. I decided to care when I bought into the idea of myself as a gardener, striving to manifest a certain vision of beauty and function. That's why it hurts when the deer come and eat something I've tended. I could just as easily decide to grow only grass, and voilà: problem solved.

But boy, am I not alone in this.

The fact that deer eat landscaping plants is viewed as a problem by enough people to merit scientific study, a steady stream of publications, and an industry's worth of repellents. Landscaping damage is also one of the problems policymakers often mention when they argue that deer numbers must be reduced. The more deer venture into human spaces to find their food, leaving mutilated shrubs and antler-rubbed tree saplings in their wake, the more the human urge to defend and enclose takes hold. Our prevailing aesthetic may not be quite as high-maintenance as, say, Versailles, but it's still tidier than any natural ecosystem would be.

Products available to gardeners are named in a spirit of indignation: Deer Stopper, Deer Ban, Deer Scram, Deer Off, Deer B Gon, Nature's Mace. If I wanted to, at this moment, I could spend hundreds of dollars on repellent spray, powders that waft unpleasant odors over the beds, coyote urine granules to sprinkle on the ground, citrus-based soap bars in netted bags to hang from the trellises, garlic-scented clips to attach to individual plants, motion-activated sprinklers, and/or solar-powered ultrasonic noise generators to stab into the earth around the garden perimeter.

There may be some wishful thinking at work for those who buy in, just as there was for me when I mixed up my own spray at home. Much advice boils down to "This doesn't really work, but you can go ahead and try it." *The New York Times* quotes an expert on the problem: "If the deer really want to get to your food source, aside from a very tall exclusionary fence, all bets at protecting it are off." *Very tall* means eight feet, since deer can leap over anything shorter. Some people also smear peanut butter on squares of foil draped over the electrified wires: training by electroshock therapy.

The futility of all these efforts—which also include endless attempts to find the plants deer don't like—does nothing to deter us gardeners. The endeavor is rarely just for the gardener's private pleasure; it's a way of communicating to other people, too. As the garden historian John Dixon Hunt puts it, a well-designed garden "confirms . . . the instinctive human goodness in its owner." That's not so much a moral goodness as an aesthetic one. We're composing with plants in order to prove our own taste, class standing, and cultural mastery. In other words, a garden is part of how a gardener shows her face to the world. No wonder we chafe when beasts tear down a living monument to the self.

🦌

To see the issue from the deer's point of view is to realize that, after millennia of wandering among a patchwork of plant communities that had planted themselves—or, in many cases, plants that had been encouraged to grow *as deer browse* by Native American burning practices—the animals have now found themselves in a world where a complex network of human intention overlies the buffet. All of our ideas of ownership, plans, preferences, and economies are totally invisible to the deer. If they wander onto my land, for example, deer might start by browsing sassafras seedlings in the woods (pretty much fine with me), move on to the half-wild red clover near the shed (considerably less fine with me, since I like to dry its flowers for tea), and finish up in our pea patch (infuriating). To the deer, it's all just food—part of the eight pounds of vegetation they need to eat each day in order to survive. A "lawn" may as well be a swath of prairie. A "garden" has no meaning.

It's the same indifference to human wishes displayed by a tornado or a tsunami. It's the Earth doing Earth things. We are not particularly good at accepting this.

🦌

The deer repellent industry might be, in its essence, a monument to human vanity. But something deeper is going on when we consider our food system. Farmers aren't just miffed, but legitimately threatened when deer enter their fields and orchards. In a 2001 survey by the USDA, farmers reported that deer were, by orders of magnitude, the most destructive of all wildlife species.

The problem is shared by growers large and small, from family dairy farms to commercial orchards to industrial-scale corn belt operators in the Midwest, where studies have found that deer can get more than half their food from farm crops.

I know a couple who support themselves and three children by running a small veggie-and-herb farm in an idyllic valley not far from my house. Ben Stowe and Heather Coiner have been running Little Hat Creek Farm since 2013, with about an acre and a half in vegetables plus a bakery where Coiner turns out loaves of crusty sourdough, croissants, and other goodies. Meanwhile, Stowe is often outside, fighting off whitetails.

"Last year was the first time we really had some serious losses, where I know we lost hundreds of dollars," he told me in 2021. What got hit the worst were the sweet potatoes. "Deer are really attracted to sweet potato vines. We've seen deer nibble around the edges before, but that time, they really ate the whole row. Two hundred fifty feet of sweet potatoes got mowed down."

Many of Stowe's other crops—leafy greens, broccoli, winter rye—are equally vulnerable. "We've had an increasing amount of deer pressure," he said, thinking back over his decade in the business.

Many of his ways of fighting back are the same tactics I've tried at home: He covers plants with a lightweight fabric called row cover (which gets expensive, and often ends up lost or torn, sometimes by deer hooves). He scares deer off by yelling at them. He uses fences (again, expensive; he recently dropped about $400 on an electric fence to enclose just a quarter of an acre).

As a commercial farmer, Stowe has another option. He can legally request permission from the state of Virginia to shoot deer on his land, even out of season. He'd done exactly that in the winter of the year we talked. It was quite easy: An officer of the state wildlife agency came over, took a look at the damage to Stowe's cover crops, and put him down for a half-year permit to shoot up to six antlerless deer on his farm. He wasn't required to do the killing personally. "We don't hunt, ourselves," Stowe said, "so I put some of my neighbors and friends on there."

He felt hopeful. But when the permit ran out, the deer were still around. Stowe's neighbors never showed up and his friends' hunt was unsuccessful. We walked together through his big hillside garden, past a long row he'd just covered with new white plastic for weed suppression. It had only been down a few days, but already the plastic was studded with holes, up and down the row, where deer hooves had punched through.

Up the hill, he showed me the amputated leaves on his sweet potato vines. "Oh, and look!" he said, discovering that they'd also clipped off the tops of some okra plants, two or three feet off the ground. "That's gotta be deer."

It was a little here, a little there, but it could really add up. Another farming couple Stowe once worked for had installed a deer fence and found they now needed 30 percent fewer transplants each year. That was how much the deer had been taking.

Stowe is a gentle guy, but a final story he told spoke to the vengefulness that farmers often feel toward marauding deer. Apparently the state officer had told him, "I once had a guy who said 'I want to bait a stump and put dynamite in the stump.'"

That, for the record, is verboten.

⚜

Of course, damaging plants isn't the only crime deer commit. They also make people sick.

Not directly; at least, not that we know of. But wherever there are deer, there are ticks. Among other diseases, ticks carry the bacterium that causes Lyme disease—more and more, a familiar sour note in the symphony of our damaged world.

Getting Lyme is no joke. Here in Virginia, it's as common as copperhead stories; everyone's either been a victim or is related to one. Personally, I've escaped *Borrelia burgdorferi* so far, but I've lost track of the number of people I know—starting with my husband and continuing through a long list of acquaintances—who have suffered the powerful headaches, the fever, the joint pain. If they're lucky, they catch it early and a round of strong antibiotics knocks it back. If they're unlucky, they end up dealing with permanent effects. "Sorry, my brain is mixed up," I've heard them say. "It's the Lyme." People contend with facial palsy, shooting pains, heart palpitations, brain inflammation, knees that swell with arthritis.

Chronic Lyme disease is controversial; some doctors don't believe it exists, and patients complain about stigma, misdiagnosis, and being told that it's all in their heads. Some go so far as to allege conspiratorial cover-ups by the government or the medical establishment. Perhaps in part due to a similar conversation around long COVID, Lyme disease is now having a bit of a moment, with public figures from Justin Bieber to Shania Twain to *New York Times* columnist Ross Douthat coming forward to talk about how long-term Lyme has debilitated them. "With my stomach, throat, and bowels all afire, I had lost 40 pounds in ten weeks," Douthat writes. "I woke up in the mornings feeling like I had been beaten by a boxer overnight."

This is a nasty disease. Part of the problem is that testing for Lyme disease is notoriously unreliable. And there's no vaccine, although several are now in development. Another strategy: Scientists near Boston are genetically modifying mice so that their bodies refuse to carry Lyme bacteria. (Along with deer, white-footed mice are a key reservoir for the germ.)

Since it was first identified in Connecticut in 1975, Lyme has exploded in prevalence. New research in 2022 made the stunning claim that up to 15 percent of people worldwide have already been infected. Lyme disease is on the rise in places that never used to harbor it: northern states in the U.S., Nova Scotia, Scotland. It can even affect dogs.

Along with vehicle collisions and landscaping damage, tick-borne disease is another top reason people see deer as a menace, especially in cities and suburbs. There are certainly studies out there suggesting that slashing deer numbers would cut down on Lyme. Although deer don't carry the bacteria, they provide blood meals for ticks, which can ultimately transmit it to humans. Almost all black-legged ticks hitch a ride on a deer at some point, so having fewer deer would seem to deny ticks a key food source.

But other research finds no correlation between deer numbers and Lyme incidence. Since one deer can carry scores of ticks, deer numbers would have to be severely reduced to actually starve them out. And the role of the white-footed mouse is a complicated factor in its own right. Deer are surely part of the mix, but it's far from clear whether reducing their numbers would really help, or how many would have to be culled.

More and more, it's becoming common to blame climate change for the rise in tick numbers. Warmer winters help them survive and spread northward, and the same is true for white-footed mice. Just like deer, ticks prefer edge habitats and are therefore boosted by human fragmentation of the landscape.

But, as one researcher pointed out frankly in the *Journal of Integrated Pest Management*, it's a lot simpler to remove deer from the landscape than to slow down climate change, or convince people to stop building houses and roads.

⁂

Meanwhile, there was the discovery, in early 2021, that deer could carry the COVID-19 virus. The first clues came from a study in which government scientists deliberately infected fawns in a lab setting and observed as they passed the virus to other fawns. Within months, researchers found that huge proportions of wild white-tailed deer in parts of the U.S. were already harboring the virus—like in Iowa, where during the winter of 2020–2021, fully 80 percent of wild deer tested were COVID-positive. Scientists surmised that deer had caught the disease from humans multiple times and were transmitting it to each other. Within months, mule deer were found to be infected too. We don't know how humans pass the virus to deer—perhaps through feeding them, or because they drink water contaminated with our waste.

All of this has vast implications for the pandemic. If deer are a reservoir for COVID, and could potentially pass the disease back to people, it means that we will never eradicate it. And within the bodies of deer, the COVID virus has even more opportunities to mutate and evolve.

Zoonotic diseases (diseases that pass from animals to people) have been around for centuries—think smallpox, anthrax, or tuberculosis. But they are symptomatic of our era. Humans and wildlife are living in closer proximity now, in many places, than we have for generations. And climate change makes it easier for many pathogens to survive and spread.

Living near deer is not without its risks for human health. But to simply blame deer for our illnesses, without investigating the deeper causes, is like putting a Band-Aid on a Lyme patient's aching knee.

CHAPTER 12

The Cull

RAGE OVER LANDSCAPE DAMAGE, DISGUST OVER PATHO-
gens, and fear over traffic accidents: These bad feelings coalesce,
in many people and communities, as a desire to take away some
of the deer. Not all of them, people often hasten to say. Just
enough to bring them into "balance." As we've seen, ecological
balance is an exceptionally slippery concept. But then, these are
not purely scientific discussions.

When local leaders propose culling, they often have in mind
hiring a professional outfit (sometimes their own local police department) that will efficiently remove a set number of animals,
out of sight of the public and with many safety measures in place.
It's arguably no different from hiring an exterminator to deal
with rats, but the removal of deer stirs up all manner of feelings
that rodents do not.

Part of the emotional charge must come from the special place
deer hunting holds in American culture. Killing deer within city
limits, without any of the traditional trappings of wilderness, fellowship, or fair chase, can strike people as perverse. It seems like
cheating—and in terms of the way many recreational hunters
understand the constraints that make their pastime a "sport," it
is cheating. Most often, the professional deer killers sit in stands
above bait piles, shooting every deer they can.

Another model involves managed hunts: recreational hunters,
pursuing deer under tight controls in city parklands, or in the
backyards of willing homeowners. This, too, can be off-putting.
Neighbors worry about arrows or bullets flying, or about

wounded deer wandering through, dying in inconvenient spots. Hunters themselves may have to adjust to a reality far less glorious than Natty Bumppo's ideal: signing up online for a time slot in a city-owned tree stand.

This is a truly modern dilemma, one our ancestors could hardly have imagined. In the early 1970s, the city of Irondequoit, New York, grappled with one of the earliest controversies over culling deer. A decade later, a similar dynamic played out in places as far-flung as Florida's Everglades and California's Angel Island. In the 1990s and beyond, the growth of deer populations and the frequency of deer-human interactions brought the discussion to an ever-growing number of localities. Like a Broadway musical that makes its way inexorably through high school auditoriums all across the land, the same words and music—both pro- and anti-culling—eventually rang out in every corner of the U.S., and in other countries as well. Today, the conversations proceed, as if following a template, in dozens or hundreds of communities, though many of them are not especially aware of each other, or of the mountains of precedent that exist. Every town or suburb that undertakes this decision process starts down a well-worn path but must nonetheless take the journey, step by painful step.

⚶

What's been happening recently? Let's begin in New York City. Deer are absent from the densest part of the metropolis; a lone deer that somehow found its way to Harlem a few years ago was cornered and taken into custody by police. But just outside that core, they abound. In January 2020, a controversy erupted on Staten Island when a first-term congressman, Max Rose, criticized Mayor Bill de Blasio's refusal to allow deer hunting there. Instead, the mayor supported an ongoing $6.6 million effort by the parks department to perform vasectomies on the island's bucks. Rose, a veteran of the war in Afghanistan, offered to personally join in the cull if it was legalized. "I'll go back to my glory days and I'll start taking down some of these deer," he said. (This proposal was not adopted.)

Travel a little farther into the suburbs and you'll find controversies bubbling on Long Island, on Fire Island, and in the Hudson Valley. Over in New Jersey, one town after another has been having The Talk. One community might be several years into a culling program, even as another is still trying to get an accurate count of its deer, while a third dithers after public controversy—like in River Vale, where the Animal Protection League of New Jersey sent residents an anti-culling mailer in 2019 and called white-tailed deer "a persecuted species."

Just outside D.C., Rockville, Maryland, finally conducted a cull in 2020 after ten years of planning but was targeted by PETA protesters, some of them apparently writing from as far away as Australia. Urban hunting and culling occurred or was proposed in central Virginia, in mountainous western Maryland, in small-town West Virginia. One community tried installing feeding stations in which a roller would apply insecticide to deer's backs to cut down on ticks. Many others called in the United States Department of Agriculture to do the shooting.

In the Midwest, the pattern repeats. Culling has taken place in little Chadron, Nebraska, and in the big suburbs around Cleveland, Ohio. It's caused hard feelings in River Forest, Illinois, where one member of the Ad Hoc Deer Committee wrote that deer culling would "normalize gun violence." When she suggested fertility control at a committee meeting, one pro-culling member accused her of filibustering.

Outside Detroit, the parks department office got a menacing phone call one day before a cull was scheduled to be conducted by park officers. A seventy-one-year-old man warned the receptionist that he would station himself in the woods to shoot the officers before they could shoot the deer. Police soon tracked him down.

In Lakeway, Texas: A neighborhood resident took a video of deer being trapped in nets before being hauled off to slaughter. The resident sobbed behind the camera. The video went viral. The trapping stopped.

186 & THE AGE OF DEER

Atlanta rapper Boosie Badazz posted a video inviting hunters to his estate. "Bruh . . . I got deer problems," he said. "I need a deer hitter."

Disagreements crop up in Canada, Maui, Australia. In the U.K., animal welfare groups opposed government plans to cull female deer in Scotland, while controversy swirled over what to do when the COVID pandemic collapsed the venison market and fueled an explosion in the British deer population. In Japan, three young entrepreneurs launched a business making handbags out of the skins of culled deer.

In reference to possible culling in Anaconda, Montana, an expert commented, "It's like mowing the grass. You have to keep doing it."

⚬

Nobody counts the grass blades cut, nor the total number of deer culled, across the U.S. Naturally, where the federal government is involved, statistics are thorough. In 2020, Wildlife Services, the division of the USDA that contracts with communities to cull deer, killed 8,035 white-tailed deer in 42 states, dispersed another 2,060, and unintentionally killed another 37.

But the numbers culled by local police departments are unclear and likely much greater. Managed hunts exist in a blurry territory somewhere between official and recreational killing. Then there are the private companies that send in professional sharpshooters. It all adds up to some unknown total. Behind that number are scores of people who—after all the talking—become responsible for the doing. Overseeing the deaths of deer is part of their jobs.

⚬

The day I drove to New Jersey felt like death. It was dim and bleak, the nadir of February. The highway up the East Coast pulled me onward, all afternoon, past apartment blocks and strip malls and long-necked machines tearing up the median. The sky was low and muted even in the middle of the day.

By the time I met up with Jim Ferry in Princeton that evening, though, the world had come alive. Mist pervaded the town, washed and sparkled by headlights. Black trees stood out in the chill. Jim, Princeton's sole animal control officer, swung his big diesel pickup into the parking lot where he'd told me to meet him. It was nearly eight o'clock, and he was just starting work.

I was here to get close to deer culling in action—as close as I could. Princeton has one of the country's more well-established culling programs. It's well known in the deer management world, both for the long relationship between the town and White Buffalo (the nonprofit that carries out the killing) and for the near-violent controversy the project caused when it began in the early 2000s. I'd already talked with a number of people involved, from Jim himself to White Buffalo's president, and had been told firmly—as I had by a number of other localities—that I would not be allowed to observe the culling itself. But I could watch everything that happened afterward. For the last four hours, White Buffalo sharpshooters had been sitting in tree stands at different spots around Princeton, killing whitetails. Now it was Jim's job to pick up the bodies.

I climbed in and we trundled through town. Jim told me that in the first few nights of the culling season, the shooters had already taken fifty-two deer. "It's a big start," he said. A hundred and fifty was the goal for the whole three- to four-week season, and the number permitted by the state. At this rate, it wouldn't take long to max out.

Jim pulled the truck over on the side of a straight two-lane road with woods on both sides. Township land, he said. On the right was an anonymous little nothing—a dirt lane with a chain strung across it. He hopped out and removed the chain, and then we started backing up, slowly, into the darkness of the flat, sunken woods. The truck's radio crackled. On and on we went. I had time to wonder what on earth I'd gotten myself into. Then a man appeared in the red glow of the taillights, wearing overalls, holding up one hand. We stopped. I got out and walked to the back of the truck. Lying on the ground was a deer with a clear plastic bag over its head.

The bag was cinched with a zip tie. A few drops of blood were spattered on its inner surface.

Here I was again, standing beside a man, looking at a dead deer and feeling like etiquette called for nonchalance.

"They're all head shots," Jim said. "We use the bags to prevent the mess."

The shooter had vanished back into the woods. Water dripped off the trees.

Jim was writing on a clipboard. "Each deer's tagged with a number so Fish and Wildlife can track them." He found the right tag—number 53—and wrapped it around the deer's rear leg, like a wristband you'd get at the entrance to something fun. The truck was equipped with a motorized lift gate, which he'd lowered to the ground; he dragged the body onto it, hit a button, and watched it rise up to the level of the bed.

A small red light was bobbing toward us through the fog. I heard grunts, and then the shooter reappeared, the red light strapped to his forehead. His body leaned forward. He was beefy, like Paul Bunyan; his face was a grimace. Each of his hands held a handle, attached to a rope, wound around the neck of a deer.

"Oh, a double!" Jim said.

The shooter threw down the handles and grabbed one deer's hoof to spread its back legs. He said, "Yearling male," then checked the other. "Adult male." Jim wrote it down. The shooter disappeared again.

"The tags are mostly for transport, like if the game warden stops us," Jim explained.

I couldn't see any antlers. "Would he have removed them?" I asked.

"Most of the time they blow off," Jim said. "But no, we leave them intact." He showed me one antler spike poking through a bag.

The red light appeared again. Then the shooter. Then two more deer, sliding heavily over the ground. "Male fawn. Adult female." Five altogether.

We gave the shooter and his equipment a ride across the main road; he sat in the back, with the deer. Near where he'd left his truck, a Princeton police officer had been parked in a cruiser, keeping an eye on the area.

The sharpshooters try to work under the radar. What they do is different from hunting, starting with the fact that they work after dark. They use night vision and silence their weapons, which require special ammunition that won't send dangerous fragments flying around the kill site. They position their stands over piles of corn, which are baited by Jim for weeks before the shooting even begins. Just before they pull the trigger, they startle the deer by flooding the area with high-powered spotlights. Aiming at the head is also not what most hunters do. But it is recommended as the most humane method by the American Veterinary Medical Association. Some of White Buffalo's employees are in fact veterinarians.

◦◦

Hunting claims the status of an honorable act based on the ethic of fair chase. If hunters are doing things right, animals have a real chance to get away. And the hunter is supposed to be feeling things—excitement, attraction, probably some measure of sadness. Our idea of sportsmanship encompasses a certain kind of gentility and self-control as much as it does love and reverence.

All of this helps to soothe the uneasiness people feel, and maybe have always felt, about killing animals. But when the killer is a professional, and in a "cold" rather than "hot" frame of mind—taking neither pleasure nor sorrow from the act of ending a life—our uneasiness returns. Isn't this a type of execution? Doesn't it leave something important unresolved?

A different question came to mind for me. If I had to be shot, would I rather it be done by an efficient professional, who'd done it dozens of times before, or an amateur with a pounding heart?

At the moment of death, would I care more about the killer being skilled, or about their caring for me?

⚶

Jim and I got back on the road.

"How many animals can you carry in this truck?" I asked.

"The other night we had twenty-three."

As animal control, Jim handles everything from feral cats to mangy foxes (best bait to use when trapping them for treatment: a Whopper Junior). But in winter, he told me, the job is "80 or 90 percent deer." Baiting the two dozen or so sites takes hours each day, and when White Buffalo comes to town, he does these collection runs six nights a week.

Jim is stocky, blue-eyed, thirtysomething; he wore Carhartts and muck boots and had some sort of powerful flashlight hung around his neck. Just as his buzz cut revealed his whole scalp, his chattiness seemed to hide nothing. I suspected this made him good at his job: He could get along as well with professional sharpshooters as with citizens who are rattled by the discovery of a dead deer in the yard. Jim will go to help them with this problem, and while he's there he'll gauge their willingness to partner with the deer program. He's always on the lookout for more culling sites. "I'll ask, 'So do you have a lot of deer coming around?' If they say 'Oh, the deer are magical, they're beautiful,' I say 'OK, thank you, have a nice day.'"

Others start complaining about ruined landscaping and poop on the lawn. These are the people who may agree to let culling happen at their homes. Jim is the one who signs them up.

We pulled into the second site. This one was behind a fenced backyard. The shooter had already brought out all of his deer—six of them—using a wheeled cart. He was tall and bearded, wide-eyed, somehow puppyish. He reported that he'd shot three before dark, then three just now, right before we showed up. "How can you get three at once?" I asked. "Why don't the others run off when you shoot the first one?"

The trick, he said, was to go for the alpha deer first. "Once you engage the leader"—*engage* being an odd term for *kill*—"the others run, but then they stop."

"Because they don't know what to do?"

"That's right. I wish there was a science to it, but there isn't."

This shooter was rough with the bodies. He whipped their legs apart. "We've got a male fawn. Female fawn." I looked at her belly; it was so soft and white, almost fuzzy. She was so little. "Adult male." This group on the ground made me think *family*. Adults and babies, males and females.

He tossed them like duffel bags at an airport. The truck was getting fuller; hooves were draped over torsos. All those perfect hooves and legs. When deer are thrown into a pile, their necks ripple like limp hoses. Wet fur was slicked down. Legs cantilevered off the pile and bobbed up and down as more weight hit the truck. Throwing deer toward the cab, the shooter stepped with black boots right on top of them. Then he loaded the cart on top of the animals.

🦌

We drove on.

Our last site was also on township land, bushhogged grass under occasional trees. Jim pulled in and circled around so that we faced the road again. Just as we approached the shooter, a car drove past on the road and Jim turned off his lights. "See, little things," he said. "Click off the headlights so the passing motorist doesn't see the carcasses."

As he did the paperwork, the White Buffalo shooter loaded up the three deer and then carefully scuffed leaves around where they'd been lying, to cover any blood.

Jim texted "On our way with fourteen" to John Hart, the butcher.

"Well, that's a carcass run!" he said. "Pretty much the same thing every time."

He'd been cheerful all night, while for me, sorrow kept knocking at the door. I'd refuse to answer, and then it would knock again. His was a job I'd never considered much, not only the deer culling, but everything else in his wheelhouse. Deer are part of his work year-round. He transports injured fawns to a rescue center. He's used the jaws of life to get deer unstuck from between fence posts. He used to be an EMT, which comes in handy when he has to evaluate a deer with a broken leg, deciding whether to euthanize it or just let it limp away.

In 2019 he got on the TV news for successfully getting a buck out of someone's house. It had crashed through a window and was trapped in the basement. It had some cuts from broken glass, Jim said, but "the legs were good." He called a firefighter friend who helped him to pile up furniture and wood to make a chute leading to the back door of the house, and eventually the deer ran outside.

"One thing that breaks my heart," he said, "people sometimes put up fancy fences, thinking they'll keep the deer out . . ."

I said, "Oh, I think I know where this is going."

"Yeah. I wish people would use a fence with the flat tops." He talked about how gory it can be when a deer is impaled on those decorative metal spikes. "I've saved a few." Others are too torn up to help. He carries a bolt gun for these situations; it's not a safe shot for a firearm when the deer is suspended in the air. Once, he rescued a person in the same awful situation—a drunk college kid who leaped over a hedge, not knowing there was a spiky fence on the other side. "We did save his life."

As we drove, I kept forgetting and then remembering all the bodies behind me. The strange light they threw on some of our talk.

We arrived at John Hart's farm and butcher shop, turning into a long, straight lane lined with oak trees. There was a white farmhouse, a tiny pond, a cluster of red barns and sheds arranged around a barnyard. Totally picturesque, even in the dark. Signs on the corner of one building read DEER DROP OFF.

I stepped out of the truck and felt a warm body near my knee. I thought of deer, then thought *No, it can't be.* I looked down and a fawn-colored dog was snuffling my hand.

A slim guy in his early twenties came out to greet us and looked at our cargo. "You guys are cleaning up this year!" His name was Sam; he wore a dark beard and an apron.

We stepped inside the shop and bright light flooded my eyes. Stainless-steel sinks. A large hacksaw hung from the ceiling. Fly-paper. Red tubs full of hooves, skinned bones, a pile of rib cages. Hairs on the floor. Some kind of scraper or squeegee. A bloody trail leading to the silver door of a walk-in cooler. Bloody card-board; bloody dog prints. While Jim and Sam did paperwork, I looked at long white deer hairs stuck to the back of Sam's shoulder blades. A young woman appeared in coveralls and boots, talking on the phone, red curls piled on her head.

Back outside, Jim opened the truck gate and I saw that blood had pooled in the corner of one of the head bags. The two young people started unloading, one deer, two deer, found their rhythm, grabbed deer by the feet, swung them onto a pile at the edge of the building. They'd halfheartedly prepared the site by laying cardboard on the ground, but the deer pile soon spilled over onto bare earth. Seven, eight, nine. The two of them grabbed, lifted, flung, talking about school. Thirteen. Fourteen.

"This is a fucking ridiculous mountain of deer," Sam declared.

🦌

It was after ten. Our last drive of the night, back to downtown Princeton. Jim told me another rescue story, about a deer that had fallen through ice on a lake. He successfully pulled it out, but then it died anyway. It had just gotten too cold.

Tomorrow he would take me around in the daylight to show me some of the sites where White Buffalo operates drop nets. Net sites, he explained, are places where there's not enough space for sharpshooting—backyards behind houses—and the method is to put out bait under a large net, dozens of feet long, suspended on poles like a wedding tent.

At the moment, the nets were "aging in"—just sitting there above the bait so the deer could get used to them and learn, falsely, that they were safe. This would take the better part of a week. Jim had been trained to operate the nets too, watching them from inside his truck or a well-placed garage and waiting for deer to show up. The job demands good timing. "You try to get everybody's nose down on the bait" before you hit a remote-control trigger that drops the net. Then you go in with a bolt gun.

A little silence. "It's a sensitive topic because the animal does struggle. You try to do it as fast as humanly possible."

"Do the deer make noise?" I asked.

"Yes, the fawns especially. It's like an *Ee-ee!* And a lot of grunts."

I remarked that in a single day, his job could include rescuing a deer, mercy-killing an injured deer, and culling a healthy deer. *How do you make sense of all this?* I wondered, but didn't ask out loud.

He answered anyway. "I understand the importance of keeping deer in check." Quite apart from the welfare of any one animal, he believed that culling meant less suffering all around. As an EMT, he had responded to vehicle crashes where a deer came through a windshield and badly injured a person; deer collisions had dropped sharply since the culling began. "That's the number-one reason." Close behind that, he said, was ecosystem health. He mentioned the effects of abundant deer on ground-nesting birds, and how they help spread invasive plants. "Understanding the bigger picture—not to be cliché, but the circle of life—I'm behind it a hundred percent."

Jim had told me he was also a hunter, but I had zero sense that he would take pleasure in violence. "I do not want any living thing to suffer. Head shots is instant death. With the nets, yes the animal struggles, but you try to be as quick as you can. We don't enjoy doing it. It's destroying a life."

My seat belt in the truck wouldn't latch, but I felt invincible riding up high in this official vehicle with someone whose whole job is to solve strangers' problems. I believed him. I wanted to believe him.

I said something about how most parts of his work, deer-

related or not, must include dealing with strong emotions. He
agreed. "There's three things people get emotional about," he
said. "Family, money, and animals."

There have always been people in Princeton who hate this
program and want it stopped. There have been lawsuits, one of
which was joined on the plaintiffs' side by Joyce Carol Oates and
supported by Patti Smith. Some people sabotaged net sites. Some
of them scooped up bait or poured vinegar over it. Back in 2000,
the mayor, Phyllis Marchand, had deer entrails left on the hood
of her car.

But the really rough times—the times when Jim's predecessor,
and the sharpshooters, wore bulletproof vests to work—were in
the past. Jim told me he didn't really hear a lot of complaints,
though he personally had apprehended a woman who was trying
to bait the deer away from a kill site. He wrote her a ticket because, except for him, no one can legally feed deer in Princeton,
but he still managed not to make an enemy of her. "I knew her
from helping her with a stray cat situation," he said. "She was
like 'Hi, Jim!' We had a good conversation."

Dark fields slid past the window. We passed one herd of deer
abroad in the night, feeding near the road. Then another.

He dropped me back at my own car, looked me in the eye—
"Watch out for deer"—and roared off in the big yellow truck.

◀▶

John Hart, who shares a name with a local signer of the Decla-
ration of Independence, stayed up until the wee hours, gutting
those fourteen deer. When I saw him the next afternoon at his
farm, he looked weary. But he was still in motion. Hosing off
the butcher shop floor. Rinsing the red tubs. Scrubbing the walls
with a long-handled brush.

"We had it all cleaned and sanitized last night," he said, "and
now . . ." He pulled a scrap of meat off the wall where it was
stuck.

Hart took me across the yard to his big barn, which smelled
deliciously of cows, and opened a flash freezer. "This freezer's at

twenty below," he said, showing me stacks of cardboard boxes inside, many of them hand-scrawled with "Prin," for Princeton. He opened one and took out a hefty package of ground meat, frozen granite-solid. During Princeton's culling season, he was driving every other day to a food bank in Trenton, donating the venison.

I looked at those blocks of meat as distillations. Of deer, first: The bones and hides and caudal fat had been removed, and only the good protein remained. The deer themselves were distillations of Princeton's soil, air, water. Of genetics and the drive to eat and reproduce. And, at the last, that meat was a concentrate of human power. Our tools and weapons. Our force and our assertions.

Back in the shop, I leaned against a table for a while and watched a butcher named Nick working his way through a bin of deer parts. He wore a metal glove, like chain mail, on his left hand. His knife was nine or ten inches long, slim and slightly curved. Frequently he stopped cutting to hold a sharpening rod against his chest and rub the knife quickly up and down it. He was solid, garrulous, with wide-set eyes. His voice cut easily through the noise of the walk-in cooler motor.

"It's very similar to lamb," he said. "Anatomically it's the same." He sliced away silver fascia from a deer's foreshank, tossing it into a waste bucket at his side. "Basically they bring them in and hang them through the Achilles tendon." After being gutted and resting overnight, a deer would have its skin peeled off by a winch. "We have a hacksaw we use to cut the hooves off. But you can cut with a knife between the joints; that's called quartering. You use gravity to pull the parts down while it's still hanging."

He showed me a beautiful, long, fishlike strip of meat that had lain alongside a spine. "This is the backstrap." He rapidly cut it into thirds and added it to a growing pile of chunks. The meat was translucent, like raw salmon, but darker.

"This is a shoulder. You can stew this meat up. This is a tendon." He excised it with the tip of the knife. "That's like shoe leather. That you discard." Bone clacked against the table as he flipped over a shank: the top of the deer's rear leg. I saw a round white knob poking out of it like an animal from a den. "That's the hip joint"—he used the knife to point to his own hip. "I like to take this little vein out, and then you trace the femur. I get myself a handle." He grabbed the bone as he continued cutting until the meat fell away completely, thick as a phone book. It was mesmerizing to watch: *slice-slice pull, slice-slice pull.* "Right in here is a lymph node. This is what you'd call the top round with beef. It's a real clean piece of meat and I like to cut it against the grain. This is the sirloin tip or knuckle in beef. It's the same exact muscle." He picked up the shank and stroked his knife down the bone. *Thump* as he tossed the meat on the pile.

Now the bin was empty; all the waste and bones were in the garbage. Nick scooped up the meat, threw it back into the bin, and upended it into the top of a grinder. Most hunters will ask their butcher to set aside the best cuts—backstrap and tenderloin— for grilling or roasting, and maybe make sausage or jerky out of some of what's left. But everything from the Princeton deer would be ground up for the food bank. Last night's cull would amount to something like four hundred pounds of venison.

He was telling me that he'd started learning to butcher deer when he was eighteen, from his dad. "I've butchered deer my whole life for friends. I've got a small KitchenAid grinder. I do that in my kitchen on my table, and I just do it as a favor. The rule is, I'm not gutting it or skinning it in my apartment."

"Seems reasonable," I said.

"Yeah!" he said earnestly.

This grinder was shoulder-high, made of cast aluminum. We watched it push out thick spaghetti strands of red and white flesh. Nick used his bare hand to guide it toward the back of the tub it was falling into. "This will be about fifty pounds," he said. "It's heavier than beef. See, it wants to tip the grinder over."

He hefted the tub onto his shoulder and I scurried ahead of him to open the cooler door. Inside there were many deer left hanging, head down, still wearing soft fur. A forest of deer. Twenty-four hours ago they'd been walking around in Princeton. Here they looked as out of place as they would under the ocean. But they weren't—after all, this was a butcher shop and they were dead meat.

I'd asked Hart what happened to all those innards from last night. They'd be composted, mixed with cow and horse manure from here on the farm. "That breaks it down real nice," he told me. Then he'd spread the compost on his fields. One of his crops is feed corn, and one of the buyers of that corn is the city of Princeton, which uses it to bait deer in the culling program. I thought of Jim Ferry's circle of life, which, as always, is also a circle of death.

Nick brought out another bin full of parts and sprayed loose hairs off them in the sink.

Somehow we got onto the topic of fetal pig dissection, something we'd both done in high school biology. I told him I'd been shocked to realize how easy it was to take apart a body.

"Yeah!" he said again. "People wouldn't drive so fast if they realized, you're just a bag of water and meat."

CHAPTER 13

Victims

TO BE A DEER IS TO BE IN PERIL OF A LAYERED KIND. There are so many dangers, even after death, and they often find their way into art. When Audubon painted black vultures, he showed them scavenging a dead buck, its tongue lolling out.

An ancient Greek story tells how the Mycenaean king Agamemnon angered Artemis by killing her sacred deer; Artemis in turn demands he sacrifice his daughter Iphigenia. In Euripides's play *Iphigenia at Aulis*, the girl nobly embraces her fate, but at the last moment—the instant of the murderous rite—Artemis saves her life by substituting a deer for her body. Reports a witness, "She was very large and handsome to see, and the goddess's altar was thoroughly sprinkled with her blood."

There is a clear and straight line between old deer-victim stories and new, real-life ones; it's one of the richest cultural veins involving the species. A carnivore ripping a deer apart, as we saw earlier, is a favorite image across the centuries. Deer serve as negative space, the counterpart to action. A Nlaka'pamux tale, from British Columbia and Washington State, describes how Old Man lures animals to their demise by getting them to jump off a cliff. The elk go first, and die; then the deer get suspicious. "'The elk are all killed,' they say. 'No,'" Old Man says eerily, "'they are only laughing.'"

Down go the deer. Maybe this isn't just about food; maybe it's about a trickster's urge to deceive, a kind of mini-theater, as much a ritual as anything else. Roman sarcophagi showed lions devouring deer "almost as a matter of course," writes the art historian Kenneth Clark, as "a symbol of the power of the soul, which triumphs over the feeble apathy of the body."

Feebleness might be an apt charge to level at a body. But apathy? That's a victor's word. No deer, no human victim, feels apathetic.

⚬

One night in December 2021, a man was driving through rural Crawford County in southern Indiana when a whitetail ran in front of his car. He managed not to hit it and watched, from his car, as it bounded up a steep hillside. Then it suddenly disappeared into the earth.

The southern boundary of the county is drawn by the beefy curves of the Ohio River, but the ground itself is unreliable, formed of limestone karst that's easily nibbled away by water. Due to this constant underground erosion, Indiana has thousands of caves. So when the man called game wardens to report that the deer had plunged into a deep hole in the ground, they were unsurprised.

"I wouldn't say it's uncommon for a deer to end up in that type of situation," Jim Hash, a state conservation officer, told me. "I've been in many caves where there's skeletons of deer or raccoons or possums." He leads his agency's special cave rescue team, which is the same crew that will come and get you if you fall off a limestone escarpment and can't climb back up.

It was nighttime when he got the word about the cave-bound deer; he wasn't about to rush underground. He considers these situations in terms of risk to human life, and it wasn't yet clear whether the deer had even survived the fall. He did know the cave, though. "It's very close to the edge of the roadway and it's about fifty feet deep," he said, adding that locals have long used it as a trash pit. "It's not a cave that most recreational cavers are going to go into. There are no pretty formations. You're going to look around and see bones, a cooler, lawn chairs, broken beer bottles, and that's about it."

The next day, he went out to the site and found that some

folks were already there, trying to mount their own amateur rescue. They'd lowered a ladder down to a shelf twenty feet below the surface and were dangling cameras near the cave floor.

In their videos, the deer was stumbling around in the dark. It was a buck, with small antlers, apparently uninjured. And there was something unusual about it—a piebald coat, with white patches over the brown. In fact, the motorist who'd seen the deer in the first place had noticed those patches, even by headlight on a dark winter night. The perennial human interest in white deer had been aroused: Posts were already going around on Facebook, talking about this special deer and its sad predicament. Hash, who'd been in this line of work for more than two decades, knew this could end badly.

"It becomes a human safety issue at that point," said Hash, whose speech is laced with terms like "viable risk" and "elevated position," the phrases of the longtime first responder. "When we have people that are untrained and aren't used to working in that vertical environment, if somebody was to take one step in the wrong place around that pit, you're going to immediately fall fifty feet." He told his crew they would have to take action.

They were well equipped with rappelling gear and pulley systems and all manner of other specialized tools, but first they had to address the fact that anyone entering the cave would be in a small, confined space with a frightened antler-bearing animal. Hash called animal control and borrowed a tranquilizer gun, rappelled down, and darted the deer in the rump.

He settled in to wait fifteen minutes as it fell asleep. Meanwhile, the officers above him were rigging up a haul system that would give them a mechanical advantage in raising the deer. Once the buck was unconscious, it was Hash's job to fashion a sort of basket out of webbing. As the 160-pound buck ascended, Hash rappelled up beside it, once or twice freeing it when its antlers or body got stuck.

Once the deer was on solid ground, the team moved it a quarter-mile away, to a field, where it couldn't fall back into the cave upon awakening. An officer returned the next day to check on it and found it still lethargic, so he gave it a reversal drug.

The story circled back onto Facebook, where Hash's agency announced the successful rescue, and users weighed in by the hundreds. Most commenters, of course, were congratulatory, thanking Hash and his team. Some people, seemingly unable to tolerate life's vicissitudes, wanted to know when the state would "close off" the cave to prevent future falls. But one person wrote, "Excellent. Now a lucky hunter can shoot this buck and make it a trophy and a great dinner."

Hash and his team had spent several hours at the rescue site, besides all the planning and follow-up. As that last commenter pointed out when other users scolded him, the agency that had devoted these resources to saving the deer was the same body that, in hunting season, would sanction its killing. When is it worthwhile to send in personnel and equipment to save an animal's life? Hash told me it's purely about weighing the safety risks—that a less beloved animal like, say, a possum, would get the same consideration from him as the deer had gotten. Then again, he acknowledged, he probably wouldn't have gotten the call in the first place.

"I don't care who you are," he said, "you probably saw the movie *Bambi*. A deer is a cute and beautiful part of nature."

◊◊

That feeling of love and attraction—laced with pity—drives people all over the world to rescue deer when they get in trouble. Over the years I've been following deer in the news, "people saving deer" has been one of the perennial stories; I once collected pages and pages of headlines, a river of the bad things that happen to deer and the good Samaritans who help them. Deer get stuck in fences and soccer nets and rabbit holes and wells and oil change pits. They get trapped in ponds and batting cages. Their mothers die, or pythons try to swallow them. And humans go to great lengths to help: risking thin ice, giving CPR, leaping into manure pits.

The mood of these stories is usually straightforward: What luck for the deer, to have been spotted by caring humans! But many of the dangers are human-made in the first place. Sometimes fawns get bundled into hay bales when they bed down in a summer field. After two men rescued a doe that was swimming around in Long Island Sound with a bucket on her head, one of them made a strange observation: "They deserve to be able to enjoy Mother Nature just as much as we do." Then again, when the dangers are "natural," the attitude seems to be that humans are nobly thwarting reality, conquering death itself.

In Wisconsin in late 2021, a hunter came upon two bucks with their antlers locked together, drew his bow to shoot one of them, then thought better of it and used an angle grinder to cut their antlers apart. After they ran off, he earned volumes of internet praise and an official nod from his state's wildlife agency. He appeared on the local news, looking very sober indeed, explaining, "I just didn't feel it was right shooting them in the situation they were in." That this should have been patently obvious according to any definition of ethical fair chase went unremarked; for not being a jerk, he got to be a hero.

🦌

There's a stunning essay by Annie Dillard called "The Deer at Providencia" in which she and some traveling companions visit a village in the Amazon and discover a deer tied to a tree, to be slaughtered and eaten at some later time. It's suffering horribly, tangled in the rope, bleeding and thrashing. They stand and watch it struggle for a while—"about fifteen minutes," Dillard coolly reports. Then she describes, with pleasure, the lunch she is served, including a venison stew, and how "terrific" she feels: "My shirt was wet and cool from swimming. I had had a night's sleep, two decent walks, three meals, and a swim—everything tasted good." She can see the deer from the lunch table.

You get ready to call her a monster, and then she flips everything around. "What surprises you? That there is suffering here, or that I know it?" None of us should pretend not to know the brutality of what it takes to continue living. "I have thought a great deal about carnivorousness; I eat meat. These things are not issues; they are mysteries."

The presence of a victim can be an occasion to feel wise: "very old and energetic," as Dillard puts it. Seeing that deer must die, simply because they live, sometimes gives us a chance to nod knowingly at the world's sad inevitabilities.

There is a certain power in that stance of sorrow that immediately, reliably, resolves into acceptance. One is, in Dillard's formulation, "moved" but not "shocked." We already knew the world was like this. We have driven past hundreds of heaps made of hides and bones; we have chatted in living rooms under the staring eyes of hunted bucks. Perhaps we also live in a town where the officials practice culling in order to maintain our human lebensraum. All of it is unfortunate, we think, but few of us are willing to really feel, for any length of time, the sorrow of it.

⚜

We've invested a lot in the idea of deer being providers—part of a natural order, hunters and prey, in which deer offer their bodies. But we also set them up as the receivers of *unjust* violence, death as a perversion of nature. The deepest victimhood results from hatred and sadism, the violent denial of the ability to consent.

When the director Jordan Peele went to the Oscar ceremony in 2018—his film *Get Out* was up for several awards—he wore a delicate gold deer antler pin on his white lapel. Many critics had picked up on the complex array of deer-related symbols in the film. An indictment of racial assimilation and the hypocrisy of white America, *Get Out* puts its protagonist, a young Black man named Chris, in a life-threatening situation at the home of his white girlfriend's parents. But first, it has the couple hit a deer in their car. Chris gets out of the car and stares at the animal in shock and recognition.

It's soon revealed that the dying deer is an analog for Chris's own experience as a young boy, when his mother was killed in a hit-and-run and, he guiltily believes, he didn't do enough to save her. Meanwhile, his girlfriend's father displays deer heads in his house—and, for some reason, rails against the presence of deer in the neighborhood. "I'm sick of it," he says, using the familiar words of the aggrieved suburbanite. "They're taking over; they're like rats." That conflation of deer with human "others" who are seen as pests becomes clearer when Chris finds himself under horrifying psychological attack while trapped in a rec room decorated with a trophy buck. As critics noted, the taxidermy is a visual pun on a racially charged term, *black buck*, applied to Black men after the Civil War—a term that expressed white fears of Black male sexuality and lawlessness.

That Chris ultimately uses the antlers from this trophy as a very effective weapon of self-defense is no accident. He is the inverse of Iphigenia: the dominant culture wants to sacrifice and consume them both, but rather than achieving agency by choosing death, as she does, Chris successfully fights for his life. His hosts had thought of him as an animal, but he uses that animal's own body to protect his humanity and selfhood.

🦌

The nice thing about having a victim in a story is how it makes everything else fall into place. We know who the villains are. We know what the lesson should be.

In 2019, a cell phone video surfaced, made by two teenage boys in Brookville, Pennsylvania, showing them laughing as they tortured an injured buck, kicking and stomping it and pulling off an antler. It swiftly made the rounds, and public outcry was quick to follow. A petition calling for criminal charges gathered over 800,000 signatures, along with telling commentary: "Disgusting excuses for human waste." "Monsters." "Subhuman." "This trash belongs in prison." Equally predictable was the public dissatisfaction when the older of the teens, who happened to be the stepson of the local police chief, avoided jail time. "They should have the same thing done to them," someone wrote.

Sometimes deer also get drawn into mayhem and the macabre. Severed deer heads get left in odd places, like the porch of a church in Lyndhurst, England, or the grounds of a Michigan high school. But far more common is the way deer-victims become the tools of ordinary people trying to vilify hunters or professional deer managers.

The easiest way to garner opposition to killing deer is to appeal to pathos, like one Cincinnati anti-culling activist I spoke to. She talked in a rapid-fire voice about the suffering of the deer ("I found a deer that had a black belly; it was gut shot, which caused gangrene") and alleged a conspiracy between bloodthirsty hunters and her local parks department. ("I started doing open records requests and making them cough up their data, and I found where they lied . . . The more I dug the more rotten it got.")

I finally hung up, feeling profoundly uninterested in whether any of this was true. What drew my attention was the pleasure the woman seemed to take in her own anger. How satisfied we are by feeling righteous. How there's something in death—its refusal of dignity, its sheer lack of manners—that we sometimes need to find a way to look at.

We may have forgotten a lot of those old stories about deer as victims, but I think they're still in our cultural DNA. And there's another story, of course, that we all remember very well.

◖◗

Jim Hash's invocation of *Bambi* was as predictable as carols at Christmastime. Is there any other wild animal that we so often call by the name of a syrupy character that animal inspired? Hawks are called hawks, whales are called whales, but in pop culture and media, deer are called Bambi.

It's hard to overstate the cultural fallout from *Bambi*, conceived way back when FDR was president and no one left the house without a hat, but still holding an iron grip on the American way of imagining deer.

Bambi is a male deer who, in the film, grows up and fathers offspring of his own. But he lives forever as a fawn, and his name, when carried by humans, is associated with the hyperfeminine—a porn star name, a trophy wife name. I don't have to tell you which is the film's pivotal moment; you're already thinking about it. The collective and primal trauma of Bambi's mother's death earned the movie a place on *Time*'s Top 25 Horror Movies of All Time, despite being a G-rated movie for kids.

In showing that death, Walt Disney was only following the plot of the Felix Salten novel on which he based the film. But of course he put the indelible Disney stamp on the story. Making the movie was a drawn-out process that began with realist ambitions—animators observed live deer in the studio and in the wild, and they even dissected a deer carcass one layer at a time to study the anatomy. But after three years of work had already been done, Disney told his animators, "I'd like to see us find things, you know, that keep us away from just the naturalistic stuff—that has a certain amount of fantasy to it."

Fantasy meant two things. One, the look of the characters (snub-nosed, saucer-eyed) and the narrative structure would make the animals arouse our protective instincts. Lead animators on the film recalled that with these choices, "the picture began to be about wonderful children who happened to be animals."

Two, the humans in the film would be faceless villains. "Walt felt they had to play up the threat of Man," biographer Neal Gabler writes, "and play down the natural hardships [animals] faced. It was Man who was the real enemy." A true complexity was being erased here: Salten, Bambi's original creator, was himself a hunter.

So the human audience was invited to identify entirely with the nonhuman characters, vilifying "Man" as destroyers who not only kill the hero's mother but are careless enough to start a forest fire. During the same prewar period when *Bambi* was in production, Disney was building a new studio in Burbank with a grassy campus where Walt sometimes sat under trees to watch deer wander through. But by the time *Bambi* was released in 1942, that peaceful vision had been shattered by World War II. The national mood had changed. Audiences stayed away, and critics

208 THE AGE OF DEER

found *Bambi* to be sorely out of step—"childish" and "entirely unpleasant."

Maybe looking through the eyes of wildlife at the threat of humanity was not a viable stance when the country was more focused on dividing the human world itself into good and evil. But *Bambi* ended up staying with us, even through the later decades when the Disney studio helped invent a different type of film about animals, the nature documentary. Such films have become one of America's primary ways of understanding the natural world. Yet, in the case of deer, they haven't replaced the *Bambi* vision that tells us deer are innocent and helpless.

And of course, *Bambi* has permanently stained the view of hunting held by nonhunters. To someone opposed to hunting, a hunter is a "Bambi-killer," a faceless and brutal murderer leaving orphans in his wake. Hunters seem to have spotted this PR danger as soon as the movie was released: *Outdoor Life* editor Raymond J. Brown called it "the worst insult ever offered to American sportsmen and conservationists."

Even more broadly, though, the movie suggests that humans are *only* destructive. It leaves no place for humans to be a functional part of the natural world.

Something complex happens when we reflexively call a deer, especially an adult deer, "Bambi." That's a major rhetorical move—to take a wild animal, graceful and tough, a survivor of millions of years of evolution, and label it with the name of a distorted fantasy designed to ignite Pavlovian parental feelings. Enjoying a movie is one thing; allowing it to shape our view of an entire species is another. But people still reference *Bambi* almost unconsciously when they are discussing deer in almost any context, whether sincerely or scornfully.

The film left us with an especially pointed pity for fawns. Every spring, wildlife agencies issue a flurry of PSAs reminding people that if they find a newborn fawn in the wild, it's best to leave it alone. And in thousands of cases, these pleadings are ignored. For a long time, I didn't understand why.

⚜

One morning in mid-June, I set out on a walk up a steep gravel driveway near my house. The day was moist but sunny; buntings and tanagers were singing their early-summer songs. The drive, almost never used by cars, is two stripes of gravel with a band of green running up the middle. As I rounded a corner I heard a little sound, thought fleetingly of bears, tensed—and looked up to find a tiny fawn, curled like a cinnamon bun, in that green center stripe.

It wasn't a very good hideaway, that three-inch-tall grass. I stopped some yards away from the fawn and squatted down, speaking softly. In the back of my mind was the question of whether the mother might appear, perhaps in the mood to defend her baby. But she was nowhere in sight, as is often true in the first weeks of fawns' lives, when they are not yet ready to follow their mothers on their daily rounds. Does leave their fawns bedded in safe places, protected by a lack of scent and their camouflaging spots, and return only occasionally to nurse and check on their young. This system serves the species well, but it tends to confuse people, who are used to thinking that a newborn alone must be in mortal trouble.

The fawn lifted its head to see me better and, because of the steepness of the driveway, actually tumbled over, rolling once or twice downhill. Then it stood up, bobbling. It was about eighteen inches tall at most. Big black nose, soft ears, velvety dark haunches under white spots. The legs were outlandishly slim and long, every tendon and bone visible beneath the skin. When it put its nose down in the clovers, I realized that its legs were actually a little too long for eating easily at ground level, but probably much better suited to reaching up to nurse.

It sniffed around the plants but ate nothing. It seemed unsure what to do—it licked its ribs, sniffed my scent, swiveled its ears. After a while it started to walk toward the woods; while it was an awkward, unsteady thing when standing still, its gait already had the superb poise of an adult deer, each foot set precisely into the grass, the finely pointed hooves arrowing straight back every time they left the ground.

At the tree line it stopped, turned, and—walked right toward me! Very deliberately, it came closer and closer—I imagined touching it, picking it up—it got within five feet of me, then suddenly veered off and headed away again, not in a panic but just a sort of instinctive prey wisdom: *No, better not.*

Then it returned to the woods, slowly eased into the jungle of wisteria that grows there, and gradually became half-veiled, its spots moving behind leaflets like the pattern on a gliding snake.

Now I was sure the mother was elsewhere. It was alarming to realize how alone this baby was, that such a young and unskilled creature could be left unprotected for hours at a time. I finally understood why so many people in this situation would feel compelled to "rescue" a fawn. That it had thought it was safe to walk right toward me! "Oh, honey," I said out loud. It seemed there for the taking, its body an instrument it barely knew how to use.

⚘

It's confusing when people find fawns in the wild. Everybody's confused. The fawns come off as clueless, and as for the humans, they often get on the phone, looking for answers. If they live in Virginia, a woman I'll call Brenda might be the person who takes the call.

Brenda is a licensed wildlife rehabilitator, one of about 150 listed by the state. (Only a fraction of those officially care for fawns; if you're an injured possum, you'll have a lot more options. Adult deer are out of luck.) I called her because I'd realized that wildlife rehabbers were the people taking on the longest, hardest work of saving deer, work that went on quietly for months and never made headlines. I wanted to see a rehabber at work.

It took some legwork to arrange; I had to first get permission from the state wildlife agency, because rehabbers can lose their licenses if they allow improper contact between animals and people. So Brenda and I spoke several times to iron out the

ground rules—I would not touch fawns or help with their care—
before I finally drove to her house one June evening.

I stepped out of the car and was immediately greeted by a
male turkey, almost as tall as my hip, parading past at a stately
pace with all his feathers standing on end. He had a lump of
blue flesh dangling from his beak and was dragging his stiff-
ened wings along the ground in a ceremonial manner. Once in a
while, with no warning, he'd gobble. We stared each other down
for what seemed like a long time before Brenda stuck her head
out the front door. "He won't hurt you," she said.

"He seems nervous," I said.

"No, he just wants to have sex with you. Hang on, I have to
put in my contacts." She closed the door again.

Besides the amorous tom, there were a couple dozen chickens,
a handful of cats, and some guinea fowl roaming the yard. Goats
stood behind a fence, and I could hear several dogs barking indoors. So far, though, I saw no deer.

Brenda soon reappeared, wiry and bottle-blond, wearing a
powder-blue tennis skirt, a white polo, and—despite what she'd
said—glasses. In her hand was a pair of pruning shears. "I'm going to pick some greens for them," she said. "Want to tag along?"

I trailed her past a garden shed and into a ragged clearing in
the pine woods as she told me about her twenty years in wildlife
rehab—starting with a nestful of baby squirrels in a bush her in-
laws cut down. Mentored by another rehabber, she'd managed to
save them; soon she moved on to possums and other creatures.
"In one year," she said proudly, "I did thirty-eight raccoons by
myself."

We were well out of sight of the house now. Suddenly, she
stopped. "You'll see a lot of bones here," she said. I looked down.
Small deer bones were everywhere underfoot. Ribs. Femurs. An
entire spine.

Brenda welled up with tears. It was the first of many times
that I'd see her cry. She'd struck me as a heart-on-sleeve person

the first time we got on the phone, and she'd already told me that a lot of the deer she takes in can't be saved. But somehow I'd expected to see babies, not bones.

"This is where I bring them," she said. "If it can help another animal survive, even if it's a coyote, and I can provide that—it's kind of a circle of life. But it weighs heavy on me."

We walked another fifty feet in silence. She put down her shears and began hand-picking stems of a slender knee-high weed.

"Everything I do for wildlife is uncompensated," she said, throwing the greens on a pile. "I grew up on a farm and we had horses, donkeys, chickens, and"—she welled up again—"I was always the one to find an animal if it was injured or dead. It's kind of a way of giving back." She shook her head as if to banish the tears. "This world is not a nice place."

It was the fawns' feeding time; we returned to the yard and found that Brenda's husband had mixed up eight big bottles of formula and put them out on the front steps. The turkey resumed his solemn display. "I put a chair out for you in the fawn enclosure," she told me. Now she only seemed concerned that I be quiet, calm, and not cause them stress. I followed her toward the fawn fence—eight feet of wire and shade cloth, enclosing a large area under pine trees—and we ducked through its low door.

And here they were: two, three, four, nosing at Brenda's hands—seven altogether. She touched one after another on the forehead, chirped at them, quickly drew bottles out of her bag. I scooted over to the camp chair and turned to watch.

First my eye was drawn to Brenda—two bottles in one hand, one in the other hand, a fourth between her knees. And then the fawns. Lord, they were sweet. Heads tipped up to the bottles, legs braced, ears laid back. Their tails wagged; loud sucking noises came from their mouths. The few still waiting for food were patient, but then I felt a warm push at my knee and found a little fawn face looking up into mine with enormous black eyes. I thought I wasn't supposed to touch her, so I sat on my hands, but Brenda called over, "It's OK! You can touch!" and I gave in to what was really an irresistible urge: caressing, talking. The tininess of her hooves was almost too much to take. One of them lightly pressed on my toe.

"Hi, Sarah!" Brenda was cooing to another of the fawns. "I do name them all," she said in my direction. "This is Diana, Amelia, Whitney, Tabitha . . ." She paused. "I have to think who has died and who has not died. Oh, that's Ferguson. And that one, her name is Paul because I thought she was a male." Her voice jumped up again. "She's got a very good poop, baby girl!"

Once the fawns had finished their feeding, Brenda spread a towel on the ground and sat on it, stretching her legs out. A black cat curled up next to her and she stroked it, saying, "I'm not supposed to have cats in here." The enclosure was nice and shady, and the fawns relaxed near a wooden shelter.

"I've taken in fifty-three fawns this year," Brenda said. "I only have fifteen left." Those who weren't in this enclosure, or dead, were staying in her garage, in what she called the rehab room— still too young or too fragile to come outside. She kept them in playpens roofed with sheets, to keep them calmer. "I play Alexa for them," she said. "At night they get thunderstorms and in the day they get woodland sounds."

There were a lot of ways they could perish. Some never had a chance. She showed me a few pictures on her phone: a female born without eyes. A male, just over two pounds, with deformed legs. "I named him Banks," she said. "He lasted five days."

Even the healthy ones could easily die from stress—no matter how safe their life was now, prior trauma could eventually catch up to them. "Capture myopathy can set in anytime," she said. I'd never heard of it. She explained that it was a stress response that could damage muscle tissue and prevent a deer from digesting. "It might be eating great, but four weeks later it's shitting water," she said.

"What can you do about it?"

"Nothing."

Some of the fawns had had mothers who were hit by cars. Some had been hit themselves. Some were what Brenda called "kidnapped"—picked up by well-meaning people who mistook them for orphans. Other people weren't so altruistic. "I have had a few calls where they say, 'There's a fawn in my yard and we have landscapers coming,'" she told me.

She sometimes got on video chat with callers to evaluate an injured fawn and see whether it made sense to transport it—in itself, a very stressful event. "Has it been following people around and crying?" she'd ask callers. "Are there flies around the baby?" She had ways of treating problems (medications to kill fly eggs, antibiotics, and so on), but sometimes she had to advise euthanasia. "You can't hang them, you can't drown them," she said. "The only way to humanely euthanize is to shoot them." What if the caller didn't own a gun? "Call animal control."

Even after refusing many cases, she still took in dozens of baby deer during every fawning season, from late spring well into the summer. (Another Virginia rehabber I'd talked to told me that every year on the Fourth of July, she'd get fawns picked up by people camping for the holiday. She called these "firecracker babies.") All these needed to be fed at least twice a day and their digestion monitored, like parents do with newborn humans. Some fawns need supplemental heat; others need to be tube-fed. A rehabber in Michigan had told me that even with four interns and two volunteer helpers, she got only three to four hours of sleep a night during the fawn care season.

The end goal was separation. "I have to have them released by the first of January," Brenda said. "I wean them off bottles slowly, and then I open the gate and let them come and go." Eventually, the fawns—now adult deer—would stop coming back, absorbed by the larger landscape, taking their chances in the world.

She told me, though I'd never have dreamed of asking, "I have two sons that hunt, but they don't do it here, and they're very respectful about how they hunt."

She petted and stroked and let the fawns lick her face. "Do

you love your mom?" she asked them, making kissing sounds, then started telling me why she avoided bonding with the fawns. "I just feed them and leave them alone. First of all, I have other things to do. Second of all, it's the worst thing you could do for them." But then she said, stroking Diana, "We're not supposed to love on them like this. But imagine never being touched, nobody ever cleaning you, someone not touching your ears. If someone wants to take my license away for touching them," she said in a tight voice, "that's fine."

I got the feeling her decision to take in fawns, in the end, had little to do with whether she was licensed or not. She'd already told me that she'd been taking them in for six years before she was officially sanctioned to do it. Looking after animals seemed as involuntary to her as breathing. Besides all the animals here at her home, her paying gig was at a horse barn.

Baby talk and all, I couldn't call her sentimental. This work required her to wade bravely through death in a way that most people, including me, would never take on. Losing well over half her fawns was par for the course; other rehabbers I'd talked to reported similar numbers. Even after babyhood, the odds were still terrible; one study found that 86 percent of fawns raised by rehabbers died within three months of release. "There are days when I go into the rehab room and I've lost three fawns," she said, crying again. "I think, 'Why do I do this?' But if I can give them a quiet safe place to lay their head down, if I can give them a safe place to pass, it's worth it."

We gathered our things. "Is your HOA cool with all this?" I asked, and her tenderness snapped back like a switchblade. "The HOA can kiss my ass."

Back in the yard, she told me to wait in the driveway while she fetched adult deer feed. She walked through her wide lawn, flinging the grain out in golden arcs. "Come on, babies!" she called toward the woods. "Mama's babies! Baby baby baby!"

She kept calling for a long time and at last told me to stay very still and look past the shed. "Oliver's here," she said. Through the trees I saw a young buck, growing his first set of antlers. He was pure white with a nose the color of bubble gum. "Hi, handsome!" Behind him, one at a time, three more yearlings appeared. They slowly made their way across the driveway, giving me wary glances, until they reached the lawn and began nosing for the feed.

Brenda had raised these four the previous year. She told me Oliver's story. "A school bus driver almost hit a doe, and then she saw this little white fawn. Instead of helping him across the road to where his mother was, she put him in the bus and he rode to school with her." Aside from his hue, Oliver was normal, and had thrived. "As far as I know, I'm the only one in Virginia in twenty years to rehabilitate and release an albino."

She sat down in the middle of the lawn, the four deer orbiting her as they fed. The day was fading. The chickens were doing their final rounds; the cats lounged and prowled; the turkey made one more bid for my affection. Oliver was a pale emblem against the green of the pines, his musculature defined like a Michelangelo marble. Brenda held out a handful of corn to him, and I watched him ease within a few feet of her, this volatile, heroic woman who'd managed to become his mother.

Part III
Craving

CHAPTER 14

The Fetish

EARLY EVENING, SPRINGTIME. UNDER A POWER LINE, I made my way on foot. A creek sang behind the trees. I glanced left and right at masses of knotweed, where goldfinches dove. Something caught my eye—a curve, a pale color, that seemed out of place.

I left the lane and climbed up the slope, stepping on rocks and pushing past the fuzzy leaves of mullein plants, until I had it in my hands. A deer's skull with two antlers still attached, a mat of dark fur clinging to the brow.

Its nose was broken off. Delicate bony sheets whorled in the sinuses. Clean molars lined the upper jaw; the eye sockets were formed from flying buttresses of bone. And the antlers: rising from knobby wreaths at their bases, sweeping back for several inches until, on each side, one tine forked off toward the center-line, while the main beams continued outward and upward, textured by small bumps and ridges but growing smoother and more austere along their length, until each one ended in three long fingers, slightly wavering, organic and self-defined like a stem or a branch.

Eight points altogether: a buck who'd been in his prime. The culminations of a lovely and improbable form, elegant as a heron's neck.

I became a pirate, as surely as if I'd been digging on the beach and my shovel hit the top of a treasure chest.

Carefully I carried the skull back down the lane and around a metal gate, holding it gingerly in both hands, afraid it would fall apart. I'd walk home and get my car. I'd come back for it right away. In the meantime I had to make sure no one else would take it. I hid it over the hill and behind a tree.

It had come unbidden and unearned. When it showed up in the corner of my eye it brought mystery with it—the deer's life and death, the unknown events that had brought his skull to rest in that particular place. The surprise of our paths' intersection on that spring evening: two beings, one on each side of the veil. But the antlers' beauty shouted that mystery down. It was as though I could hear thousands of human voices, talking fast in my ear about souvenirs and possession, and I listened, and thought I owned that deer.

❦

Trophy Category: Score:

Hunter's Legal Name:

Guide's Name:

Taxidermist's Name:

Location of Hunt:

Date of Arrival / Date of Departure: Mode of Transportation:

Kill Date: Time: At a Distance Of:

Gun Caliber: Bullet Type/Weight:

Make and Model of Scope:

Weather at Time of Kill:

[Signature of Hunter]

❦

If you want to have a trophy deer scored, after filling out a form like the one above, you have to sign an affidavit stating that the animal was taken under rules of fair chase, submit photos of the trophy and copies of your hunting license, write a narrative about the trophy's condition and how you acquired it, pay a $40 fee, and get a sanctioned Boone and Crockett Club measurer to inspect the trophy and fill out a score chart, which both of you must sign and date.

In exchange for all this, you will receive the chance to have officials at Boone and Crockett headquarters in Missoula, Montana, review your entry and—you hope—include the trophy in one of its publications listing recent trophies and all-time records. (These records cover dozens of species, including jaguar, bighorn sheep, and antelope, and some may stand for quite a while. The largest known Atlantic walrus tusks, for example, were submitted for scoring back in 1955.)

I was sitting at a conference table in Elkins, West Virginia, with two people: official measurer Robert Tallman, and a hunter who already knew he wouldn't get into that book. Tallman knew it too—he's certified to score all thirty-four categories of big game, and has been at it for a dozen years, so he saw it as soon as the guy walked in with the antlers—but both men were curious anyway. They had the trophy and they had the tools: a black box the size of the Oxford Shorter with BOONE AND CROCKETT on the lid and opening to reveal, on a bed of foam, a folding ruler, a steel cable, two different tape measures, and a green alligator clamp. The hunter swiveled his chair back and forth while Tallman went over the paperwork.

"Who's your taxidermist?"

"Chad."

"He does good work. Did you use a compound bow?"

"Crossbow."

"Did you use a guide service?"

The hunter scoffed. "No."

"Do you mind if I make pencil marks on here? It'll rub right off."

Tallman took the metal cable and stretched it along the length of a main beam, the name for the primary member of an antler, which begins at the knobbly pedicle just above the skull and proceeds to the antler's foremost tip. On this beam he marked the bases of the other points. Most grow upward, some down, but in the hands of a measurer, the entire trophy—two antlers and whatever part of the skull remains between them—will be turned over and over, sky and earth tumbling, the logic of the animal's form giving way to numbers.

"The whole system is based on symmetry," Tallman had told me before the hunter showed up, as we talked in the Elkins field office of the West Virginia Department of Natural Resources, where Tallman is a biologist. The mountains I'd driven through to meet him were quiet and blurred, swirled with fresh snow. It was January, which is a busy season for scoring. After shooting deer in the fall, hunters must wait at least sixty days before having a trophy measured. During that period, the skull dries and its sutures—which look like very tightly meandering streambeds—slowly cinch together, reducing the width of the space between the antlers.

The human eye loves symmetry, but very few living things achieve it perfectly. My right hand looks older than my left. Each of the trees in my yard invents its own version of *poplar* or *walnut*, with its branches forming a characteristic but surprising illustration of division and reach. Deer antlers are no different: there is a pattern, a sort of Platonic rack with the most typical and predictable traits, and then there are all the deviations, small and large, that living antlers undertake as they rapidly put on mass and length during their season of growth. These can result from injury, malnutrition, or genetics: the real world, always fraying at the edges, expressed through the stacking and queering of bone cells.

These particular antlers on the table in front of us had five points on the left side and four on the right. This is not unusual, especially since that extra left point was quite small. But the scoring system values even development. A high score comes from sheer size, but also from regularity.

Tallman measured the extra point first. It would only affect the score if it were at least an inch long. "I don't think it's an inch," he said, putting the cable on it. At the tip of the point, he clamped the cable, then laid it along his ruler. "Oooh, it is," he said. "It's one and an eighth." He turned to his colleague Russell. "One abnormal on the left antler."

This would hurt the final score. Russell—wearing a brown sweater with an agency logo patch on the breast—tip-tapped the data into a laptop.

I liked Tallman. He was self-possessed but affable, with light blue eyes and a fuzzy red beard. He seemed to approach all this business sensibly, without any particular attachments.

He was one of about twelve hundred certified measurers across North America, many of whom are private citizens rather than state employees. I asked him why scoring trophies was part of his state job.

"West Virginia's not Iowa or Texas," he said. "We don't have a tremendous number of animals that meet the standard. But it's a way to recognize the work we do."

This was a version of the hunting-as-conservation paradigm that Boone and Crockett itself, along with many others, promotes. If B&C scores can put a limelight on the most impressive bucks taken in a particular state, that's one way for the state to show that it's successfully stewarding the species, using funds that come from hunters' license fees. Plus, the agency likes collecting the biological data on the animals. Antler size is one way to monitor herd health.

As for hunters, their focus has changed. It was around the 1930s that media reports began to emphasize the size of racks taken by hunters. Whereas for my grandfather's generation, counting points was often enough of a thrill (*I got an eight-pointer*), trophy envy today is finer-grained. Now, said Tallman, "They like to be able to say *I got a 150-class buck*." That is, a B&C score of 150 or above. People also sling around specific measurements. *He had eight-inch G-twos.*

"I see a greater number of bucks coming to be scored," said Tallman. He doesn't really think the deer are getting bigger, but hunters are changing their tactics. They're passing on smaller bucks, hoping they'll live a few more years and grow a bigger rack. They're scouring record books and contest results to figure out which states and counties might hold the biggest trophy bucks. And they're keeping a virtual eye on their hunting spots, often year-round.

"I have friends who put out twenty or thirty game cameras a year," Tallman told me. "They'll say 'I have a picture of this deer from the last four years—look how it's progressed.'" Hunters will notice a certain buck on their cameras when he's young. They'll scout him and try to spot him in person; give him a name, like a pet. Possessiveness creeps in. There have even been cases of poachers who had illegally killed trophy bucks being ordered to pay restitution to neighbors who had been scouting the same deer—as if taking pictures of a big buck, fantasizing about killing it, constituted some sort of deed of ownership.

Twenty or thirty game cameras, by the way, represents an investment of, on the very low end, $600—far more if you spring for the cams that send images right to your phone. Not to mention all the time spent choosing sites, hanging cameras, changing batteries, reviewing images.

Tallman added, "Here in another month, those same folks will be out hunting sheds"—the antlers bucks drop in the winter. "They're obsessed."

After waiting, perhaps years, to shoot a buck, then another sixty days for the antlers to dry, hunters often walk in and ask Tallman for a number even before he starts measuring. He has a line ready for these situations. "I never guess. I just say, 'We'll find out here in a minute.'"

This hunter didn't ask for a guess.

He was slight and fortyish, dressed more for Starbucks than for the woods. "I thought that thing was bigger than it was," he said. "It only dressed out to one forty-eight or something." He meant the weight of the whole deer.

"Ground shrinkage?" said Russell, laughing. "That's still a big deer. Average is a hundred twenty or a hundred twenty-five pounds."

"We do a lot of food plots and supplemental feeding at our other property," said the hunter. "The does are about one-oh-two, one-oh-three over there."

Tallman was busy measuring.

The actual calculations reminded me of doing taxes. You add up all the pluses: the inside spread of the rack, the lengths of the main beams and their circumference in four different places, and the lengths of the "normal" points. From this gross score you deduct the minuses: in this case, the length of that small, abnormal point, plus all the differences between the two sides—the little punishments for asymmetry.

I looked at the antlers and noticed how many different hues of brown and ivory striped their surfaces. The tips of the tines were smoother and lighter, the bases darker and rougher. They invited my grasp, but I didn't touch them; they didn't belong to me. I had a sense—which would later strike me as silly—that it would have been a rudeness to the hunter to touch without asking.

Some record-holding antlers are owned by people who didn't kill the deer—an heir, or a collector. Big-box outdoor companies buy up some of the biggest trophies to display in their stores. And technically, the scoring process has nothing to do with hunting; I could, for example, have brought in the skull I found to have its antlers scored.

But there are many ways for a trophy to become ineligible, and a perusal of the Boone and Crockett rules hints at the shenanigans that must go on—tampering, trying to bribe measurers, attaching shed antlers to the skull of a different animal. The regs detail a procedure to be followed in case a dispute must be settled with X-rays.

More simply, Tallman told me, some hunters try to argue with his numbers. "Most everybody has already scored their deer their own way," he said.

The biggest rule about trophies is that hunted animals must be taken according to the principles of fair chase. This is a flexible concept; one state may allow baiting deer while another bans it, to name just one issue addressed by fair chase doctrine. Maybe most relevantly for the trophy-scoring world, deer cannot be killed within an enclosure. That eliminates a whole category of hunting: the ranch excursions on which people pay large sums of money to shoot at bucks carefully bred and raised for their oversized antlers.

If the final score for a whitetail is 160 or above, it can be submitted to Boone and Crockett for review. Of the couple hundred trophies he scores per year, Tallman only sees a handful that are big enough for that. (Record-holding typical whitetails mostly score a bit over 200.)

This deer on the table in front of us wasn't as big as that, but it was handsome and respectable. The buck who'd worn these antlers had never seen them; they'd ridden out of sight on top of his head from the time they emerged in spring to the day in early October when the hunter killed him. He'd rubbed their velvet off on trees, leaving marks that rivals would have seen and smelled. He may have used the antlers to battle those bucks. They were advertisements of testosterone and expressions of his ability to contribute to the gene pool. Does would have noticed them. Maybe other hunters did, too. This buck's meat was in the hunter's freezer. His guts had likely been eaten by scavengers within hours of his death. As for his bones and hooves, who knew? Had he survived the hunting season, he would have carried these antlers a few more months before finally letting them go, maybe getting to lay eyes on them at last when they tumbled, one at a time, to the ground.

Tallman was finished. He looked at the hunter. "What'd you come up with?" he asked.

The hunter answered, "One twenty-nine. The gross was one thirty-five."

Tallman said, "One twenty-five and two-eighths final. One twenty-nine and one-eighth was the gross score."

The hunter asked, "What's the minimum, one twenty-five?" He wasn't referring to the Boone and Crockett minimum, but to West Virginia's standard for its state big buck contest—a lower, and equally arbitrary, benchmark. Another way to make meaning.

"You made it," said Tallman. "Just made it."

On his way out, the hunter got a little chattier.

"This is the only buck I shot this year," he said. "My eleven-year-old daughter missed one—literally shaved some hair off it."

He signed the score sheet, telling us about his son, who was eight. "Oh, that's right, I did shoot another buck. I probably wouldn't have done that, but my son was with me and he really wanted me to shoot something."

The conference room had wide windows. We were up on a bluff overlooking a big bottomland, and all the air between here and the next line of mountains was full of snow. Early afternoon: The building seemed to be flying through whiteness. It was the kind of day when animals bed down and hold on, making no tracks until later, after the snow has stopped.

⸙

In myth, antlers have the power to capture the sun. Around the world, stories tell about a stag who crosses the sky, carrying the sun away in its antlers. As it runs, warmth drains from the earth. Darkness thickens among trees.

These stories voice our impatience with winter, and each contains a hero—a hunter—who chases down the thief and restores the sun. Someone remembered around a fire, carved onto a rock, or stepping out of a truck, wearing camouflage.

From a sober biological standpoint, the deer of autumn is running simply because it's in rut. Just before winter clenches down, the temporary madness of fertility drives its movements.

The fall rut is also prime time for the hunt. There are practical reasons for this, but perhaps seeing life flare up in deer, at the very moment that the green of the world dies back to nothing, has also inspired a mixture of envy and longing in humans, quickening our bloodlust. It feels both obvious and a little naïve to say that underneath that lust for a big trophy rack lies an ancient awareness of what antlers have symbolized: seasonality, fecundity, quiescence. In historic art and stories, antlers have been depicted mimicking the sun's shape, or burnished with gold; they branch like trees, veins, rivers; their formation and shedding follows the growth cycle of the plants deer use as food.

In fall, they are literally and frankly horny. But antlers—as any biologist would hasten to tell you—are very different from horns, even if *horns* remains in fond, folksy usage among some hunters. Animals like goats and sheep employ fingernail-like keratin to grow one set of horns in a lifetime. But an antler is a bone, grown and discarded annually. Antlers are also a defining characteristic of the Cervidae family of mammals. In all cervids except reindeer and caribou, antlers are the exclusive province of males.

There's excellent reason that they're so firmly connected to the idea of life force and vitality: Antlers are the fastest-growing animal tissue in the world, sometimes adding as much as half an inch of length in a day, and their size is an index not only of a buck's genetic gifts and testosterone levels but also of his diet. In wild deer, antlers are truly an expression of the land and system of which they are a part. But given our crops and landscaping, and hunters' food plots, whatever antlers are out there these days often reflect not only a natural habitat but human intentions as well.

During that season of growth, a deer's antlers will look rounded, almost furry, covered with velvet, and they are soft and vulnerable to injury. Blood vessels thread through the velvet tissue, delivering oxygen to the growing bones, making them hot to the touch.

As summer curdles into fall, the blood supply slows and stops, the velvet dries up, and bucks rub their antlers against trees and branches to strip away the softness. Underneath is naked bone, soon hardened by the drying and polished by the rubbing. The antlers are full-grown and ready to be used: as announcement, as badge, as weapon.

⚶

No one's sure why males in the deer family shed their antlers each year. It's an evolutionary mystery, and it makes deer, in a strange way, akin to trees.

For millennia, other animals, like mice, have gnawed on shed antlers for the calcium. Years ago, I found a three-point antler covered in tooth marks; its smaller tines were all but gone. Someone had gleaned significant nourishment from this discarded prize before I picked it up and brought it home, where it lives on top of the piano.

In collecting this object, just like when I picked up that antlered skull, I'm sure I knew I was part of a very old human ritual: taking possession of biological tokens. Is this about homage or mastery? The first Queen Elizabeth enjoyed receiving antlers, as symbols of her own authority, from the North American lands some of her subjects were exploring. I'm not after political power, but I certainly feel the lure of scientific dominion, the feeling that a natural history collection represents a kind of mental encompassing of the world. (In the U.S., there are at least two museums devoted entirely to displaying antlers.)

But I don't think I realized, when I picked up those antlers, that I was also taking part in a fast-growing activity called shed hunting. Just within the last couple of decades, the intentional search for shed antlers, during the late winter and spring when they've just been dropped by bucks, has become a big, internet-fueled trend and a kind of off-season companion sport to hunting. Elk antlers are the most valuable finds. But plenty of deer hunters, too, now incorporate shed hunting into their annual cycle of excursions. The hunting media pitches the hobby as a way to up one's game, proclaiming that shed hunting goes hand in hand with scouting for deer trails and sign, intel that hunters can use to their advantage next fall.

Just like a deer killed by bow or gun, a shed antler makes a trophy. People get especially excited about finding matched sets from a single buck. A skull with both antlers still attached, like the one I found, is called a deadhead and carries even more cachet.

Besides information and glory, hunters can gain something more tangible from shed hunting: cash. The freshest deer antlers can fetch $10–$14 per pound when sold to an antler broker, who will in turn supply the medicinal market, or sell them to furniture makers, taxidermists, and dog treat companies. One eBay seller I found was offering dozens of different antlers, ranging from a set of asymmetrical antlers still attached to the skull plate, offered at $925, to a small single antler for $20.

Where there's money, there's competition—and the potential for bad behavior. Game wardens in Wyoming started to document increasing numbers of unscrupulous shed hunters in the 1990s, leading them to partially ban the practice. Apparently, people were harassing mule deer whose antlers were still attached, chasing them over fences with ATVs or sending packs of dogs after them, trying to knock the antlers off. The area covered by the ban had to be expanded in 2019.

As a culture, it seems we are becoming less inclined to simply let antlers lie where they fall and slowly break down; we look at them like coal in a seam, wanting to take them all for ourselves.

⚘

I have a neighbor who's gradually been adding to a roadside display of antlers along the front edge of his property, and it always grabs my eye when I drive past. I've never spoken to this man, but I like the way he's arranged the antlers along the ground, throughout the branches of a small tree, among birdhouses and whirligigs, making a sort of folk-art tribute to his woodsy surroundings. Every set of antlers is as unique to an individual animal as a human fingerprint, and yet, looking at them in a group, one senses pattern: an ancient habit underlying their forms. The spirit of what my neighbor is doing feels loving. Celebratory.

Less so the language used by trophy enthusiasts to describe what they call nontypical antlers. That inch-and-an-eighth tine I'd seen Robert Tallman measure was a small aberration on a mostly symmetrical rack, but some antlers—again, for genetic and nutritional reasons—are much more irregular, and are scored using a whole different system. They may have "drop tines" that point toward the ground. They may have "kickers," "spikes," or "cheaters." Antlers can resemble a knobby cactus or a dripping candle; some tines have blobby tips. Deer antlers can be palmate, like moose antlers, or a set may be wildly asymmetrical. Third and fourth antlers are not unheard of.

All of this could be seen as beautiful, and certainly nontypical antlers are valued in their own right, but the collective name for their traits is, degradingly, "junk" or "trash," and the animals that carry them are "freaks." One headline I found read "Here's a quadruple drop-tine giant with more junk on his head than a used car dealership." Big trophy bucks get ugly names: "goonies," "hawgs," "slobknockers," "stink pigs," "mega-toads." The ones with tiny antlers are "dinks."

There's a bullying edge to all of this sizing up and labeling. It's odd that there's no term for a *pair* of antlers that isn't denigrating—we only have "trophy" and "rack." One can't help but think of the way women have been summarized by our measurements, our bodies reduced to parts that are there for the naming and the taking; "rack," of course, gets pasted onto both bucks and women.

⚸

"Fainting I follow," wrote Sir Thomas Wyatt in the 1500s about a hind he poetically hunted who was also, or actually, a woman—possibly Anne Boleyn, later beheaded.

The line reminds me of a European fairy tale called "The White Doe," in which a princess is turned into a deer by a fairy's curse. She regains human form every night, but in the daylight she is followed by the prince to whom she'd been betrothed. When he sees her he reacts with a hunter's instinct, immediately sending several arrows in her direction. He misses, she flees, and they embark on a multiday pas de deux of desire and fear.

He searches for her; she finds him asleep and awakens him with a kiss; he pursues her and she flees. She runs until she's near death, and he tenderly cares for her and brings her water. But when she runs again he becomes angry, a thwarted hunter. "'She shall not escape me again . . . If I hunt her every day for a year, I will have her at last.'"

The next time he sees her he shoots an arrow into her leg.

The wound is the key that unlocks the magic; the pain of being shot is "the last part of the punishment." Finally the princess sheds her curse, and the two are married.

Through blood, the woman earns the right to her own body. Through an admixture of tender violence, the man takes possession of his wife.

This is hardly the only such shapeshifter story—doe as woman, woman as doe, hunter as lover as claimant. Deer-women may be victims or they may themselves victimize men. A treacherous Deer Lady trots through various Native American stories, including a prominent role in an episode of the TV series *Reservation Dogs*. Like her counterparts in older myths, the Deer Lady looks like a beautiful and seductive woman, until you look down and see hooves instead of feet. In the show, she conducts silent vigilante killings of criminals—the kind of person she calls "bad men." "Be good," she tells a young boy, in a tone both nurturing and ominous. It feels like symmetry when the same series shows a young Native woman killing a big buck.

If a man chasing a doe is a potent motif, then something about the quest for a big buck contains even more inherent tension and torque. Being prey animals, deer of any sex embody wariness, a propensity to hide or flee. When that passivity is combined with noble virility symbolized by the mature buck, it creates a perfect stage on which human masculinity and dominance can perform. Buck hunting is a stag party—traditionally a males-only event— and it's a chivalric contest. The buck is taken at the height of his maleness, in the midst of pursuing mates. In spring, he may not look terribly different from a doe, but during hunting season, he's complete with antlers in all their phallic expression of generative force.

For decades, deer hunting in America mostly meant shooting bucks. This came about as part of the conservation movement, the idea being to protect does and leave them free for reproduction. After deer populations recovered and the task became about controlling, rather than boosting, their numbers, managers wanted to bring back doe hunting. But hunters objected, sometimes fiercely. They usually did so on biological grounds: *You'll destroy the herd*. But there was a reactionary element, too. Hunting females had come to seem downright perverted.

Doe hunting is more accepted these days. Meanwhile, hunting has become commercialized. Like other industries, it mixes money and desire, and in this case, the desires of deer themselves are part of the brew.

🦌

I'd suspected that there was a bit of an erotic aspect to modern deer hunting, though I'd always immediately think, *Nah, that's going too far*. But even my first casual stroll through a big-box hunting store offered evidence for the theory. Frank and ample evidence.

Exhibit A: the little potion-sized bottle of Cherry on Top— cherry-scented powder for a hunter to sprinkle over a bait pile, promising to get deer "licking their chops and begging for more." Then there were attractant scents made of beet, apple, and mysterious grain by-products, with names like Head Rush, Meltdown, and Acorn Rage, offered in both powder and spray form. There were tiny bottles of doe urine: Screamin' Heat, Code Red, and one promising "Powerful Sexual Attractor: Bring in Bucks—AROUSED," with a sexy cartoon doe on the package.

You could also lure bucks with buck testosterone: Buck Fever Mature Buck Blend, or Buck Fever Full Rut Formula ("Make Bucks Hunt You!"). There were big candy-like chunks of mineral lick, encased in plastic.

There was even cologne for hunters: many feet of shelving devoted to products that erase the human odor from body, clothing, and gear. You could get a deodorant stick, a laundry detergent, a body wash/shampoo, boot and storage powder, or a general "field spray" for anything not covered by the other products.

The average American hunter spends $2,100 per year on the sport, totaling $26 billion across the industry—numbers that feel jarring when set against the frontiersman tradition and mentality that pervades hunting culture. Of course the same store contained thousands of other products, from binoculars to clothing to weapons to fillet knives. One might say this is just capitalism at work, leveraging our desires in the service of the market. We prove our desire for other people by spending money on them, and the same goes for deer. But if the desire wasn't there in the first place, there'd be nothing to leverage.

Hunting starts with looking, especially for such a visual species as humans. The poet Marianne Moore called antlered deer a "candelabrum-headed ornament" on the world. And if one of antlers' purposes is to catch the eyes of other deer, they never fail to attract people, too. It's something else we have in common.

CHAPTER 15

For Show

I COULDN'T BREATHE VERY WELL INSIDE THE HUNTING and fishing expo. People flowed past me as I hesitated near the entrance to the big hangar-like building, trying to get my bearings. The pandemic was on; I had a brand-new N95 pinched hard over my nose. This put me in a tiny minority.

It was Friday afternoon: hour one of a three-day sport show near my home. Behind their tables, the vendors seemed juiced for conversation. The lights were bright; the air smelled like vanilla-roasted nuts. Wooden turkey calls *awk-awk*ed continually.

My breath hot inside the mask, I dove down an aisle. A sign on a booth: THE MOST INTIMIDATING BLINDS ON THE MARKET. That seemed odd. A deer blind is a structure in which a hunter can hide; they're meant to make the hunter invisible, the opposite of scary. I stepped away and was immediately buttonholed by a man selling supplements pumped up with extra protein and minerals to encourage antler growth in wild bucks.

Hefty antlers poked up everywhere: in logos for hunting ranches and gun companies, in framed prints of wildlife art, in photo after photo of hunters with their kills. In every direction was animal death and essence. An African safari outfitter had draped the sides of his booth with zebra skins. Mounted deer heads—every one of them a big-racked buck—sent their blank gazes ricocheting all around. Little kids passed me holding ten-inch trout enclosed in Ziploc bags, like goldfish from the pet store. I came around a corner and found myself facing the centerpiece of the whole show: a giant taxidermy display, dozens of different specimens, filling a low stage and the tall wall behind it.

There were two or three whitetail bucks on the wall, but they looked small next to the moose and elk, and downright boring compared to the alligator, grizzlies, and wolverine. Some kind of small deer lay dead—well, all the animals were dead—under a triumphant male lion. Pressed against the stage, a little boy was talking on his mother's phone, listing what he saw. "A bobcat catching a turkey . . . a buffalo . . ." The one I couldn't stop staring at was the giraffe. It wasn't the whole animal, just ten or twelve feet of neck soaring up from a truncated chest, ending in a long, sad, and infinitely patient face.

Deer played a small role in this arrangement, but in general they lay at the heart of the show, as they do in American hunting culture. Although there were a lot of things for sale, the real point of this event seemed to be not money, but feelings.

Feelings of amazement: Five record-breaking mounted bucks displayed in a sort of mini-museum, behind a velvet rope. They were deer with antlers so enormous—some balanced and graceful, others wildly irregular—that instead of hanging in somebody's man cave, they were traveling the country like Van Goghs, accompanied by plaques explaining their significance.

Luke BREWSTER Buck

327 7/8 P&Y

World Record Killed in Illinois in 2018, by Luke Brewster of Virginia. The Brewster Buck is the largest whitetail ever killed by a hunter! He was pursued by Luke and neighboring hunters for 4 years! Luke had 4 years of trail camera photos, detailing the history of the growth of this phenomenal buck!

Feelings of dominance: Brands of arrowheads called Dead-meat, Swhacker, Barbarian (Built to Give a Beating). A teenage boy—the kind who looks almost like a man by the time he starts high school—with solid limbs and big work boots and a knife on his belt, taking laser shots at a paper target.

Feelings of patriotism: In a large booth hung with paintings of wildlife, Native Americans in traditional dress, and white Daniel Boone types, there was an image I couldn't quite parse—a modern bowhunter crouched over a buck, with the ghost of a soldier just behind him, holding an American flag.

Religion: In the official program, God was mentioned four times in a brief letter from the show's producer. Stacks of pocket-sized Bibles were available for free in many booths, with camouflage covers: *The New Testament, Military Edition.* A big banner for a gun company: "Where Faith, Country, and Firearms Matter."

And—inexorably—politics. Here was a large stand selling T-shirts, staffed by an older couple whose two tiny terriers rested in dog beds right on their countertop. Occasionally, the woman would lean her face down to them and get a kiss on the lips. Trying to be inconspicuous, I copied down some of the T-shirt slogans in my notebook. "Stand for the flag / Kneel for the fallen." "I have a pretty daughter. I also have a shotgun, a shovel, and an alibi." Rebel flags; Don't Tread on Me flags. "Strike Back / Silent War." "Trump 2024." "Guns Save Lives."

The deeper into the show I went, the weirder things got. A group of Mennonites was selling fancy binoculars and spotting scopes, plus some sort of magazine. A young, pink-faced woman in a long dress and white cap told me, robotically, "It's a nature magazine the whole family can enjoy! It has . . . stories . . . and articles . . ." She trailed off. I turned around and found myself staring at a poster for a live grizzly bear show that would be starting in an hour. *Ladies and gentlemen, boys and girls*, someone sound-checked behind a curtain. *Ladies and gentlemen . . .*

A few more steps to a giant white tub in which a couple hundred trout were circling, slowly, all of them moving in the same endless direction. I watched a kid hook one on a tiny pole while a man beside me told a friend that his son had recently killed himself. Then I looked up and found eight live raptors—hawks and owls—arrayed before me on railings, leashed by their feet. Their presence shocked me; I didn't want to look at them. A woman stood six inches from a hawk and said loudly to the proprietor, "Didja ever have one jump up and grab somebody's nose when they got too close?" A man near me answered, "Only if they're a Democrat." He turned and stared at the trout, musing out loud, "I bet if you surveyed everybody in this place you wouldn't find two of 'em."

I decided to take a breather outside.

On my way out, a guy handed me a homemade CD with "How to get to Heaven" written on it in Sharpie.

There was only one other thing at the expo that I wanted to see— the Big Buck Contest—so when I finally reentered the building, I put my head down and made a beeline for the back room where scorers were waiting behind long tables to receive hunters and their trophies.

It was a relief, after my uneasy survey of the expo, to just talk with a human—Dale Wenger, contest judge, a tall and personable man with a salt-and-pepper beard and a big laugh. Unlike Robert Tallman, whom I'd seen score that trophy in West Virginia, Wenger was neither a biologist nor an official Boone and Crockett measurer. He was a taxidermist.

There were only about a dozen entries so far, but there was still lots of time for folks to enter the competition. Wenger expected about seventy in total. Prizes were modest—you could walk away with $100 and an unframed certificate—but like everything involving antlers, emotions could run hot. One year, a hunter came in with a giant buck and plunked it down on the table along with his Boone and Crockett paperwork. Wenger slapped his hand down loudly to demonstrate. *Whack!* "He was one of these guys, you know"—he hooked his thumbs under his armpits and puffed out his chest, imitating a thundering voice. "He said, 'That's what it scored.'"

"I said, 'I'll still have to score it.' He said, 'Are you a Boone and Crockett scorer?' I said 'No, I'm the scorer for this contest. I have to score all the deer. I'll be durn close to that score.' And when I was done, I had actually added half an inch to his score. After that he was my best friend. He hung around the whole weekend, he was just so afraid someone would bring in a bigger buck."

Just then a hunter appeared beside me with a deer. A nice big one; Wenger was impressed. "Has anybody scored it yet?" he asked. "No, sir," answered the hunter. Wenger said, "If I hunted him, I would have scored him right away," and laughed his big laugh. "This is a really, really nice buck."

"My buddies were freaking out when I shot him," said the hunter. "They couldn't believe I was as calm as I was, but I was just in shock."

He was slim, middle-aged, wearing a little fuzz on his cheeks, an orange ball cap and a hoodie. When you looked at him closely, he didn't quite fit the stereotype. His T-shirt said something about New York City. He wore little hipster eyeglasses.

Wenger got to work scoring and I asked the hunter if he'd done anything special to get this buck. Not really, he said. Just four or five years of hunting the same area, figuring out which tree stands worked in certain winds. "I had never seen him on my cameras," he said. "And there's a hunt club over the ridge—they had never seen him either."

The craftiness of bucks—their ability to seem invisible, or to show up as though out of thin air—is part of the legend hunters weave around them. The older the buck, the more worthy an opponent he's assumed to be, since he's already survived numerous hunting seasons. A five-year-old buck, tough and full of testosterone, doesn't make the best eating. But tender young females are puny trophies.

The wily-buck legend serves a ritual purpose—it makes the animal, in the words of one writer, "a worthy opponent in a game of life and death"—but it also has some biological basis. Most people who observe deer near their homes will spot does far more often than bucks. Because bucks are preferred by many hunters, they stand a greater chance of being killed. If they do survive, they learn to stay out of sight. (One study put six hunters in a one-square-mile enclosure with seven male deer and recorded how long it took for the hunters to even spot a buck: 124 hours.) They congregate in smaller groups and feed covertly. Their existence is a more elusive version of the deer lives we usually witness.

The hunter pointed at a small, sharp tine at the base of one main beam. "This is the most interesting part of the deer to me," he said. "Just from loving deer, watching their behavior . . . This is a knife. It's an evolutionary advantage—to have something low like that." He was thinking of how bucks spar during the rut, charging each other with antlers pointed forward. "That's probably had eyeballs hanging off of it."

Wenger announced the final score: "One sixty-four and two-eighths."

"All right! Nice buck!" said the hunter—ironically, perhaps.

Two guys standing behind me marveled out loud: "I can't believe it's not more than that."

"Your gross score was five inches higher," Wenger said. "I only like net scores for contests. It doesn't tell you what he grew on top of his head. I like the saying, 'Nets are for fishermen.'"

"The gross is the hunter's score, right?" agreed the hunter. "It's like, 'Look at that big mess on his head.'"

He posed for my camera, holding his deer. Wenger coached him: "Hold it out from your chest! Make it look big."

◊◊

Two days later I returned to see how it all turned out. On the way in, I got behind a giant pickup with a big sticker on the rear window: SORRY BOUT YOUR NECK.

The expo was almost over, and now the buck contest wall was fairly full of deer. Lined up in ranks, they surprised me with their variation—in the antlers, of course, but also in other ways. The longer I looked, the more individual they seemed. One was light in color, almost lemony around the muzzle. Another had a neck as thick as an old-fashioned washing machine.

"Imagine fighting *him*," somebody said beside me, pointing. "He'd mess you *up*."

I got to chatting with Wenger again and he showed me what he thought was the best taxidermy job in the contest. It had a nice natural look, he thought, and was positioned in a "stealth pose," with the head stretched forward as though the animal were alert, but not frightened. "That's the type of look I go for most often," he said. His only quarrel was with the position of the left ear: too far forward.

The room filled in with people. A few minutes after four, an announcer took the mike and said two bizarre things in a row. First, "Thank you for bringing your heads in." Then, "We can give everybody a hand for their kills this year."

Polite applause. The contest had a number of different categories; I felt glad, for some reason, when the hunter I'd met won second place in his category. But the announcement of winners, for all the hand-shaking and photo-posing, was anticlimactic. People seemed more excited about a raffle drawing for a guided hunt in Illinois, known for its corn-fed trophy bucks. I tried writing down the details of the winners' appearances and found myself making the same notes over and over: *Flannel shirt, boots, ball cap, goatee.* Two of the younger winners had "Hunter" as a first name. There was supposed to be a ladies' category, but no ladies won anything; apparently none had entered.

Someone took a group shot: a dozen white men holding a dozen sets of antlers.

Then everyone claimed their trophies and began to filter out of the room. I wandered the expo one last time. The turkey call noises had finally stopped. The T-shirt woman, lapdogs still pacing the counter, was packing up her designs into folders marked WOLVES, CHRISTIAN, OLD CARS AND TRUCKS, GIRLS—NEON & MISC.

Men carrying deer heads in one hand. Men cradling deer heads to their chests. Men standing around talking, their deer heads resting on the floor, rocking back and forth as the men's fingertips rolled over the antler tips. A man outside in the parking lot, in the raking warm light of late afternoon, carefully loading a deer head into the bed of his truck. The woman with him wore tight jeans and a leopard-print top. I could just see the deer's nose poking up as he drove away.

⚚

Standing outside of deer-hunting culture, as I do, maybe it's a little too easy to cast an ironic eye. It can be a bit of a knee-jerk response.

Hunters, for their part, are not apologizing, not trying to ingratiate. In surveys, nonhunters prefer that hunters chase meat rather than trophies, but meanwhile, hunters are over in a different room, nurturing and absorbing a culture saturated with the mythology of the big-racked buck. Though most hunters do eat what they kill, and plenty kill female deer, the outward-facing expression of the sport is firmly connected to a lust for antlers.

Big buck contests take place all over the country; in some areas, there's another tradition called the "buck pole," a ritual for the opening day of hunting season. Hunters bring their kills directly to a central spot, like a gas station or an outfitter, and string them up in a line alongside other freshly harvested bucks. Antlers and weights are compared and a winner declared.

More simply, there are endless trophy photos, and endless storytelling. Anyone who partakes of the hunting media, even lightly, is guaranteed to view a parade of very conventional, very repetitive images: the hunter kneeling on the ground, the freshly killed deer with its head held upright, a little (but not too much) blood. The vast majority of the deer in these photos are bucks, the hunter's hands grasping the antlers as focal point and proof.

I found a newspaper story once that explained how best to set up a trophy photo. "Make sure you are wearing the clothing you had donned when you harvested the animal," the advice ran. "Do not rest your gun or bow on the deer's antlers; it is disrespectful to the animal. Put the deer's tongue back in its mouth. Display reverence for the deer by kneeling beside or behind it, and smile."

I doubt reverence can be so easily prescribed. Maybe there are better and worse ways to take a trophy photo. But why take them at all? What do they commemorate? What do they prove?

⚶

My own feelings about hunting are awash with dissonance. Certainly I went most of my life without feeling much interest in hunting or sympathy for hunters, but I knew that to understand our relationship with deer, I'd have to look hard at hunting. And

I knew that, through family ties, hunting was already a part of me, a kind of dormant animal within. In fact, it's part of everyone; we all have hunters for ancestors. Hunting is a flash point in our society—for academics (anthropologists, feminist theorists, environmental philosophers), for pop culture (witness our fascination with the survivalists of *Alone* or *Yellowjackets*), and for politics (think gun control debates). The act of pursuing and killing wild animals can't help but feel like a set of ethical questions. As our prime game animal, deer are the major doorway into these dilemmas.

The standard got-a-big-buck headlines ("Hunter Downs Velvet Brute"; "Goldman Slams Freak Buck in Dad's Backyard") carry forward a tradition that sustains itself by simplicity and sheer repetition. But hunters are a small sliver of the U.S. population, and mainstream culture—nonhunting culture, that is—increasingly equates animals with pets and talks a lot about kindness. All of this means that it's getting harder for nonhunters to understand the brashness, the pleasure in domination, of the big buck hunter.

American hunting culture is peculiar to this country; hunting looks very different in other places. In Germany, for example, traditional rituals of reverence are still practiced. When people hunt in large groups, they end the day with a ceremony called the *Strecke legen*: carefully laying out the game in a prescribed pattern, surrounding the carcasses with tree branches, and playing special songs and signals on horns. Herbivores are also given a "last bite," a small branch placed in the animal's mouth, followed by a prayer of thanks to Saint Hubertus, patron saint of the hunt.

It's not that American hunters are the only ones interested in trophies; it's more a question of tone, and of the cultural strains that flavor it.

Talking with hunters one at a time, I've often sensed a solidity and groundedness that feels deep and real. I've thought, *Here is a person who understands something about life and death.* I've experimented with the belief that by entering into such an intimate relationship with an animal—a relationship that transcends the visual to involve all the senses, that incorporates the animal's habits and perceptions into the hunter's own mind, and the animal's flesh cell by cell into the hunter's own body—hunters may be able to claim a knowledge of the world that is unique and, in a sober-eyed way, very beautiful.

Then I'm turned away by the trophy photos, the headlines, the politics. To me, the paradox continues to rub: that individual hunters can possess exactly the virtues their conservationist forebears would have predicted—self-reliance, self-restraint—while the culture that caters to them seems focused on a different, and brutal, set of values.

Maybe it's possible for individuals to enter a space of deep relationship if and when they allow that culture to fall away—when they are in the field, immersed in a place, sharpening their senses, and consciously practicing an ethics of carnivorism. When they move away, at least partially, from the trophy mindset. But that's a lot of baggage to leave behind.

⚹

Many nonhunters probably have no idea about some of the things people do to kill big bucks. Like the food plots they plant so they can hunt from stands right above the crops that draw deer and spur antler growth. They might not realize that one can buy a timer-activated, solar-powered feeder that holds up to twelve hundred pounds of feed at a time, using an infrared meter to measure how much feed is left in the barrel and Bluetooth the information directly to one's phone. They may never have heard of LED arrow fletching or night-vision rifle scopes. They might not know that trail cameras have brought to deer hunting a level of video surveillance that rivals what's happening in urban downtowns—cameras everywhere, recording exactly who comes and goes, when, and how often. They likely have no idea that people pay top dollar for land in areas known for big bucks, land they intend to use solely for hunting. Or that there exists a metaverse of cable shows, social media, and podcasts that tell hunters how to hunt and why it matters.

Where it concerns the actual biology of deer, a lot of this amounts to boosting natural processes—like putting fertilizer on your garden, or targeting workouts to specific muscle groups. They are ways of seeking optimal results within what we understand to be natural limits of physiology. There's a floating goal of taking a buck larger than the largest known, but there is also, in theory, some outer limit to what's possible. Human aspiration, ego, competition nudge against that biological curve.

But then there are deer farms.

⚶

I knew that deer farms existed (according to one source, they are a billion-dollar industry); I'd heard the industry's complaints about having to comply with chronic wasting disease regulations. But well into my research, I still hadn't really wrapped my mind around *why* people would breed and sell deer like cattle.

Domesticating deer isn't exactly new. In Siberia, Mongolia, and Scandinavia, reindeer have been kept for meat, milk, hides, and even riding for as long as three millennia. But other cervids are part of a modern and growing global industry. New Zealand farmers breed deer and elk for meat, antler velvet, and hides. Musk deer are farmed in China for the production of musk, an ingredient in perfume. And in America, since the 1970s, deer farms have existed to produce grotesque, exaggerated antlers.

These farms make money in a few different ways. One, they sell live bucks to high-fence hunting ranches where they will be shot for trophies. Two, they sell bucks and does, or semen and embryos, to other breeders who are also trying to produce bucks with enormous racks. Finally, they find lucrative sidelines in the sale of venison, antlers, and deer urine—the latter to be used as scent attractants in hunting.

Multiple parts of a deer can be commodified, but if they didn't happen to grow antlers on their heads, I suspect the American industry would be much smaller if it existed at all. I set up a video call with Josh Newton, a deer farmer and industry spokesman in Pennsylvania, to get this strange business explained to me. I told him, "I need *Deer Farming for Dummies*."

He chuckled. His bearded visage was topped with an antler-logo ball cap. Behind him was a picture of his farm, snow-covered, mountainous. It looked like a lovely place. "Every deer farmer I know," he began, "is a hunter first—always a hunter first. This is a hard business, extremely hard. It's very capital-intensive up front. What makes somebody want to do that? Hunters love deer so much, and they love interacting with deer. They want more." As a seventeen-year-old hunter, he himself was hit with a bolt-from-the-blue desire to enter the business. "Hunting was what I lived for; that's all I did," he said. "I visited my uncle's deer farm and I was like this is crazy—I want to do this. It took one day, and I was game on. I was just so fascinated with deer."

This romantic story soon gave way to a more nuts-and-bolts discussion. Compared with cattle, Newton explained, deer can physically fit into as little as a tenth of the acreage, while fetching similar profit margins per animal—and they can be raised on steep terrain where cattle could not thrive. Meanwhile, the techniques and economies that breeders have developed for other kinds of livestock—artificial insemination, tinkering with the timing of ovulation, buying and selling semen all around the country—can readily be applied to deer.

Even though farmed deer are under human control, they retain more of their wildness, and are harder to handle, than cows or goats. Most people who are unfamiliar with the deer farming phenomenon have an instinctive reaction when they learn about it: that it just feels wrong. That a farm is a place where a deer should not be.

Yet deer have several traits in common with animals, and even plants, that were domesticated by humans long ago. Like many species from pigs to wheat, deer are opportunists and edge creatures—brilliant adapters. The author Stephen Budiansky describes "long, loose associations between free-living partners before a full-fledged domesticated relationship appears." This describes our connection to deer quite well: We live as neighbors in environments that offer advantages to both of us.

In Budiansky's view, domestication is not a process of enslavement—humans grabbing control of and exploiting another species—but simply part of evolution. It's a mutual adaptation that serves both parties. If numbers equal success, that idea bears out: The total biomass of land species on earth is becoming more and more weighted toward humans and our domesticated species.

↟

Talking to Newton, I had questions about everything, and the answers had a way of wandering away from any sense of real animals; it was like talking about a peculiar combination of intensive care and car repair. How can you collect embryos from a pregnant doe? "You have to cycle the doe, get her in heat, get her bred, let a buck live cover her and/or artificially inseminate her. Seven days later, you take saline solution and physically flush embryos through the system. You filter to catch them, put them under a microscope, pull them out of there and then freeze them." How do you then get the embryos into a different doe? "Laproscopic embryonic implantation. You put two embryos in every deer." And how do you collect semen from a buck? "You sedate the animal, clear the rectum of any feces, and you take a probe—it's called an electro ejaculator—and you stimulate the process with electrolysis and they deposit semen in a collection vial."

He turned off his virtual background to show me several mind-blowingly huge racks of antlers on his wall, plus a squat white cryogenic tank on his office floor in which, he said, he was storing "six hundred straws of semen and a couple of embryos." The former could fetch between $100 and $1,000 apiece, while embryos might go for up to $5,000. But prices have plenty of room to inflate. Newton had once seen a single buyer pay

$140,000 for five straws of semen "like it was nothing," he said. As for live animals, a highly desired breeder buck (ranchers like to give their studs names, like High Heat or Majesty) can command more than $50,000.

I asked Newton what he feeds his deer. He said that although Purina and other big feed companies do make deer feed, he personally uses a grain-and-pellet mixture from a local mill. He also imports alfalfa hay from western states, where arid conditions make for a finer stem. "And our pastures have plenty of clover," he added. "Greens are good for them; that's what they're meant to eat. Ruminants aren't meant to eat grain."

Then why do you feed them grain? I asked.

"Performance. Performance," Newton said. "If you don't give them a nutrient-dense feed, they won't reach their genetic potential in the time you want them to. I want to raise my animals as fast as I can in an ethical and healthy manner."

Bucks can grow big antlers on their own, in woods, farmland, or suburbia, just by eating acorns and browsing trees and shrubs. They can do it without trucks hauling bales of alfalfa halfway across the continent, without being vaccinated for disease, without having been sired or birthed under human supervision. But wild bucks will never grow to anything like the dimensions of farmed bucks. Whereas a wild buck is considered very large if it has ten or twelve antler points and measures more than 150 in the Boone and Crockett system, farmed bucks may score at 300, 400, 500 inches, with many dozens of points.

Bucks raised on farms look like they are carrying Manhattan around on their heads. They look like aircraft carriers. They look like diseased trees, exploding in a frenzy of extra branches. Their antlers are shaped not like antlers but like bunches of peonies, or gymnastics equipment, or very inventive and unworkable sex toys. They make Barbie look sensibly proportioned. They are like sea creatures growing at the bottom of the ocean on a mound of nuclear waste.

⚶

Budiansky makes one other point about the process of domestication: It hinges on a trait called "neoteny," in which adults of a species retain some juvenile characteristics. This can mean physical appearance—think of the foreshortened faces of some dog breeds—or it can have more to do with behavior, like when a pet cat begs for food. If adult deer learn to expect and even ask for food from humans, perhaps they are exhibiting their version of neoteny. I think of Canela and her crackers as much as Newton's deer and their daily rations.

But humans, too, have neotenic tendencies. We are curious and open to learning new behaviors, even as adults; this is part of why we've been able to enter novel and complex relationships with other animals in the first place. So if deer find opportunities on the fringes of our world, they also find humans ready to imagine ever tighter connections with them. Some spread corn. Some disallow hunting. Some even provide a place to sleep and assistance making babies.

Domestication eventually results in animals that are genetically dependent on humans; you cannot turn a sheep loose from a farm and expect it to survive. We imagine deer behind fences and we squirm because we know so much about the trade-off they may, as a species, be on the precipice of making. A strict evolutionist might say there is nothing inherently wrong with the loss of wildness if it means greater survival and adaptation. Most of us aren't prepared to go quite that far.

In the deer farm world, unlike the rest of the world, the best time to take a photo of a buck seems to be summer, when he's in velvet and his antlers appear even heavier. In a lot of these photos, too, the bucks are positioned with their rumps toward the camera, clearly showing off their testicles, the repositories of their lucrative genetics, which are employed in deliberate inbreeding to exaggerate the desired traits. Their heads look dwarfed by the antlers they have been forced to grow, eyes seeming tiny, staring out from inside a biological prison.

Farmed deer, like certain purebred dogs, are the living inscape of human desires at their outermost borders. They are a brazen example of the biology of artifice: beings who are alive, and having an experience of being embodied on earth, while enclosed in forms that, cell by cell, prove the overreach of our clever, but misdirected, minds.

⑪

And where is the endpoint of all this effort? It's in Texas, the state most famous for high-fence ranches, the hunting preserves where the biggest artificially bred deer live out their destiny as targets and trophies. Texas has enough acreage behind high fences that these ranches amount to a real ecological force—millions of acres, though no one tracks the number precisely. Texas is also a stronghold of American hunting culture.

Searching for a ranch I could visit, I contacted the Texas Deer Association, the Texas Trophy Hunters Association, and a number of fenced ranches, all of which responded with silence, suspicion, or both. Several ranchers asked me directly whether I was anti-hunting; one demanded to know whether I personally eat meat.

Finally, I found a rancher who seemed completely open to being interviewed. I am grateful, and I opted to change her name so as not to punish her forthrightness. Jody, as I'll call her, chatted easily with me on the phone and agreed to let me and my family visit her ranch. The place is owned by her in-laws and overseen by Jody and her husband, both of whom hold degrees in wildlife biology. They're all native Texans.

Around 2008, the family decided to enclose 1,700 acres of the several-thousand-acre property within an eight-foot fence. High fences cost $3–$9 per foot, but the way she told it, this fence, and the animals it contained, had started out as nothing more than a family amusement, and turned into a business almost accidentally.

"My in-laws thought, 'We'll put some critters in here we like to see, and if we want to hunt we have a place that we can,'" she said. "With high fences generally it starts off like something like that. You have a few animals here, a few animals there, you throw in some different species, and over time you've created your own little planet in there. Things can't move out or in, and at a certain point you have to start managing it." Inviting paying clients to hunt inside that fence was simply a way to keep the family animals from multiplying too fast.

We made arrangements for a visit, about which—given all the suspicion I'd encountered elsewhere—I felt both victorious and nervous. I didn't really buy that origin story, though. Once I saw the ranch in person, it would seem even less plausible.

On the appointed day, my husband and kids and I found ourselves approaching the ranch gate on an arrow-straight dirt road. It was close to a mile from the turnoff to the office where Jody had said we'd meet. From a plain but neat metal building, she emerged, smiling: slight, about thirty, with a dark pageboy haircut, subtle makeup, an official ranch T-shirt, and rubber boots over jeans.

We all shook hands and then my kids noticed a strange animal behind a fence. Her pet wallaby, Jody explained. She called him Steve. He hopped over and sniffed her fingers, then used his forepaws like hands, fetchingly, to groom his dark fur. He had tiny, rabbitlike teeth.

The paneled office inside had a taxidermy theme: a stuffed swan, a mountain lion, and several deer heads with abnormally large racks, like the ones Josh Newton had showed me. This was May, a slow time for visitors. But Jody told us that the ranch was booked by six or eight groups of clients per month from October through December. Most hunts lasted three days. Guests would come from as far away as California and Alaska, eat catered meals, use the fire pits and pool tables, and pursue their chosen quarry in the company of a professional guide.

That could be a whitetail (priced by rack size, with the biggest going for $7,000 or more); European or Asian deer (fallow or axis, $5,000; red deer, $7,000); or something really exotic, like oryx, ostrich, or zebra (price on request). I'd never even heard of some of the animals on the ranch's website. What was an eland? I had to look it up. *The cow-like eland is the world's largest antelope.*

These prices, though not pocket change, are not the highest out there; apparently, on some ranches, shooting a trophy whitetail can cost up to $20,000. Nor was Jody's ranch even close to the most elaborate. Another, the Ox Ranch in Uvalde, harbors more than sixty game species and offers its own private airstrip. When they're not hunting, guests can drive and fire a World War II–era Sherman tank.

The high-fence phenomenon in Texas began in the 1930s as a way to contain exotics imported for hunting. But it was only in 1985 that Texas allowed ranchers to enclose land specifically for breeding deer. These animals are the legal property of the ranchers and are regulated as livestock, rather than held in trust for the public like wild deer. There are now over eight hundred high-fence ranches in Texas, but it's not the only state with such an industry; Pennsylvania and Michigan allow them, too, though they're banned in Montana, Wyoming, and many other states.

Despite all the ranch's exotic offerings, white-tailed deer were the only animals that Jody and her family were actively breeding. They had to in order to command those prices. Unlike exotics, whitetails are easy to find outside the fence.

From the office, she led us through the deer barn, where we watched a tabby cat sniff at two brand-new fawns nestled on a mound of clean bedding, warmed by the red glow of heat lamps. Then we stepped outside between a pair of tall, straight chain-link fences. Actually, they were more like walls, being lined with plastic tarps. It had been raining, and we tiptoed along the muddy corridor. At the far end, we went through a gate into one of the ranch's deer breeding pens.

"You see those fawns?" Jody said, pointing. Two of them curled in long grass along the fence, almost invisible though they were just a few feet away. But the does kept their distance. There were maybe eight of them, each bearing plastic ear tags, and they bounded down the fence line at the far end of the rectangular pen, which I guessed was about a half-acre in size. Bounded and stopped. Bounded and stopped.

The does could see into other adjacent pens, but not outside to the buildings or driveways. Those tarps on the fence blocked their view like blinders on a horse, keeping them from getting spooked. "When deer are frantic, they tend not to use their brains—what little they have," Jody said. "They tend to run right into the fence."

They looked like normal deer when they ran. It wasn't a matter of brains. They were exercising their four-million-year-old instincts, which told them running was the best way not to die. But the rhythm of their movement, inside this metal geometry, was unsettling. They ran one or two at a time, collected in the corner, stared at us, erupted into movement again, and tumbled back the other way.

"These girls are not super happy we're in here," Jody said, in her unhurried way. "But it's different when the food cart comes."

These were breeder does, one group of several on this ranch who would spend their lives in pens, eating alfalfa and commercial feed and producing fawns. Each fall, about eighty of them would be impregnated with the sperm of a big-antlered male. Most of them would raise their own babies, but those two fawns we'd seen inside the barn—they were just a few hours old—had been pulled from their mothers because the ranchers judged them too runty to survive outdoors. They'd have to be bottle-fed.

After the babies were weaned, they'd go into special pens for yearlings. Yearling males would get at least a couple of years to hang out and grow antlers under the ranchers' watchful eyes before being considered huntable. If they had really remarkable antlers, they might be retained in the breeder buck pen, prized more for their genes than for their value as targets. Otherwise, they'd go out into the high-fence portion of the ranch, live some semblance of a wild life (though their ear tags would stay in, and their antler scores would be carefully noted by their human managers), and await the day when a trophy hunter would show up with whitetail on his mind.

On the phone, I'd formed an impression of Jody as friendly, if laconic—maybe even innocent of the fact that many of her fellow ranchers would regard a writer as an enemy. But as we talked, I realized I'd been wrong. It was just that she and her family had decided to bet on hospitality instead of defensiveness.

She wanted me to notice the lush grass in the deer pens, for example—different, she said, from the bare dirt at some facilities. She used fond words, like "boys" and "girls," for the deer. The ranch, she emphasized, complied scrupulously with CWD regulations.

I asked her about the guests. Were they experienced hunters? Yes, mostly, she answered. "Pretty much everybody's interested in the meat," she said. "If we have a hunter that comes in with the mindset of 'I just want the antlers on the wall,' that's not the kind of person we're trying to get out here." (However, the ranch charges only $200 to take a female deer.) I wondered if anyone came to take more than one trophy. "It's not strange at all," she said. "We have a few companies that use this as a retreat, and they'll give us a budget and I can build them a combination of different animals." It was as though I were suddenly talking to a caterer or a florist. But the wares were large living creatures—in Jody's term, "hoofstock."

We all stood there, watching those does charge back and forth. She was in her box, and I was in mine. Back at home, every single time I'd told somebody I was going to visit a fenced hunting ranch, the person had responded with something along the lines of "That's gross. What kind of hunting is that?" It was a reaction I tended to share. We'd come all this way, and although it felt very awkward, I had to voice some version of that question. "Your website mentions 'ethical harvest' and 'no canned hunts,'" I said. "Can you help me understand the difference between a canned hunt and what you offer?"

She nodded, as if to say to herself, *Ah, here it is.* Then she answered, "The high fence is just under two thousand acres. If an animal has a home range that fits within that space, it's not canned. They may not even know there is a fence." Not all high-fence ranches were the same, she added. "Some places have a hundred-acre pen, and the day the hunter comes they throw the animal in. Here, our animals have time to acclimate and they have the opportunity to evade us. There are plenty of places for the animal to hide and escape."

I asked if any of the clients went home empty-handed. It would make a big difference to the ranch's bottom line, because if a hunter killed nothing, they'd pay a much smaller fee.

"I think it's only happened once," she said.

⫙

It hadn't surprised me at all that most ranches I called wouldn't talk to me. I knew they felt unfairly targeted. Even the very pro-hunting National Deer Association opposes all deer breeding, and the Boone and Crockett Club pointedly calls what happens at these places "shooting," not "hunting."

Yet some people call them an ecological boon because they give landowners a reason to return the land to a more natural state, instead of using the acreage for cattle—which beat up the land by overgrazing—or crops that require irrigation and pesticides. In rural areas, they argue, people need a way to make a living from their property if they're to avoid selling out to developers.

It all makes sense within the framework of human dominion— if your basic question is, What's the least harmful way we can *manage* the land? But the more telling argument is the one that says trophy hunters are just buying a service—the experience of an exciting and gratifying hunt. They pay handsomely to avoid all the waiting, the hard work, the failure. If some hunts happen over bait piles, that's not unique to high-fence ranches. If the animals are listed with their prices, as baldly as items on a breakfast menu, that's just a more naked version of the fact that hunters everywhere pay for land leases or real estate where they think the bucks are bigger. If the hunter is really just a customer, the ranch can't complete the transaction without the fence. It protects the investment and it affords control. It's the key tool for satisfying the customer's claim to what he's paid for. It's also a way that wildlife—which we usually define as belonging to the public— can be remade into private property.

Jody's argument boiled down to the ranch being, in some sense, a natural hunting scenario. But the fence contained animals who'd evolved on distant continents. The whitetails among them, though native to this habitat, had spent their early years in pens, having their oversized antlers sawed off, eating commercial feed, and being pushed through a chute to receive vaccinations. This business must have required a tremendous capital outlay— for the land and animals, the man-made ponds, the vet bills and purchased semen, for the employee whose job was to keep an eye on the back gate and prevent "road poaching."

And even if the guests did eat the meat of the animals they killed, they were the antithesis of the subsistence hunter. They were consumers in a very filigreed sense. Padded with money and thrilling to images of pioneer forebears, Hemingway in Africa, their own corporate careers as heroic explorations. Consumers of jet fuel, of a story about a landscape, of antler and horn. They were killer tourists.

These things are never really that tidy, though. For days after visiting the ranch, I would keep turning it all over in my mind, pricked by that other rancher's question. *Do you eat meat?* A deer in a pen, a cow in a slaughterhouse: I couldn't say they were fundamentally different. The ranch wasn't far from the Chisholm Trail, where cattle had been driven to market in the cowboy days, before barbed wire confined them. Fences have been one of humanity's most basic means of controlling nature, and high fences are only a recent iteration of that long, metal-hard history.

After we finished in the deer pens, we got into a late-model pickup truck and went four-wheel-driving all over the ranch, spotting exotics like blackbuck, Père David's deer, and a mixed herd of zebra and gemsbok. It was certainly a beautiful place, reminiscent at times of the African savanna, where some of these animals were native. It was much more interesting than a zoo. There were some genuinely thrilling moments: watching a group of oryx pour through a gap in the trees like liquid, or spotting two red stags, as big as elk, as they crossed a meadow.

I hoped that my "wows" and "That's beautifuls" wouldn't be misunderstood as an endorsement of the business model. But who could avoid saying "wow" when a zebra wandered into view? Some of the photos of rifles on the website were, in a similar way, irresistibly pretty. What I meant was that the animals were lovely, and so was the land. The one time we stepped out of the truck, our daughter found a perfect white arrowhead on the ground, and Jody let her bring it home.

⚹

I wrote the above and then went to sleep, and in my dream, I was standing at a compost bin in my yard that was built of a dead buck's body. It had been there for months and I was used to it, but this time something was different. His forelegs, stretched across the front of the bin, seemed unusually vibrant, their fur brighter-colored than I'd expected. I stroked them, gazing at his head—and realized his eyes were open. And that his chest was rising and falling. He had antlers, modest ones, maybe four points or so. I stepped back in fear, but the feeling quickly changed to pity. He'd been gutted months earlier when he died—I thought maybe I was the one who had done the gutting. He was missing all his innards and his abdomen was wide open, but he was breathing, moving, looking around; I was afraid to meet his eyes. He struggled to his feet and began to walk, then run. I worried he would run into the road and be hit by a car. But he didn't; I saw him, his altered profile, cantering behind trees, moving off into the provinces of wild deer, those shadowy places where the trees melt into the background of the hills.

CHAPTER 16

November Dawns

MY BROTHER IAN AND I STOOD ON A LONELY DRIVEWAY, our boots marking its lacy sheet of snow. We faced down into a wooded ravine, hoping to see movement in the thin light. He had a rifle over his shoulder. "Do you think you would ever want to hunt, yourself?" he asked.

I said, "I don't know." And inside that answer was a whole forest of questions—trees among which I had been gathering clues.

⁂

Faulkner: "He was running. Then he was standing over the buck where it lay on the wet earth still in the attitude of speed and not looking at all dead."

He is Ike McCaslin, age twelve; he has shot his first deer under the wing of Sam Fathers, a man whose mixed Black and Chickasaw ancestry is as expressive of the Mississippi Delta as the slaveholding committed by Ike's own people. "The boy," Faulkner goes on, "drew Sam Fathers' knife across the throat and Sam stooped and dipped his hands in the hot smoking blood and wiped them back and forth across the boy's face."

Deer and land are already wedded. It's story and memory that weave deer, and the hunting of deer, to *places*—to the human sense of location and dwelling. Ike's first kill is a lodestone that calls Faulkner back, over and over, throughout the linked stories of *Go Down, Moses*. It's a late autumn hunt, a land-bound rite that carries Ike through his life from boyhood to senescence:

seventy years or more of pilgrimage to a recurring moment within a place and a season.

Into Faulkner's oneness with Mississippi, deer hunting dissolves like salt in water. And yet deer hunting—through all the turns of the herds' fall and rise, through the swift changes of human time—is just as inextricable from the North Woods of Wisconsin as it is from the Delta. It is quintessential to Texas, to the Adirondacks, to the Scottish Highlands, where centuries ago a Gaelic poet sang the onset of autumn. "I have tidings for you: the stag bells; winter pours; summer has gone."

And to my own Pennsylvania, where my grandfather was one of many World War II veterans who came home and walked into buck hunting as though it were a bridge back into civilian life. Like thousands of others, he hunted in the northern part of the state, where the deer were then most numerous. He and his brothers built a little camp on the Allegheny River.

In Pittsburgh, the steelworkers' unions once bargained for them to get time off in deer season. My grandfather wasn't one of them; he was a Punxsutawney electrician. But like them, he made hunting, along with football, a central anchor of his twentieth-century life. When I was born in the 1970s, although I would not come of age by killing a buck, I nonetheless inherited a texture, an unspoken essence of my home, embroidered with the lives and deaths of deer.

⚶

When I was a girl, some of my friends' fathers had trophy heads on their walls, or a gun cabinet in the corner. I deeply connected the gruffness of these men to guns and what they were used for, a sort of dark affirmation of a home's being equipped, that it housed a particular class of skill and competency. Some of my cousins and my brother Ian learned to hunt. Ian's wife, Ashley, grew up hunting, too. But hunting was alien to my education (which ran more toward Brit lit and classical music), and when I left home at age seventeen, the proximity to hunting culture was one of the things I left behind.

But oddly enough, I now find that the arc of my life may have been leading me, through a very roundabout route, toward a new view of hunting. First there was vegetable gardening. Then layer hens. Then broiler chickens. Two decades after our first garden, John and I have in our household stores everything from frozen whole chickens to quarts of sauerkraut, from pints of fig preserves to frozen currants. We are invested in a vision of human life that prevailed for thousands of years, and still does in many places: the small-scale domestication of food.

For anyone who gardens with history and ecology in mind, and who appreciates the physical engagement with food, it becomes equally logical to cast the mind even further back in human history. Agriculture is a human invention. If growing a garden is better for the self and the planet than shopping the supermarket, then wouldn't it be even better to avail oneself of foods that grow themselves? What is more truly human than plucking a wild fruit or killing a wild animal?

No hunted animal in the U.S. provides more food than deer. I look at hunting now and—at least in the abstract—I feel a certain unexpected envy, like I am looking into a roomful of people who know something very basic and original about life on earth. Something that nobody ever invented. This is another clue.

ⅉ

At the same time, I have yet to take the step of killing an animal for food.

We have raised broiler chickens for about five years at home, and I have always gratefully leaned on my husband's willingness to do the actual cutting of jugular veins. He kills and plucks the birds outside, then hands them to me in the kitchen, where I cut off their heads and feet, remove their organs, separate the useful parts like hearts and gizzards from the offal like intestines, and rinse the birds very thoroughly before putting them in the freezer. (My daughter enjoys peeling the feet.)

I have a peculiar love and dread of this whole operation. Writing this now, thinking of the smell that rises from the offal bowl,

I'm feeling a little nauseated. But I know that when I have my hand inside a chicken, using my fingers to carefully peel away fascia from between the meat and the guts, I will experience a type of focus and calm that rarely comes to me. My hand will be a visceral tool used on viscera; my whole body will understand how bodies are put together. I will even have fleeting relief from fear of the inevitable breakdown of my own body. When we eat this chicken we'll all remark on how *good* it is, and that will not just be because of how it's cooked; it will be because of our work.

Talking to hunters, I found myself eager to mention these experiences—maybe because hunters are sometimes suspicious that any nonhunter asking questions is actually an anti-hunter. Or maybe I was reassuring myself that I had some kind of business writing about this. Several of these people tactfully suggested that raising livestock is not on a level with hunting wild animals. "The hunting experience is so much broader," one told me. But our little chicken project is the closest thing I know to a true reckoning, or wrestling, with the act of eating meat.

In the view of the hunter and scholar Mary Zeiss Stange, that reckoning is a process. She calls it "coming to terms." One *comes to*, but never *gets to*. Elsewhere in my reading, I found similar language. "Paradoxical type of love." "How to cope with being ethical murderers."

All of this carries an undeniable lure, especially because of the long mythical echoes, the deep human history at play. I can read about hunting all day, swept away by the ideas around it. But I also know that, curled on my couch, I might as well be reading about Victorian furniture design; I'm still light-years from actually hunting.

Reaching adulthood without ever having killed for food is, maybe, a very modern condition. (Even for women; it's a myth that only men in hunter-gatherer societies hunt animals. Women in such societies regularly kill small animals as part of what's termed *gathering*.) Maybe there's something important about crossing this line as a child, before there is time to stand apart from the question and make it abstract.

Doubts about carnivorism go back a long way—to Pythagoras, to venerable traditions of Buddhism and Hinduism and Jainism, and in the modern West, at least to the 1600s. But eating meat became a more urgent moral question in the nineteenth century. Amid an American culture in which the upper and middle classes counted hunting and fishing as their most beloved amusements, Thoreau and the Transcendentalists articulated a vision of being outdoors, communing with the sacred, with no intention to kill. They considered this a moral evolution. The historian Roderick Nash relates a stunning scene in which John Muir scolded Teddy Roosevelt, on excursion in the Sierras, for his famous love of hunting. "'Mr. Roosevelt,' he asked . . . 'when are you going to get beyond the boyishness of killing things?' . . . Taken aback, the President replied, 'Muir, I guess you are right.'"

The sense of wilderness as temple is still present, if often muted, in the outdoors culture of today. Hiking, kayaking, backpacking: These are specific cultural acts usually associated with urban and left-leaning people who are also more likely to see killing as profanity.

But replacing gun with camera does not spell the end of moral or ecological questions. Even a casual hike is consumptive, if the hiker has to drive to the trailhead, and especially if one has amassed a variety of special gear (wicking fabrics, titanium trekking poles, etc.) for the occasion. To imagine our own gazes as impact-free is a fiction.

As much as I like hiking—which befits my demographic—I have at times experienced a certain sense of vagueness about it. Getting to the top of a hill feels good, but is it really as meaningful as standing over a deer you killed and will eat? There have been plenty of hikes on which I was lost in thought or conversation, largely blind and deaf to the surroundings. "The sportsman," wrote the Russian novelist (and hunter) Ivan Turgenev, in an argument that's still echoed by hunters today, "enjoys a communion with nature denied to those who simply roam the fields or work in them."

Hunting itself has its own definition of appreciation. The *experience* of the hunt—along with all the ritual and performance that's gone along with it—has often been at least as important as the goal of securing meat or trophy. Whether in seventeenth-century England or the North Woods of 1950s Wisconsin, hunting has been a way to feel things, show things, affirm things. And it's been ripe for aestheticizing. "Deer will be slung up when blast of powder / driveth dark-blue lead thick into their pelts," wrote an eighteenth-century gamekeeper in Scotland, brutally and beautifully.

As such, it's been as slippery a concept as any cultural phenomenon. The boundaries around why and how to hunt have morphed over and over again; at various times, hunting *only* for meat and hunting *never* for meat have each been considered the superior approach. And the same style of hunting can be perfectly acceptable in one milieu, but condemned as barbaric elsewhere. British nobles had formed huge circles on the moors to drive deer into the center, then killed them with dogs and spears. But the American conservationists who were their progeny had complete disdain for these ways, painting them as butchery practiced by groups they despised: Native Americans, freed Black people, pot hunters, and market hunters.

Ultimately, whether or not one is fundamentally on board with the concept of killing animals, the very fact that hunting is a question attests to the comfort of many of our lives. Hunting is optional for us, even though the vast majority of Americans eat meat. Our industrial food system is a site of secrecy and emptiness. Our disengagement from killing subconsciously needles us, an unresolved dilemma.

The world of the subsistence hunter is one of beautifully porous boundaries. In the great children's novel *The Yearling*, Jody Baxter is growing up on the late-1800s North Florida frontier, hunting almost constantly, moving within an endless round of death, eating, using, loving. Bucks and does transform into scabbards, fishing lures, bootlaces. Jody's father, like a medieval healer, draws out snake venom from his own arm with a doe's hot liver. The boy ponders the mystery of how a deer's body can make him "sickened and sorry," even though once butchered, it "maddened him with hunger." Walking over a deerskin rug, "he half expected to feel it start under him."

⫯⫯

Ian had come down from Pennsylvania in October to visit us, while I was immersed in my research on hunting. He brought us frozen venison sausage and backstrap from the previous year, and we ate the sausage with scrambled eggs for my birthday breakfast. He also brought photos from his game cam: a big buck wandering through his camp in the mountains.

That year, he planned to do both bowhunting at the camp and rifle hunting with our relatives in Mom's hometown of Punxsutawney. Though that crew had also traveled to Colorado to hunt elk in a wilder setting, they do their deer hunting in fairly small wedges of woods, behind houses and stores on the edge of Punxsy (as the locals call it).

Hunting these days can take many forms—on public land or private, with a guide or without, over a food plot or on a farm. Like any other subculture, hunting has its fads and trends, its diehards and disruptors. There was no way I could experience all of these niches. But Ian and I made plans for me to come up to Pennsylvania in November, so I could, for the first time, see some form of hunting in person.

⫯⫯

The night before that first hunt, my top concern was staying warm enough.

My brother and I stood in his kitchen, looking at piles of camouflage clothing stacked on the table. "Let me see what you brought," he said.

I opened my backpack and took out five or six shirts, a running jacket, a hoodie, a puffy coat, a puffy vest, and several pairs of pants. "And I have long johns," I said.

"Let me see them."

"What?"

"Let me see them."

I handed them over and he examined the tags, then nodded. My sister-in-law came in with even more camo in her arms—sweatpants, hoodies, fleeces—and added them to the table. The two of them had a long discussion about which camo pieces I should add over the layers I'd brought so that the next morning I could sit in a tree stand for hours and stay reasonably warm, and invisible. Ian and I were going to the mountains before sunup. It would be in the upper twenties.

We went outside to the shop, which is what Ian calls his enormous three-car-plus garage, with a vehicle lift and its own bathroom. On a shelf of heavy bins, several were labeled HUNTING. All his own clothes were stored here, away from the house and its fragrances of little girls and detergents. Instead, they smelled like wet soil, thanks to small plastic scent disks hiding at the bottom of the bin.

He pulled out a big camo backpack and a smaller camo front pack meant for binoculars and other gadgets. There was a "doe bleat," a deer version of those cans you find in toy stores that moo when you flip them over, and a plastic device that could be shaken to make a sound like antlers clashing. If a passing buck could be convinced that two other bucks were fighting nearby, he might come to investigate. "Some of these things are gimmicks," Ian acknowledged. But they might confer some advantage, too, and the plastic rattler was easier to carry than real antlers, which Ian also had hanging on the front wall of the shop.

The packing wasn't over yet. He pulled out a rat's nest of straps, a harness that would keep me from falling out of the tree stand. "Here, you're smarter than me, figure this out," he said, and left me to untangle it while he gathered packs of hand warmers, more scent-killing spray, hunting gloves, camera cards. And, of course, his bow and the case into which it zipped.

I did manage the harness, but otherwise I felt pretty impotent, watching him go about his business. Ian is someone who can change a transmission, back up a trailer, talk you into purchasing an impact driver, buy and sell ATVs. Hunting with him, the best I could do would be to not hinder him too much.

Ian started hunting back in the late '90s, when he was fourteen and our uncle Jim, from Punxsutawney, invited Ian and our cousin Dave to come along on a deer hunt. Jim had been hunting for years with his own son, Mark, who was in his twenties, and along with some local friends, they had largely perfected the art of the deer drive. It's a way of hunting in groups that involves some of the hunters (the pushers) scaring up deer so that they run toward others (the shooters) who wait to intercept them. Because deer follow predictable paths when they flee an area, it's possible to get pretty precise about where the shooters are positioned, and deer drives can be an efficient way to harvest a large amount of meat to share among a group.

"I remember the whole first day really well," Ian told me. Jim had sent him to hunter safety class, loaned him a rifle, and supervised his target practice in the shale pit behind Jim's house. Mark had taken him turkey hunting, too. "They said I was a pretty good shot, so that was a confidence booster."

Before dawn on a freezing morning, during buck season, Uncle Jim and Mark took the boys to a nearby spot they'd hunted before—a pipeline clearing, where the shooters could see a long way from one ridge to the other. They split up, with Jim and Dave as pushers. "Mark kept telling me, this is where they'll come from," he said. "We were watching groups of deer. It was cold as hell, sitting there with the rifle on my knees. He would tell me, there's some, look and try to pick out at least two points on one side." (At the time, in Pennsylvania, antlers had to be a minimum size for the buck to be legal.) Eventually he saw a group with a four-pointer out in front.

He felt the rush of a long-awaited moment. "I shot at it two or three times. One of the shots, I could tell I hit it because it stumbled. Mark shot at it too, and hit it to stop it. It fell before it got to the woods."

So, on the very first morning of his hunting career, Ian had shot a buck at something like two hundred yards. I don't even remember hearing this news at the time; I was away at college, busy deconstructing some ideology or other. But now—it was strange—despite my own ambivalence about hunting, despite never having handled a weapon myself, despite not even being sure I knew what "two hundred yards" looks like, I felt, upon hearing this story, an unmistakable, unexpected pride in my brother.

He told me, along with the excitement of success—"like say you hit a home run"—there was a feeling of relief at not having disappointed Jim and Mark. He'd done it, and they were pleased. "It wasn't like, 'We're going to buy you ice cream, fella.' But they were happy."

Ian offered this without being asked: "I don't know that I really considered the whole life and death thing . . . There wasn't any part of it that weighed on me. I knew that's what we were there to do. People that start hunting later in life, it can be an emotional thing. But when I was fourteen, it just didn't sit with me. It just didn't register."

Later he sent me a photo from that day: himself, baby-faced, sitting in the back of a pickup truck in an orange vest and Jim's oversized flannel shirt, holding the buck's head by its rather slim antlers, his elbow resting on its back. There's a little blood on his jeans. He looks happy, and far away.

⁂

Ian and I rose at five the next morning and ate breakfast standing up. Then I started getting dressed. It was completely dark outside,

Ian was back out in his shop, and the only sound was layer after layer of fabric sliding over my body. Suddenly I stopped and thought of the mountainside where we'd be sitting. Was there a deer somewhere in that forest, just rising from its own bed, getting ready to move and feed in its familiar places, destined to die today by an arrow from Ian's bow?

It gave me a feeling I recognized from the mornings of our chicken-slaughtering days at home, a dread of the very near future, but this time that future was not inevitable, like an execution; it was pliable, like a courtship.

🦶

We drove for an hour to get to his camp. From the low hills of our home county, we crossed the Monongahela and climbed toward the aloof ridges of Pennsylvania's Laurel Highlands.

The night felt very deep and black, punctuated by occasional islands of fast-food lights and tollbooths. Ian was talking about hunters who are mostly in it for the trophies—how some of them will shoot a buck and then parade it around for a few days in the truck. "Hey, Bill, look at this!"

Prizing the venison, Ian likes to take his deer directly to the processor or butcher them himself. He doesn't like the thought that the fresh meat he'd obtained would be handled alongside that several-day-old trophy buck. This made complete sense to me from a locavore perspective: all the time and energy spent in order to provide oneself with food, potentially spoiled during one of the last steps in the process. It would be like my garden tomatoes, fertilized with horse manure and fish emulsion, getting mixed into a sauce with somebody's Miracle-Gro mutants.

"I'd say we're about fifteen minutes late," he said as we turned into his property. A sliver of dawn light was invading the trees. We shook out handwarmer packets. When he turned off his truck, he said in a whisper, "This is about as loud as we want to be talking from here on out." I nodded and closed the passenger door as quietly as possible.

In another minute or two I was following Ian down through

the woods, along the little creek, concentrating hard on my foot-
falls. We didn't speak. It took maybe five minutes to reach the
tree stand, a two-seat platform fifteen feet above the ground,
with a metal ladder snugged against the tree trunk. We climbed
up, we clipped in, and just like that, we were hunting.

After that first buck, Ian hunted with Uncle Jim and Mark every year for several more seasons. He took a few years off, but
then for a while in his early twenties, he was living with Mark
and helped him butcher a deer that Mark had killed on one of
those Punxsy deer drives. They ate a lot of venison together. Ian
started to think about hunting again.

"I bought my first gun on my own when I was twenty-three or
twenty-four," he said, and tagged along with friends who knew
good spots. It would be a few years before he started having any
luck—our relatives had set him up for early success, but now he
was hunting in a more difficult way, usually without the benefit
of a pusher to send an animal toward him. But he kept at it.
Amid the demanding years of starting a business and a family,
he gradually found more time to get out in the field—hunting
not only deer but turkeys, squirrels, grouse. By the time I finally
tuned into the fact that my brother had become pretty good at
this whole hunting thing, he was putting venison in the freezer
every year. And he was a key part of the deer drive group in
Punxsy.

Talking with him about it, I felt my own outsiderness—the
subtle ways that I was missing the argot, the context. Hunters,
for example, don't say "I saw some does"; they use "doe" as a
plural. They say "buddies," not "friends." They say odd things
like "pushing deer around" and "blowing out the woods." I kept
asking questions—"Does it work like this?"—and Ian would say,
always patiently and kindly, "Well no, not really like that."

He asked me if I wanted to come and watch the annual deer
drive with Jim, Mark, Dave, and some other cousins. "Would

that be weird for me to come?" I asked. "Oh, no," he said. "It's not like anyone's gonna say, 'Who brought the chick?'"

◑

We sat in the stand and the day slowly lifted off its lid.

On my right was a steep drop-off down to a larger creek, and I imagined that if deer were to arrive, they would come from that direction. The woods were open, fairly young, their floor speckled with bright red maple leaves and club moss, its new growth lime green and standing upright as candles. I was cozy in all my layers. Ian had hung his bow off the side of the stand.

He pointed a laser rangefinder—a little black device shaped like a video camera—at a few different trees, to get an idea of where a deer would have to stand in order to fall within his effective range. A bow can deliver a fast, powerful shot at about forty yards, sixty at most. That means a bowhunter has to be much closer to a deer than a rifle hunter to even attempt a shot. Being in a stand is part of what makes this possible; if a hunter is lucky and the wind is right, a deer may walk under the stand and never know the hunter is there. But if that were to happen today, it would be a first for Ian; he'd been hunting with a bow for only three years and killed just one deer with it, and that was from behind the first row in a field of corn.

Bowhunting carries a certain mystique, the image of a hunter in deep attunement. Noise and scent become more crucial. Knowing the habits and behavior of the deer might be more important. And there is an association with antiquity—a technology in use for thousands of years. Yet Ian's compound bow looks different enough from a traditional bow that Robin Hood might not have even recognized it as being a tool for archery; it's roughly rectangular and includes two pulleys and tiny fiber-optic cables to assist with sighting. A different version, the crossbow, is even more powerful and is fired with a trigger, like a gun. For at least some hunters, the main reason to choose a bow is that the season opens earlier, lasts much longer, and offers the ability to hunt in tighter spaces where a gun wouldn't be safe. Many of them also put piles of bait under the stands, just like cullers do.

Ian took out a little bottle labeled WINDICATOR and squeezed; it puffed a small amount of fine dust into the air and we watched it drift away.

A long, storyless time commenced. The soft light of dawn yielded to sharp shadows and glowing trunks of trees. A jay stabbed the air. We heard a faraway growl that Ian said was the sound of a gas compressor.

Then he nudged me. "There's a deer." He was looking to the left, the opposite of what I'd been expecting. I leaned to see behind him and, near the path we ourselves had followed in, I caught sight of the flick of a tail, a tiny gesture: in that moment, it was the center of the vast, leafy world.

We kept watching as she—a doe—slowly proceeded up the slope. I soon saw a second doe behind her. "If they keep going that way, it could work out pretty well," he said.

They were still far off, in and out of trees, and at some point we realized there were even more in the group—maybe five altogether. But they were so perfectly a part of their world, so quiet and quietly colored, that it was hard to tell.

After a while it was clear they weren't coming our way. They were angling away on a trajectory of their own. They trailed each other up the hill and out of sight.

◖◗

Ian had a game camera positioned on a tree near the one in which we sat. It had, over the past couple of months, recorded a number of deer. But he'd just bought this property ten months earlier, and was still figuring out the lay of the land and how the deer tended to move through. Putting the stand in this spot was a guess.

"I don't know what to make of this wind," he said. It was a very still day, so it seemed the only air movement was a result of thermals, the warming of the day as the sun rose higher. They seemed to shift each time he checked.

As the hunter, he was constantly calculating. Time of day.

Slopes. Creek crossings. Where the deer would be looking for acorns. Cause and effect. Whether we should leave the stand and try moving around instead.

But as the observer, I had the luxury of treating the entire day as one long meditation in a theater of light. There were very few events (a noisy leaf falling; a brief performance by a squirrel). Instead there was the delectable movement of time. I felt the exact moment when my eyes stopped having to labor to see, and the exact moment when the temperature slipped from cold to chilly. I'd always fantasized about spending a whole day sitting in the woods, just watching. Now I was doing it, and the cleanness of purpose felt deeply calming. Our quest was entwined with being; our job was to pay attention, be still, be quiet. All around us was a sense of large lonely space, from which, at any moment, important characters might emerge. The whole place was potential. Every mossy log and sailing raven vibrated with significance.

But hunger and stiffness did become more and more insistent. It got to be ten o'clock, and Ian judged we should take a break. The stand was making his legs cramp, and he struggled to unclip his bow. I'd been plenty warm in the stand, but on the walk back to the truck, I began to shiver.

When we got there, both our phones binged at the same time. Our brother had sent us a picture, from his backyard on the edge of Pittsburgh, of a ten-point buck reclining in the leaves. A well-fed, unhunted, unthreatened city deer. "I open the window and yell random stuff and he just stares," Seth wrote.

◆

We spent lunchtime strolling on the road, looking at the big views from the top of the ridge, drinking beer with our sandwiches, and laughing. I called Ian Jägermeister: Master of the Hunt.

Finally we headed back out to the stand for another long sit.

"Now, if I do get something, you might feel some things," Ian said, trying to prepare me. "I think I always have some remorse at taking a life."

"Is it remorse, as in regret?" I asked. "Or just sadness?"

"Yeah, it's sadness," he said.

I noticed that with him, as with people I'd interviewed whose jobs involved culling deer, I felt squeamish about using the word *kill*. I'd say something like "if you *get* a deer" or at most "if you *shoot*." It wasn't out of my own discomfort, I believed, but out of a strange kind of worry that the one doing the killing would not want that fact stated plainly. But if the ethics of hunting were never addressed directly within our conversation, they could nonetheless become very real at any moment. No matter how experienced the hunter, every shot taken is a fresh decision.

I could also feel exactly why, sitting for long hours, a hunter would start to think of ways to gain an advantage. Why not this year's new $400 boots, if they'd allow another half hour of comfortable waiting? Why not the most up-to-date game cam? Soon after we started our afternoon sit, Ian pulled out the doe bleat and sounded it. Its noise seemed impossibly small in the silence, but at least it was something to try.

All the gear was part of the strategy. Yet it was an encumbrance too: the broken buckle. The malfunctioning card reader. The camo pants Ian had bought online, not realizing how lightweight they were. He was starting to shiver. He added gloves, then a neck gaiter, then another jacket. We kept ourselves entertained telling possum and bear stories, but I could feel his frustration mounting a bit. "I'm not sure what else we can do here," he said, and then later, "I just find it surprising that with all the pictures on that camera, we're not seeing anything."

We kept talking. Swedish meatballs. Tattoos. What a "turkey choke" is. I wanted to elbow him with good news from my side of the stand, but there was none; the pale potential deer in my imagination never materialized. I listened for a long time to the shush of the creek, and the thin ringing of my own ears. I felt the aching gladness of being alive among other living things. I looked at backlit leaves, mustard gold and rust-edged; the woods felt graceful and large, and filaments of spiderweb shimmered here and there like harp strings. In the mellow golden hour, the opposite ridge was washed by sun.

By the time that light had narrowed to a fingernail, Ian started cursing the deer a little. "Sons of bitches," he said, half joking. His legs hurt again. "This is a shitty place for a tree stand." He'd already described how hard it was to put it up in the first place, so I knew he wouldn't be eager to move it. Darkness approached, then arrived. He told me one more story—about hunting with Ashley's brother, using flintlock rifles, on a negative-eight-degree morning—and with that, we called it a day.

We'd spent over six total hours in the stand. I wasn't deflated, but the day had illustrated the hunter's basic subjection to what the world offers or doesn't. The big buck in Seth's text was the last deer we'd seen.

Later, just before sleep, I saw that tail flick again, and my final glimpse of those morning does as they slipped out of sight, unaware of our eyes on them and our desire reaching toward them. They were *wild*, a word that comes from *willed*, as in *self-willed*: passing their own time on earth. They were still alive.

⚬

It had been my first time hunting, and I was changed. I wanted more—to get up before dawn, to sit and look, to feel the aliveness of the land that had always been there, though I'd too often seen it as inert.

I wasn't sorry not to witness a deer get killed. But strangely, when Monday came and I saw the usual deer-season headlines about hunters getting big bucks, along with the victory photos, I understood them in a way I never had before. They were, to some new and tiny extent, relatable.

Back in Virginia, we thawed a brick of ground venison sausage and made a soup out of it with carrots and kale. Ian encouraged me again to come and watch rifle hunting in Punxsutawney.

I had realized that although he does eat all the venison from his kills, like many hunters he harbors a mix of motivations, including an interest in antlers. All else being equal, he'd rather shoot a buck than a doe. But from what he'd told me about the deer drives, meat really was the prime motivation. He wanted me to have a chance to see a successful hunt—even as I wondered about that whole idea of "success." I'd enjoyed our bowhunt so much I half wanted to declare that it was enough in itself. Maybe this, as much as anything else, said that I was not a hunter.

⚜

A few days later, I had an evening phone interview scheduled with a bowhunter named Melissa, who lives in a different part of Virginia. I called her at 6:00, but she didn't answer. At 6:49 she emailed: "I shot a buck tonight and am on the way to the processor." Immediately I was flooded with a sense of things happening out there, in the November dawns and dusks. We were in the height of the rut and the height of bow season. Deer were on the move; hunters were on the move; the season held all of them like a net stretching over the dark, wide continent. Stories were unfolding in real time. I didn't want to miss it.

A hunter killing a deer is an interaction that happens between our species more than six million times every year in the U.S. If my goal was to understand this, being invited to a deer drive really was golden.

In truth, I felt trepidation about going to Punxsy because I knew I'd feel wildly out of place, awkward with my notebook, reappearing at the scene of something from which I'd long ago excused myself. To be all but assured of seeing deer die—this was a little fearsome. And yet it was nothing more than going home.

CHAPTER 17

Craving

A WEEK LATER, I ROSE VERY EARLY IN MY MOTHER'S house, where Thanksgiving leftovers still stuffed the fridge, to drive the two hours north to Punxsutawney. There was a scrim of snow on the ground when I pulled into Jim's driveway at 6:30 a.m. I saw Mark hurry out the back door and jump into his truck. Sunrise was due at 7:17, which meant the year's rifle season would open at any minute.

This morning, once again, I had on my warm layers—this time topped by a blaze-orange hat and vest—so I could join in with a group of nine: my brother; Uncle Jim; three cousins (Mark, Dave, Jared); Mark's two daughters, Maggie and Eleanor; and two of Jim's neighbors. The "orange army," Ian called it. Different versions of this group had been hunting cooperatively on the land around Jim's house every year for decades. They had deer drives down to a science.

Mark was the natural leader of this group. He grew up here, taught Ian and several other cousins about hunting, and still directs these hunts, figuring out where everybody should be and what jobs they'll do. His work as a high school teacher seems an extension of his role in our family; he's generous and gregarious and wears an easy authority.

He's a couple of years older than me. In one of my earliest memories of big family gatherings, he and I—maybe seven and five—pulled on opposite ends of the wishbone from the Thanksgiving turkey at our grandfather's house. He got the bigger piece, then immediately gave it to me.

Before the drives, we were going to do some "still hunting," which is the odd name for hunting while sitting and/or creeping around. This was mostly because Mark wanted a chance to sit in a tree stand with Eleanor, age twelve, the way Ian and I had done at his camp—appreciating the morning and having time to react if they saw a deer standing or strolling. It was Eleanor's first time as a shooter. The drives, which get deer moving faster, would happen a little later in the morning. For now, the group would split into pairs, go to assigned spots, and hope for the best.

Ian and I were to go up the hill behind the house and skirt the neighbor's yard toward a place where a powerline intersected a gravel driveway. Like much of Pennsylvania, Punxsy possesses a rumpled, hilly terrain, with lots of small-scale ridges and ravines. From here we could see several stretches of woods, an old gas well, and a big patch of land that had been cleared and, for some reason, flattened. It was the sort of habitat we'd be hunting all day: humble and hard-used, the backstage places, right outside town, that people drive past constantly but hardly look at. There was a Walmart just out of sight past the trees. It was no wilderness, but it was thick with deer. (Mark would later tell me about a prank he'd played years ago—chasing twenty-six deer into a hotel parking lot just as some hunters, visiting from Pittsburgh, emerged at dawn on opening day.)

We weren't alone out here. Gunfire started at the very edge of legal shooting hours, and it continued at a constant pace as the birds performed their muted dawn chorus and Ian tried to figure out the best place for us to stand.

"This gun," he said—he carried what he told me was a .30–.30 on a strap over his shoulder—"is dead-on at a hundred yards, but not after that. I can see that whole powerline but seventy-five percent of it, I wouldn't shoot." He moved us uphill a little, then back down. "You're always giving up vantage points," he said. "There's no perfect spot."

We could see no people, but the landscape felt strangely crowded. We heard more shots from other directions; every minute or so, more fire. There were all manner of restrictions on what was possible. At one point, a big buck trotted past us, very close, oblivious to our presence—"That's incredible that thing didn't see us or smell us," Ian said, breathing hard, after it disappeared—but he couldn't have shot at it safely because it was silhouetted above us on a ridge, and whatever was beyond it was invisible.

◊◊

Eight hours later, I was back in my car. Driving south into freezing rain. Trying to sort through everything I'd seen.

There'd been the group gathering behind Jim's house to strategize, a little like a military brigade or a football huddle with Mark and Jim explaining the plan for the first drive, how we'd be working a ravine below the main road into town—a narrow, irregular patch of woods. Mark, Maggie, and Jared would start walking from one end of it, hoping to stir up deer and get them moving toward a powerline, where four shooters, Ian and three others, would be posted in different spots on the hillsides, waiting.

There'd been the moment when Ian and I were descending that slope, stepping through light snow and muck and brambles, and Jared and Dave winked into view at the top of the opposite ridge, their blaze-orange vests popping out like hyperreal flags from the gray-and-white landscape.

There'd been Uncle Jim coming in behind us and setting up in a high spot overlooking everybody else.

Stretches of waiting, watching, standing, shifting.

There'd been deer too far off to shoot at, looking as tiny as emojis on faraway hillsides, or glimpses of orange behind distant trees: an awareness composed of distances that turned things unreal.

Ian always spotting deer several seconds before me. Once he sniffed the wind and said he could smell them.

A deer streaking across the powerline across from us, the sound of a shot that echoed off a big metal building, and then Ian getting a text and saying, "All right. Dave got one."

Church bells carrying up to us from the town below.

The reduction of the entire landscape to people, deer, and shooting lanes.

More waiting. More waiting. Crouching. Whispering. An abandonment of time.

And three deer swerving toward us through a swath of half-logged woods, tacking around the brushy tops of downed trees. This recorded perfectly in my memory: their forelegs doubled as they leaped, coming exactly toward us. Then turning broadside. Me scooting behind Ian and putting my gloved fingers in my ears. The *pop* of the rifle. Not as loud as I'd feared. Another *pop* and the smallest of the three fell and flailed. Several silent seconds with my ears plugged. The other two turned and doubled back. *Pop.* The leader, a big one, fell. Flailed with her head, uselessly moving and moving and moving in circles.

My involuntary *Oh my God* and not crying, I really wasn't, but water from my eyes and nose. Heart pounding now as I write this.

And then a third on the opposite hillside, running, a *pop* from another shooter, and it slumped against a log.

A lack of words, an inability to locate a reaction.

Hearing myself say stupidly to Ian, "Damn, I hope I never get on your bad side."

Mark appearing way above us on the hill, Ian calling to him, Mark and Maggie descending, Mark saying "Let's get to work, all right?" They quickly discussed how to divvy up the job of cleaning. But first: Ian standing fifteen feet above the still-flailing doe, shooting her again.

Passing the first one on my way to the second, not enough time to take her in.

The second, her tail still flexing, Maggie saying in confusion "She moved," and Mark explaining that sometimes deer move just before they die. "Eyes closed is a bad sign," he said. "They close their eyes when they're still alive." This one's eyes were open. He bent down, touched her face tenderly. She was still.

Thinking *I hope she really is dead* as Ian's knife neatly punctured the skin of her belly. The process of gutting exactly analogous to what I already knew about cleaning chickens, but bigger, *so much bigger*. The organs of a ruminant: baglike forms laced with what looked like white veins. Dark acres of liver, deep ponds of blood. Steam in the chill. Ian heaving the doe a little uphill to get a better angle on her. Swiping at strands of fascia with his knife, putting his arms inside her up to the elbows. She was dead less than ten minutes, her body like a small wet cave, still full of brightness and energy. Ian grunting as he tried to free up the windpipe. Her front legs curled limply. She lay next to her guts. A few stray hairs on the liver.

Ian wiping his knife on the snow, then on his boot.

No way to be delicate in dragging a deer, a body the size of my own body: one person grabs the right front leg, another grabs the left, and the two people pull with all their might and the deer slides forward, her neck flung back. Getting back up that powerline. One step, one yank at a time. Panting. The last impossibly steep stretch and across a few yards of gravel and one more big heave up into the bed of the truck. Then staggering back for the second one.

Pulling back into Jim's. Someone telling us, "We've got a stack going, over there." Four does already lined up, nose to toe, in a random patch of gravel. Someone saying in a mock-TV voice, "Saving drivers on Route 119, each and every year." Ian adding the two from his truck to the stack. Deer like sheaves of wheat. A tangle of deer; a bouquet of deer.

Eating lunch without tasting it.

Dave telling me how his gun had jammed the first time deer had passed. "I was so pissed." He hated to waste the pushers' effort. "I don't want to let these guys down; they're out there busting their asses, for me. They're not doing this for their health."

Circling up again, talking through the next drive. All the planning was crucial: It drew on the many years Jim and Mark had been hunting here, all their experience with the land itself and the intelligence of the deer, their escape routes and habits.

This day was "crunchy," Mark said, because of the snow, and that made us less stealthy, so he'd adjusted his calculus, his estimations.

Into the truck with rifles laid across the back seat.

More drives. Walking in a straight line through the woods, Mark distant on my right, Ian distant on my left, to rouse deer out of their beds on the south-facing slopes, where it's warmer. Mark would later tell me that he and Maggie had walked as much as seventeen miles in a day, pushing deer.

Walking down a creek bed. Walking past a barn, past a man-made pond, past a logging road.

Ian's phone humming, as it had all day, with tiny bits of news from other people in the group. "Big buck coming." "Dave's in the tree stand." "Jim is ready."

Asking several times how they used to do this before cell phones. No one able to remember.

Jim kneeling over a six-point buck, seeming about as far from the proud-hunter stereotype as one could be. As far as he was concerned, it would have been better to get two of the does that had run past in the same group. More meat.

Mark cleaning the buck. The penis and testicles cut away, tossed on the gut pile. "He won't be needing those anymore." "Poor booger." Mark squeezing feces downward in the truncated colon, then tying it off in a knot. The buck's body, lying belly up and collecting pooled blood, like water in the bottom of a canoe. After cutting out the anus and pulling all the guts away, Mark lifting the deer from the front end, using the blood to wash downward and out and rinse any contamination from the body. It came out studded with bright yellow kernels of corn.

The cornfield we'd walked through at the start of that drive.

The junkyard near there, where Mark said the deer love to sleep. A neighbor's yard we walked through with Jim; the pine trees he pointed out that he'd planted there, decades before.

⫘

Back in the car, as something between water and ice pattered the windshield, I drove and listened to the wipers, both exhausted and very, very awake.

I was trying to sort through all these new clues. I was thinking about the deer drives: their matter-of-factness. Their almost agricultural cast: a reaping.

Ian wasn't the only one who'd shot more than one deer. And the gutting had been done so quickly, with so many hands to pitch in. For me it had been another of those standing-over-dead-deer-with-men experiences, when the social norms prevented me from really feeling the weight of the deaths.

Yet the amount of meat they'd gotten was wonderful—hundreds of pounds they wouldn't need to purchase in the form of beef. The group of ten people had gotten eight deer, a success rate roughly double the average of American deer hunters. Their costs were low, too, because of their efficiency and because they did their own butchering. (Many hunters, after gear and travel costs, find their venison has cost more per pound than filet mignon.)

Cooperative deer hunting might be trending downward in popularity, burdened by class associations that reach back to the nineteenth century, but the methods that are ascendant now—bowhunting, food plots—don't promise to replace the sheer efficacy of a tight-knit group of people hunting together on land they know well. In fact, many of the methods historians say were used by Indigenous people in North America—sometimes involving fire or water, fences or horses—were group efforts, not solitary quests.

I'd heard the famous hunter Steven Rinella say on his podcast, a few weeks earlier, "Deer driving is very blue-collar. It's very scrappy. You don't do a deer drive and then go have a glass of red wine."

In this case: cans of Bud Light.

A deer drive has little to do with glory, trophies, mystery, or awe. A deer drive is a system for pulling animals out of the woods and turning them into food. "Tacos and burgers and chili, oh my!" Dave had said.

When Uncle Jim was growing up, Mark told me, there were hardly any deer and they were hunted hard. Things had not always been easy for our family. Our grandfather's dad had owned a bar and a hotel, but Prohibition put him out of business. He and his wife had twelve children. There are stories of her working so hard to can tomatoes in summer she had to crawl up the stairs to bed.

We are better off now by far, but we all still need to eat.

Late afternoon: an ATV pulling two more deer back to the garage. Beginning to feel, ever so slightly, part of the team as I helped Jim lay big sheets of cardboard out on the garage floor, and Mark brought in the first deer for skinning.

The tendons behind the ankles pierced so that hooks could go through and lift the body on a winch to be skinned. The head and forelegs sawed off. Mark slipping into his teacher mode, explaining the different cuts to me as he did the skinning. He pointed to the loins up inside the carcass next to the spine: they were once called "preacher meat" because, as the very best cut, they were customarily offered to clergy. "The second best is the backstrap," he said, pulling the hide down over the neck, then letting it rest like an inside-out cape over the head. Eleanor watched, in sweats and Crocs, from a nearby folding chair.

Jim was born in a small house a few hundred yards away from his current one, which he built in the late '6os. This is his patch of the earth. The meat in his freezer comes from the land within a very tight radius of his home, and it grows itself; it is wild food. This is—leaving aside the trucks and cell phones and synthetic fabrics keeping us warm—a very old, communal way to get meat. Ian gave Mark, who'd been a pusher all day and hadn't taken any shots, half of his venison. An ancient ritual: sharing the spoils.

Families share food. My aunt Jean had chatted with me during lunch, and then she made me a copy of my grandmother's recipe for orange-rind cookies.

Mark and I got on the phone a few days after I was in Punxsy—actually, he was cutting up the deer while he talked to me—and he told me about a few of the ways he would cook it for his girls. "We do a Crock-Pot roast," he said, "or we do this recipe with the backstraps, where we sear it in a cast-iron skillet and then bake at three-fifty. And I save the loins—that's like filet mignon on a cow—and we cook them for Christmas."

Knowing what to do with venison in the kitchen is a bit of a cultural litmus test, though not a straightforward one. Mainstream cooking magazines and blogs don't tend to offer venison recipes, so home cooks have to consult hunting media or their own family traditions. Because deer meat has to be acquired either through hunting or by purchasing an expensive imported product, it functions as a down-home ingredient on the one hand and a luxury item on the other.

Somewhere in the middle, you can find the stars of modern hunting media—people of my own generation, who came of age along with the empires of Martha Stewart and Whole Foods—offering recipes like Venison Bulgogi or Guava-Glazed Venison Heart Skewers: deer meat as a hip, globally influenced, versatile ingredient for the adventurous cook, miles from the tough, gamy survival food many people imagine. That venison implies hunting gives it an extra layer of significance, a locavore-foodie vibe pushed to its limits by a spirit of outdoorsy self-reliance. There's room in the zeitgeist, it seems, for hunting to equal curiosity, live-your-best-life optimism, and an enthusiasm for travel and gear. Just like hiking does.

◖◗

Venison is a place where the two Americas might meet, and sometimes do. "Hunting for food is consistent with liberal values," Jackson Landers told me. I had wanted to talk to him because, a decade ago, I'd seen his how-to book on deer hunting, aimed at an educated, locavore readership, and I remembered that for a while in my area he was teaching courses for adults who wanted to learn to hunt deer. He himself—after being raised vegetarian—had figured out how to hunt deer as an adult. In 2010, almost as a lark, he offered a deer-hunting course and discovered he'd hit a nerve.

"It filled up immediately," he said. "I planned field trips: We'll go to the shooting range, everyone's going to learn how to safely handle a gun, we'll have a fresh deer on the ground and everyone will learn how to gut, butcher, and cook it. People loved it." He added a second course. Then he landed on the front page of the *New York Times* food section. "From the time that article ran, I got three hundred emails a day from people all over the world who wanted classes."

His students were "predominantly New Yorkers, but not exclusively," he told me. Lots were female, queer, Jewish. He had paleo students; he had entire classes booked by CrossFit gyms. "It was really fun watching the students. There was a married lesbian couple from Brooklyn, and then these three guys from somewhere in Pennsylvania—they were like stockbrokers or something, and they were looking at these girls like *I don't want to go near them*. And then while we were butchering, one of the women picked up a raw deer heart and took a bite out of it like an apple, and these guys were in utter awe."

Landers wasn't the only promoter of a new hipster-hunter amalgam. Others have spoken to that audience too, even as Americans continue to awaken to the true costs of eating beef. *Epicurious* quit publishing new beef recipes in 2021, citing environmental concerns. Meat substitutes are a growing business.

This is all another way of answering the ethics questions around hunting. It's a locavore answer: Venison is nutritious, wild food that could let us bypass factory farms—deer as the most viable wild substitute for cows. It's an answer that says if we want to eat meat that doesn't cook the planet, we are willing and able to kill it ourselves.

◖◗

My answer to Ian's question on that morning in Punxsy—*would I ever want to hunt?*—would have been an easy *No* for most of my life, but the more I read about hunting, and deer, the less certain I was about that answer.

That same fall, I'd encountered a writer at an online reading named Christie Green. She was a white fiftysomething hunter who lived in New Mexico. She read part of her essay about hunting deer in Texas, butchering them, bringing them home and making a sort of backyard altar from their skulls. As she read, she wept. Here was something new to me: a hunter openly grieving the animals she'd killed.

I wrote to her, she wrote back, and we began exploring each other's work. I learned she was also an artist, landscape architect, and grower of food. I read about a dinner party she'd thrown, the dishes accompanied by little printed notes about the individual animals being served, and a beautiful arrangement of their body parts, right on the tabletop. A deer's skull, a grouse's foot. I looked at photos: Christie's strong hands holding a feathered body. Knives sticky with blood. Pale teats on the belly of a hide.

Soon we got on the phone and I was asking her the hard questions—this time, no squeamishness at all. Questions about killing.

Her voice was soft and searching as she answered. "There's something that happens in the moment of choosing to take a life," she said. "There is something exactly akin to giving birth. This ultimate bodily experience."

Christie had grown up in Alaska. Although the men in her family hunted, she didn't learn how until around age forty, from her then husband. She soon found she preferred to go out alone. Sometimes on a hunt, she did not know, right up until the moment she pulled the trigger, whether she would decide to kill. She told me about five days she'd spent hunting elk and passing up every opportunity she'd had to shoot. "I had a shot at a hundred and thirty yards at a cow," she said. "I had the crosshairs right on her, and in that moment she had a calf that walked out. The first thing that went through my mind was my daughter; I thought, 'I cannot take this shot.' In some ways it was devastating because I went home without any meat."

She added, "The death doesn't happen instantaneously even with the best shot. There's still life trying to happen in the body. It's bearing witness to that, that liminal space; being with that animal as he or she moves towards death. Then the actual body itself is still soft and warm. Here's this whole body, it's a beautiful animal. You make the first cut, you see the intestine, the hide, the blood."

It sounded like a sacrament, but she was not prepared to accept the comfort of believing that the animal gives itself to the hunter. "I don't know that they looked at me and said 'Please take me from this world.' I just don't know. I feel like that makes me bigger than I am, but I'm not as big as they are." She addressed the animal: "I'm not big enough to take your life, and yet at the same time I do it."

I wondered aloud whether it made any difference to the animal what the hunter's ethics, or methods, might be, if death was the result in any case.

She answered me mostly in the form of more questions— posing them not to me but to herself. "Do skill and reverence go together?" she asked. "I've hunted with a bow, but I'm not as experienced as I am with a rifle. Is bowhunting more of an ethical kill because of the effort? The last elk I shot, she was very close in range to me and it all [happened] within a matter of seconds. Does she know how I felt? Does she know I was crying?"

She repeated my answer to Ian as a refrain: "I don't know. I don't know."

So much of what seemed off about trophy-hunting culture was the way it inflated the hunters themselves. But for Christie, the parts of the animals' bodies that she kills are not prizes; they are not stories about her own experience; they are stories about the animals' lives.

"It's so exquisite how it comes through the body," she said. "Every story is in every part of every body. The least I can do is revere or be curious about every part of this body that I can. None of it's about me at all. How can we see these animals as something more than what we can consume?" And she immediately acknowledged the irony: "I'm consuming every part of them."

More photos. Christie peering through a skull, her blue eye positioned between the teeth. A heart wrapped in red tulle and red twine. These were images of love and reckoning. I wanted to look at them for a long time, not to push them away from my eyes, like all those many, many images of hunters grinning over their kills. She had written, "Her body is in my body now, as nourishment, matter."

🦌

In his book *Eating Animals*, an otherwise cogent critique of meat consumption, the novelist Jonathan Safran Foer dismisses the possibility that such choices can rescue what, for him, is an inexcusable act. "Very silly," he calls it. "Killing an animal oneself is more often than not a way to forget the problem while pretending to remember."

Certainly a lot of hunting culture, even when it allows the question of *how* to kill a deer, almost totally obliterates the question of *whether* to kill a deer. But I think Foer misses the possibility that some hunters have committed to a never-ending engagement with what he calls "the problem." This is a marriage to discomfort: a well of doubt that becomes more acute, not less, the longer you gaze into it.

🦌

Venison can be a food of necessity, refinement, sustainability. I had experienced it as a food of luxury on my trip to the vineyard, then as a food of mercy when I spent a morning handing out donated venison to clients at a food pantry. I had experienced it as a backstrap that John rubbed with oil and garlic and cooked up in the cast-iron skillet: tender like a beefsteak, but with its own wild flavor. Maybe that taste came from both the life of the self-willed animal, and the knowledge that its death was the labor of someone I love.

After hunting, I began to experience deer, very subtly, in yet another way: as a craving.

I started to desire deer, both in living form and as food, and those two guises were not entirely separable. I began getting up early, walking around outside, hoping to see them. My plans for these walks were vague and changed with the wind, with fleeting glances at possible trails, with sounds from between the trees that I couldn't identify and that didn't repeat themselves.

I began learning how to keep my footsteps quiet, to roll each foot along the outside edge, to step on rocks and avoid the twigs. I had always seen deer so often, so easily, that they felt like a given. Now I had crossed some strange line. It wasn't looking *at* but looking *for*. I had become a seeker of deer, a wanderer and quester, glad for every track, every nibbled stem. Hearing a snort, then some resonant hoofbeats through the tangled vines, and knowing I'd just pushed a deer forward with the noise of my own footsteps, a line of sound connecting us forward and back. Putting my finger carefully on the little ridge of soil running down the middle of a hoofprint. Touching the ends of chewed saplings, frayed by deer's teeth.

For the first time it seemed incredibly unlikely, miraculous even, that I might actually see one. That a deer, and I, could be here together. What I felt when I did see one was very clear: wanting to move past the connection by eye and toward some kind of deeper communion. What kind of clue was this? I felt the longing on my tongue. I felt, *I want you.*

⚬⚬

I'd told my brother, "I don't know if I'll ever get that far down the path." But certainly, I was on the path, and certainly, I wasn't standing still.

⚬⚬

During that fall I'd hunted with Ian, there was one other hunter I'd watched up close.

Midmorning, I'd been sitting on my bed and working when I

looked up and saw a man in full camo mounting the steps to my front porch. A little white SUV was parked in the driveway.

I answered his knock, feeling self-conscious in my writer's uniform of pajamas. He introduced himself as Michael and explained that the evening before, he'd shot a buck with a crossbow about a quarter-mile away. It had fallen, but when Michael approached, it jumped up again and ran off into the dusk. He believed it was on my land. Could he track it?

I said yes, of course, and asked to go along. Michael—who had an elfin face and an instantly likable demeanor—agreed right away. I dressed as quickly as I could and joined him in the driveway, where two more people had emerged from the car: a young black-haired woman named Crystal, and Tommy, a lanky, taciturn man with a long beard. All three were booted, with camouflage jackets.

They fanned out and I followed Michael south through a part of our land with few trees but lots of tall, brittle wildflowers. Michael pointed out a track, a small disturbance on the ground, a near-invisible difference in the angle at which some leaves were lying. I would never have noticed it.

He was troubled. The night before, he'd waited fifteen or twenty minutes after shooting the buck before he moved toward it, standard practice to avoid spooking an animal out of the spot where it had fallen. But in this case, that wasn't long enough, and when Michael got up the deer had taken off with a crash. Because it was getting dark, he'd called a friend whose dog was trained to track wounded deer. By six thirty or seven, the dog, wearing a GPS collar, had followed the trail to our property and stopped. Michael had thought it was too late to go knocking on doors, so he'd waited until the morning. But he'd had a restless night, feeling unsettled about that buck somewhere out there, unclaimed.

From fifty yards away, Crystal called, "Anything?" Michael answered "No." We kept moving slowly and talking quickly, in

294 THE AGE OF DEER

a strange twist on the usual host-guest relation—he knew both more and less than I did about where we were. "You have a big old game trail here," he said, and I explained that the path we were following was used not only by deer but also by my daughters. We stopped at a juncture in the trail, looking around at thick brambles, an old stone wall, a pile of brush, with no clues to guide us. From here, I knew how to get to the landmarks that usually matter to me, but this was a different mission altogether. We stood together in confusion.

Then Crystal called out "Blood!" And Michael instantly transformed. "Oh God!" he cried in a shaking voice, and took off at a run.

I could see Crystal's black hat, moving fast up the hill toward a stand of Osage orange trees. Michael was crashing through tangles of vine that grabbed at his clothes, then mine, as I tried to keep up with him. He and Crystal kept calling back and forth and the pitch of their voices was rising and he said "Blood! Oh God!" as we rushed past red spots on a boulder and then he was moving so fast I lost him altogether and then I caught up and saw him and Crystal and Tommy standing over a big, big buck, a prone body vivid in three dimensions, a brown form in vibrato on the plain brown ground.

His head, with a generous set of antlers, was toward me, and his eyes were open. It was astonishing to take in his presence. He was sleek and perfect and seemed more alive than I was, but there was a gaping wound in his side, six inches wide, through which his ribs looked back at us.

Michael was in tears. "Oh my God, he's gorgeous." He knelt and touched and examined the buck. One hand came up covered with blood, and he said, "He blessed me."

It was a reunion of two beings that had met, hours before, in a fateful instant. All night they'd been separated, one dying, one grieving; now I could almost see Michael's heart reaching out of his body toward this animal. He put his hand on the buck's flank. "Sorry, buddy," he whispered. "Thank you. I'm sorry."

There it was—what Ian had called remorse—mixed indelibly with gratitude. And there was tremendous relief. And pride.

"I told you he was a six-pointer!" Michael said to Crystal. "He's a stud. He's a grown deer." Tommy remarked, "It's the biggest six-pointer I've ever seen." They estimated, by the size of the antlers and the outline of the body—a thickened neck, in particular—that this buck was fairly old, probably five or so. Dark streaks stained the insides of his rear legs, a hallmark of the rut season, when bucks urinate on the tarsal glands at their ankles in order to advertise their scent. I got down and put my nose right next to it: creaturely, strong, but not unpleasant.

As for that wound, Michael wanted me to know that it wasn't from his arrow. He'd shot the deer on the opposite side; this circle of missing flesh was due to some other animal who'd scavenged in the night. Not a bear, which would have done a lot more damage and probably dragged the carcass around. Not the tracking dog, who'd returned to its handler with a clean muzzle. More likely a raccoon or possum. Whoever it was hadn't taken much.

Michael was still patting and stroking the deer. "We eat a lot of venison," he said. "I don't trust the meat you see in the stores." Every few minutes as we talked, he'd well up all over again. "It's an emotional roller coaster," he said. "I tossed and turned all night. Hunting will take you to the highest of highs and the lowest of lows. You never do a drug that gives this kind of high." And he talked about the moments before he'd released his arrow, sitting on the ground facing downhill, watching a rutting doe trot past with her tail tucked, glancing behind her like she was being followed. "I could hear him grunting," Michael said, looking again at the buck at his feet, and then it all seemed to crash over him again and he put his hand to his chest: "Oh my! My heart!"

The buck seemed to flicker between life and death right there on the leaves. He was so beautiful and whole, but so still. His life had left him, yet it hung all around him, just above him, flowing back and forth between him and this man I'd never met before, who'd killed him, but loved him. But then the buck would seem to turn into a corpse again, as when Michael lifted his head by an antler and the shift caused the torso to release a farting smell and sound that went on and on. Later I petted the buck's side, and again he came alive as I fingered the short bristly hairs around the base of his antlers.

It was a sunny day. As Crystal pointed out, the temperature was climbing, threatening to spoil the meat. "I'm so happy we found him," she said. "Something just told me to turn, and I saw a spot on a leaf, and then I saw lots more." The three of them flipped the buck over to his other side. Now we could see the arrow wound in the center of his torso. "I'm not happy with this," said Michael. It was farther back than it should have been; hunters usually aim for the heart and lungs, just behind the front leg. "I got liver," he said, pointing at the quarter-sized hole. "See how dark this is? If it were heart or lungs, it would be brighter red. They can live five or six hours and go a mile with a liver shot." It was a painful thing to imagine.

The buck was his first deer of the season. "I usually have a notch in my belt by now, but I've been passing on younger bucks. They won't breed as much, but this one—he's going to sow his oats everywhere. He's a giant."

I looked at the buck again. If Michael was right, this animal had fathered many fawns in the last few weeks, some of which would die in their hunted mothers' wombs. Others would be born next spring and try their luck at living, perhaps walking through my yard, perhaps bedding near where we now stood. There was a refreshment of a basic surprise: the land had produced this big animal, just like it produces acorns, wild turkey eggs, grasshoppers, morels. The word *harvest*, applied to what Michael had done, seemed righter to me than it ever had before.

"I could lay down right next to him and be happy," Michael said. "But we've got work to do. A lot of work."

⚬

All along, writing this book, I'd wondered why I didn't have a good origin story for it, no singular epiphany I could recount. I'd figured my motivations were rational, that I was just drawn by an interesting topic, looking for ideas, not mysteries. But it came to feel less and less that I was taking hold of something, more and more as though I were following something.

One thing I hadn't expected to learn, a signature my relations already knew: what deer *smell* like. I'd come to feel that deer *were* my relations.

I'm grateful that, after so many large animals have disappeared with the advance of human beings, there is still this one—an exquisite and mysterious creature—that I can see, often, in my Anthropocene life; one that, despite our caricatures, remains a survivor, a supreme example of life among the ruins. And that we can pause, at this point in our history, and ask these questions about how to proceed. We have good tools for doing that: science, art, and dreams.

For now, we still have the chance to encounter each other. For now, we can still get together.

Later, after Michael and his friends had left, I went back out and followed both the trails by myself. There was the trail of life, the series of blood spots the deer had left on rocks and leaves as he made his way uphill from the road. And there was the trail that Michael and Tommy had made as they dragged him, by the antlers, back down. The two trails intersected at the edge of our land, and the death trail ended with a broad, unbroken track of blood and gore that had wept from the scavenger wound as the men pulled the buck across the road to load him into Crystal's waiting car. The line of crimson ran straight and then formed a hook at its end, where they'd lifted the animal away from the earth it had walked when it was alive. There had been a brief, awkward struggle to fit the buck's wide antlers and long legs into the car, while a woman driving a very new Jeep waited on the road behind. I'd wondered what she was thinking, whether she felt disgusted, or fortunate, or just annoyed at the delay. Before driving away, Michael had thanked me for the umpteenth time for allowing him onto the land, and offered to bring me some tenderloin after processing the deer. I told him I wouldn't take the best part of the meat, but that we'd love to have some ground venison, and we promised to be in touch.

I walked back to the spot where the buck had died, under a small redbud tree. There was an impression of his heavy body, larger than my own, and some scattered white and brown hairs. And there was a red-soaked spot on bare earth where he'd lain on the arrow wound, bleeding right into the soil.

Like Michael, I hadn't slept well the night before, but I hadn't known why. An animal—not a human, of course, but I suddenly and completely felt that it was right to say "a person"—had come to our land, wounded, suffering, leaving blood in great quantity; had made it this far, and then lain down into death.

There was a casual breeze, yellow leaves remaining overhead, the sound of a distant engine. There was the lonely weight of blood drying in the sun.

In the months to come, I would keep an eye on that hook-shaped trail of blood on the road. It lasted a very long time, growing darker, rustier, through many rains and snows, until it finally became hard to see. But even the following spring, when it was invisible, I could walk a few yards away, turn and look back, and find it again—silvery, ghostly—on the pavement.

Acknowledgments

A LEGION OF PEOPLE HELPED ME WITH THIS PROJECT.

I'll start with my brother Ian Howsare, who went beyond being a crucial source and acted as a generous, loving guide to a whole world I needed to explore. I'm not sure how I could have entered it without him.

It was sweet to spend this time with my relatives in Punxsutawney. Extra special thanks to M.

Jim Ferry in Princeton was very generous in the access he granted, not to mention a pleasure to talk with. I hope I've repaid his willingness to let me view a sensitive operation up close.

Marcelo Jorge and his colleagues in Arkansas made room for me and my family in their evening's work—a true adventure that's now part of our family lore. Likewise, the ranchers we visited in Texas, and Angharad Jones at Creswell Crags, were gracious to all of us. Mary Kate Claytor and Misti Furr provided crucial leads that moved my research forward, Gino D'Angelo and Bridget Donaldson opened numerous doors, and Thom Almendinger, Jay Kelly, Meesha Goldberg, Bernd Blossey, Brice Hanberry, Josh Barnwell, Katherine Edwards, and Earit Powell all went above and beyond in the time and attention they granted me. It's been a treat to explore creative realms with Christie Green and Madison Creech.

I gleaned information and background, and often the satisfaction of good conversation, from a long list of people. Some appear in these pages and others, only because of the realities of word limits, do not. Thank you to Hawk Hurst, Jeff Gottlieb, Hub Knott, Robert Tallman, Philomena Kebec, Nicola Allen,

Will Waldron, Gwen McCrea, Earl Calhoun, Alex Royo, Duane Diefenbach, Gary Arrington, Joe Folta, Katrina McDougald, Lois Poole, Charles Smith-Jones, Jeff Pritzl, Kate Knott, Mick Brooks and all the hospitable people of Abbots Bromley, Jonathan Clark, Jackson Landers, Kate Ahnstrom, Jimmy Mootz, Joyce Forbes, Carolyn Porter, Holly Nielsen, Randall Francis, Laura Galke, Dafna Reiner, Truman Bells, Aaron Mark, Ben Stowe, Heather Coiner, Eric Morris, LéChan Christian, Tim Moore, Toby Boudreau, Jim Jordan, Joseph Colbert, Marian Keegan, George Timko, Jay Boulanger, John Zampini, Odin Stephens, Ryan Butler, Luke Leonard, Jeannine Fleegle, Terry Carroll, Thomas Nelson, Wayne Dehn, Andy Albertson, Matt Knox, Jimmy White, Millie Schafer, Alan Saunders, Cheryl Connell Marsh, Gina Saro, Anthony Worley, Jim Hash, Scott Bates, Amanda Eicher, Chad Tuttle, Bret Wallingford, Wendy Gehlhoff, Josh Newton, Lindsay Davenport. Thank you also to Julia Brennan at Caring for Textiles, Madison Creech, and Meesha Goldberg for providing images.

I'm grateful to the hundreds of people whose own writing, scholarship, journalism, and storytelling shows up explicitly or otherwise in these pages.

It was delightful to discover, with the help of many friends and acquaintances, examples of deer lurking everywhere. Priscilla Melchior opened my eyes to a Henry Taylor poem in which deer possess "an absolute purity of style"—what a line!—and many other folks sent stories, clippings, dictionary entries, and photos. Annie Kim shared Sir Thomas Wyatt's hind and also helped me as a very early and encouraging reader, and she and Sally Ashton were incredibly gracious about reviewing chapters of this book in what was nominally a poetry group. Their feedback was smart, loving, and invaluable.

Kate Zuckerman has been an especially supportive and wise friend throughout this project. Elise and Preston Lauterbach, and Brian Gresko, were generous with their guidance and help, and Earl Swift and Jenni Ferrari-Adler offered key advice. Thanks to Melissa and Corinne for essential counsel. Thanks to Anna Sullivan, Megan Bloom, Ethan Zuckerman, Rachael Keast, Leigh Anne Keichline, and Augusta Jacobs for cheering me on. Rain Perrie has been something of a muse for this book and has pointed my way, in many ways, over the years.

Love and gratitude to writing companions past and present, who are also dear friends, especially Mary Phillips, James Cochran, Zoe Krylova, Gwendolyn Bright, Jen Tynes, Kate Schapira, Adam Tobin, Susan Scarlata. The writing path winds through many habitats, but it's all one continent.

Tyler Carter appeared near the end of this process with wise feedback and writerly understanding, and showed the way to an entirely new dimension to the project—all in all, a gift.

My time studying with Thalia Field at Brown forms an indelible backdrop to this work, and my time working with Cathy Harding gave me skills that made the working possible. Thanks to both for their fierce examples. Alison Hawthorn Deming's workshop through *Orion* gave me space for productive reflection on the book. Thanks to the editors who have supported my work in various guises—journalism, poetry, and what I end up calling "Other."

Veronica Goldstein was the first person to share my vision for this book and has been an astute reader, a tactful diplomat, and a tireless champion. Megha Majumdar gave the book a home at Catapult and encouraged its development with great kindness and enthusiasm, and Kendall Storey brought it to fruition with grace and dedication. Clare Bullock made it possible for the book to find an audience in the U.K. through Icon Books, and she's been a delightful partner in the writing process. Thanks to Victoria Hobbs, Tajja Isen, Summer Farah, Elizabeth Pankova, Katherine Kiger, and James Lilford for their insights and support, and to Nicole Caputo, Olenka Burgess, and Anna Morrison for their lovely design work.

My parents, Susan Phillips and Marty Howsare, were the very first supporters and sounding boards for my writing life, and have made this book and so much else possible in countless large and small ways. Thanks to Seth Howsare, to John and Heidi Gulino, and to all my family members. My daughters, Elsie and Rosa, helped me spot deer in life and in art ("Deer!"), allowed me space to work alone when needed, and came along for the ride when possible, always bringing their inventive curiosity with them.

It is a miracle to have a partner as true as John. Thank you forever.

Notes

INTRODUCTION
xxii **warriors and saints:** Christian saints including Eustace, Hubert, and others famously encountered stags bearing crosses between their antlers.

CHAPTER 1: DANCING

7 **We've been bound by mysterious ties:** More than a million and a half years ago, *Homo erectus* hominids in Dmanisi, Georgia, occupied a plateau for at least eighty thousand years, leaving behind the remains of multiple species of animals they hunted in the valley below. Of these, deer and horses are the most abundant. Rob Cowen writes, "It's reckoned that between *Homo sapiens* and our ancestors, we've probably hunted animals similar to deer for as long as two million years . . . That's a long time to have known one another."

8 **deer, water, and renewal:** Christ was sometimes also connected with stags and hinds in Christian texts, emphasizing the connection between deer and regeneration.

8 **To carefully lay out:** Paul Shepard writes, "In the ethos of the ancient conjunction of 'to prey on' and 'to pray to,' the hunt is not a seizure but a voluntary immolation. Hunters preserve a lore of wild things who oversee the ethics of their own transformation into food, observe atonements, and return again and again."

11 **Cree people tell stories:** As the scholar Howard Norman explains, "The word *deer* may be seen to represent what the Cree refer to as the 'old agreement.' This agreement provides a symbiosis between the Cree and food-animals. It is the basic moral and physical framework of the Cree's subsistence. Animals give themselves up if the Cree attend to them properly. When Wesucechak forces on someone a linguistic amnesia, makes that person forget an animal's name, the animal is insulted . . . It can upset the overall equilibrium by . . . causing a break in communication between

Cree hunters and their environment. The slighted food-animal may not 'come around' for a considerable period of time."

11 In the Sonoran Desert: People wearing antlers in life or art, often while dancing, is a phenomenon that recurs from England to France, Siberia, Japan, and Bhutan. Yet antlers have also designated cuckolds.

15 a broader world: Scythians had meaningful contact with other groups as various as the Celts, the Greeks, and the inhabitants of Hunan China. (It was Greek metalworkers who made the amphora, to Scythian specifications.)

15 The Scythians themselves: In the fifth century B.C., Herodotus described Scythians as nomads who roamed the steppes.

15 Another stag: Scythians even bestowed antlers on some of their horses. In Scythian barrows, ornate leather masks, shaped to fit a horse's head, have been found topped with antlers, some culminating in flamelike tufts of golden hair. It could be that the masks symbolize the fact that when horses were first tamed by these people, they took on some of the significance that deer had previously held: In an earlier age, the Scythians had once been reindeer keepers.

17 crowned with antlers: Perhaps not unrelated is the fact that for centuries, people captured and collared stags to signify their own status.

19 In 1834: Earl A. Powell calls this series "the most ambitious artistic undertaking yet conceived by an American artist."

CHAPTER 2: GOODS
27 The Mantle may have: You can spot it being worn in the Terrence Malick film *A New World*.

29 The pales were constantly: L. Cantor and J. Hatherly write, "To enclose new park land at a time when people had run out of options for bringing new land under the plow and when crop yields were failing to meet the basic needs of the population was a blatant expression of extravagant consumption."

30 That inviting, human-friendly: A deer park also provided the tranquil setting for the Buddha's first sermon, at Sanarth, near Benares, around 400 B.C.

31   There would be a steady: The term for poaching was "park breaking."

31   This is a fantasy: Karl Jacoby writes, "The parks and forest preserves of the Old World might appear to be peaceful pastoral landscapes, but such institutions in fact precipitated numerous episodes of social unrest. Among the most notable of these were the actions of the armed poachers known as 'Blacks,' who roamed Great Britain's woods during the 1720s, to which we might add the 'Captain Swing' riots that flared up in England in 1830–31 and the 'War of the Demoiselles' staged by French peasants in the Pyrenees against the National Forest Code of 1827." Jacoby also mentions less organized peasant poaching of "wood, fodder, game in 1800s Prussia, which attracted the attention of a young Karl Marx, whose first published articles included a defense of Prussian peasants prosecuted for the theft of wood."

32   In 1642, for example: Philip J. Deloria also recounts how royal control of deer forests was in places eclipsed by commoners' customary rights to the land and game, though in the late seventeenth and early eighteenth centuries enforcement was stepped up and spurred rebellions mounted by poachers in blackface.

44   *hunting shirt image*: This particular garment was made in the late 1700s for Dr. Jean Pierre le Mayeur, a French dentist who treated George Washington, and was restored in 2016 by Caring for Textiles.

46   Though not all: Daniel Justin Herman writes, "The image of the 19th-century hunter-hero—wearing moccasins and buckskins, carrying a Kentucky rifle, and educated in the school of nature—suggested a new aborigine. This man—the American Native—became the symbolic heir of the American Indian."

Chapter 3: The Graph
51   As for the deer: White-tailed deer fossils have been found dating from the late Pliocene into the Pleistocene.

57   The earliest European explorers: William Cronon writes, "In the course of their migrations, [the first North Americans] failed to bring with them many of the illnesses that were common elsewhere in the world. Their low population densities and their having lived for extended periods under semiarctic conditions served to filter out microorganisms which required large host populations and more temperate climates to survive. Their lack of domesticated animals . . . also helped to reduce the number of pathogens they brought with them from Eurasia . . . For hundreds of generations, Indian babies had grown to adulthood with no experience of these illnesses."

57 When more European colonists: William Cronon writes, "Their refusal to lay up stores for the winter meant that many starved to death."

58 Rather, there was: Holly Haworth writes, "In 1588's *A Briefe and True Report of the New Found Land of Virginia*, one of the voyagers who crossed the wide Atlantic to establish the first English colony in Virginia breaks down the habitat, of which he knows very little, into a list of extractable commodities, including 'a kind of grasse in the country vppon the blades whereof there growtheth very good silke in forme of a thin glittering skin to bee stript of . . . Deare Skinnes . . . Mayze . . . Beanes . . . Peaze.' He goes on and on."

60 By 1642: Louis S. Warren writes that the English repeated this complaint with satisfaction; it was a sign of their own power.

60 The word *wilderness*: Daniel Justin Herman writes, "Below the breezy tale of New World contentment, meanwhile, burned the coals of anxiety . . . Only after Adam's fall had God sanctioned hunting by turning man and animal against one another, remaking nature into a place of disorientation, confusion, danger, and anarchy. The name for this realm, wilderness, was what the New World often seemed to be . . . The idea of the New World as wilderness, together with its opposite, the New World as paradise, bespoke profound contradictions in colonial thought . . . If Europeans were to reign in the New World, they would do so by wedding themselves to a powerful instrument of authority, the gun."

62 These conditions did boost: There were other, less obvious ways deer benefited. In New England, the killing of beavers for the colonial pelt trade caused many beaver ponds to fill in and revegetate, creating rich zones of fresh deer browse. Also, depopulation of Native Americans in the Deep South allowed deer to move into fertile bottomlands previously full of people, who had left the lands partially cleared—from the deer's point of view, ideal habitat.

62 They repeated again and again: Phrases in this paragraph quoted from Halls, *White-Tailed Deer: Ecology and Management*; Mighetto, *Wild Animals and American Environmental Ethics*; Nelson, *Heart and Blood: Living with Deer in America*.

66 **Kublai Khan:** In Europe, thinkers had begun to warn against resource exhaustion at least back to the English Civil War.

Chapter 4: Value
74 **one that needs to eat:** This is about the same amount of food American adults consume, by weight, annually.

Chapter 5: Kinfolk
79 **The White Hart:** A white stag was the personal badge of King Richard II (probably the monarch in the story of Herne the Hunter); apparently, during Richard's time, many pubs elected to honor the monarch in their names.

79 **But humanoid gods:** Paul Shepard's words are "idiographic and alphabetical." Shepard also outlines intermediate stages in the change from animal to human deities: composite animal-humans, humans wearing animal skins, humans riding or being drawn by animals, and animal familiars that accompany humanoid deities, like the goddess Artemis and her sacred deer.

84 **Compared with bacteria:** Alison Pollack writes, "The kingdom Animalia, in which we reside, is an offshoot of the domain Eukarya, which includes every life-form on Earth with a nucleus—humans and sea squirts, fungi, plants, and slime molds that are ancient by comparison with us—and all these relations occupy the slenderest tendril of a vast and astonishing web that pulses all around us and beyond our comprehension."

88 **Can we avoid:** Ursula LeGuin puts it this way: "I guess I'm trying to subjectify the universe, because look where objectifying it has gotten us . . . It may involve a great reach outward of the mind and imagination."

Chapter 6: Capacity
105 **These days, the leading edge:** Even in Leopold's time, at least one thinker implicitly suggested that the model of a stable ecosystem might be too narrow. Alfred North Whitehead argued in 1925 against an overly mechanistic view of the world, emphasizing qualities of relatedness, indeterminacy, unpredictability. Four decades later, the Harvard ecologist Hugh Raup advocated looking at forests without the expectation that they would reach some stable climax state. Instead, he saw them through a lens of uncertainty and flexibility. "The systems are open, not closed," he wrote. Carolyn Merchant writes, "The appearance of chaos as an actor in science and history in the late twentieth century is not only symptomatic of the breakdown of modernism, mechanism, and, potentially, capitalism . . .

Chaos theory also fundamentally destabilizes the very concept of nature as a standard or referent. It disrupts the idea of the 'balance of nature' . . . Chaos is the reemergence of nature as power over humans, nature as active, dark, wild, turbulent, and uncontrollable (fallen Eve) . . . Chaos theory suggests that natural disturbances and mosaic patches that do not exhibit regular or predictable patterns are the norm rather than aberration."

107 **They are "cosmopolitan":** I borrow these terms from Del Tredici, *Urban Plants of the Northeast.*

107 **They are "protean":** I borrow this term from Flores, *Coyote America.*

CHAPTER 8: MANAGEMENT

121 **the fate of rural land:** The Boone and Crockett Club pursued bans on commercial hunting, favoring a vision of parks showcasing wildlife.

123 **The agencies were:** State wildlife agencies are supposed to conserve all species. But deer, and the sliver of the population that hunts them, provide nearly all the funding for these efforts.

124 **Blossey's study found:** He also found that sterilizing female deer did nothing to restore the forest. The only thing that made a difference was to have volunteers sit over bait piles and systematically kill as many deer as possible. Blossey himself takes part in an annual cull around Ithaca, personally shooting fifty to sixty deer a year.

127 **immigrant newcomers:** Interestingly, the perception of difference between "true" American hunters, who understand conservation and stewardship, and those from other places, who wittingly or unwittingly violate the sportsman's code, may still be alive and well. In 1995, the psychologist and hunting apologist James A. Swan wrote about California's "diverse multiethnic racial mixture with many people who do not hunt or who come from parts of the world where there are no game laws. More deer are shot here by poachers than by legal hunters. Every week or two you read in the paper about some new immigrants caught hunting squirrels in a park or fishing with illegal nets or lines."

127 **Fair-chase, recreational:** Daniel Justin Herman writes, "Progressive era hunters bequeathed to modern hunters—as well as to environmentalists, who share with hunters a common cultural ancestry—an ethnic identity. So tightly did Roosevelt and his fellow hunters weave together stewardship and ethnic identity that it is all but impossible to separate them a century later."

128 By appealing to anti-Black: Today, critics charge that the North American conservation model not only continues to deny Indigenous people access to land but also is entangled with racial violence. (Gun and ammo taxes are a primary funding source for conservation; gun sales rise when racial resentments bubble up, as they did during the Obama presidency and again in 2020; therefore, the argument goes, racism is fueling conservation.) If this all seems far-fetched, there are segments of the hunting world that sense the critique from urban, left-leaning quarters and react defensively. The mission statement of the Pope & Young Club (a Boone and Crockett counterpart that focuses on bowhunting) bristles with a don't-tread-on-me tone: "Anti-hunters and activists continue to work to destroy our heritage and redefine our way of life . . . We will not forget our history." Twenty-three states have felt the need to amend their constitutions to protect the "right to hunt and fish," most of those since 2000.

131 both deer and wolves: It's far from clear what that would mean for deer. But one clue comes from a 2018 study that involved lands managed by Kebec's community and other Native groups in Wisconsin. The study asked how forests were doing on those lands, compared with those managed by the state. The short answer was "better": tribal lands had fewer deer per square mile, more diverse plants, fewer invasive plants, and better regeneration of trees. In tribal forests, the researchers wrote, deer were hunted "assertively." That didn't mean frenetic hunter recruitment. It meant a whole different hunting culture, focused more on community needs than individual success, with the rules "enforced socially, not by wardens." Some tribal lands had no hunting seasons or bag limits. What's more, wolves were welcomed as ecological partners. Rather than persecuted, they were revered, and hunters would leave portions of the deer they killed as gifts for the wolves.

CHAPTER 9: SHOULD NOT BE

135 Animals, too, can be refugees: Philip Armstrong writes, "The expanding population of unwanted animals—homeless pets, infected livestock, feral pests, or inconveniently placed wild species—are the by-products of those modes of animal consumption that define modernity: the enclosure of ever-greater areas of land for animal farming, the trade in pets, the eco-touristic taste for encounters with wild species. And thus the principle of organized containment is applied even to the populations of so-called wild species: whales, seals, elephants, wolves, bears, all are culled when their numbers begin to overflow the space allotted to them within the current geo-economic pattern. Indeed the oxymoronic phrase 'protected wild animal' sums up the tension identified by Mirzoeff, between global capitalism's demand for certain kinds of mobility and certain kinds of restriction, as they pertain to the non-human world."

CHAPTER 11: PESTS

177 Native American burning: Though, to be clear, Native Americans also faced the necessity of keeping deer out of their own agricultural zones, sometimes posting the young or the elderly as lookouts.

178 In a 2001 survey: The author Richard Nelson points out that vegetarians may not be aware that even their plant-based diets involve the deaths of animals, since many farmers shoot deer to protect their fields of corn, soy, and vegetables.

182 Zoonotic diseases: Even malaria has been found to be harbored by white-tailed deer in the U.S., though they cannot transmit it to humans.

CHAPTER 12: THE CULL

189 something important unresolved: James Serpell writes, "Throughout history, those directly responsible for killing animals have been regarded with a curious mixture of awe and disgust, not unlike that normally reserved for public executioners."

CHAPTER 14: THE FETISH

229 Around the world, stories tell: There are examples of this theme—the hunter who restores the sun after it's been carried away in the antlers of a deer—from Siberia, Mexico, and other places.

231 a natural history collection: Daniel Justin Herman writes, "Sportsmen's trophies were . . . not so different from the costumes and faunal totems of American Indians. Although Indian regalia made from deer, bear, or buffalo signified the status, character, and prowess of individual bearers, these emblems carried a mythological significance that whites labeled superstition . . . By paying tribute to science over superstition and civilization over savagery, sporting cabinets seemed to make sport hunters cultural proprietors of the continent."

232 the medicinal market: In China and Korea, traditional medicines call for ground antlers, or velvet, to boost energy and vitality—a practice that still fuels a brisk international trade in those materials. Often these are produced on deer farms in the United States and New Zealand.

235 a chivalric contest: Daniel Justin Herman writes that hunting "recapitulated . . . the mano-a-mano combat of knights . . . Hunting became more popular in seventeenth-century England as newcomers to the ranks of the nobility and gentry reenacted (and reinvented) the chivalrous codes of old."

CHAPTER 16: NOVEMBER DAWNS

264 Mary Zeiss Stange: Specifically, "coming to terms with the extent to which each individual life is founded upon the deaths of vibrantly alive creatures."

266 seventeenth-century England: Dan Beaver describes how English sporting etiquette was thought to derive from Sir Tristram, one of King Arthur's knights, who codified its principles, language, and music.

266 painting them as butchery: William Byrd described a similar hunting method in frontier Virginia and also reflected on its long history around the world. "They fired the Dry Leaves in a Ring of five Miles' circumference, which, burning inwards, drove all the Game to the Centre, where they were easily killed. It is really a pitiful Sight to see the extreme Distress the poor deer are in . . . This unmerciful Sport is called Fire Hunting, and is much practic'd by the Indians and Frontier Inhabitants . . . What the Indians do now by a Circle of Fire, the ancient Persians performed formerly by a circle of Men: and the same is practis'd at this day in Germany upon extraordinary Occasions, when any of the Princes of the Empire have a Mind to make a General Hunt, as they call it."

CHAPTER 17: CRAVING

288 Venison is nutritious: It has been noted that fatty meats from domesticated animals are not what the human body evolved to eat; lean game meat may be better suited to our physiology.

Bibliography

Abel, David. "Can Genetically Engineered Mice Permanently Curb Lyme Disease?" *Genetic Literacy Project*, May 5, 2022. geneticliteracyproject .org/2022/05/05/can-genetically-engineered-mice-permanently-curb -lyme-disease/.

Abram, David. *Becoming Animal: An Earthly Cosmology.* New York: Pantheon Books, 2010.

Adams, Clark E., and Cassandra LaFleur Villarreal. *Urban Deer Havens.* Boca Raton, FL: CRC Press, 2020.

Adams, Duncan. "Urban Wildlife: Problems Arise with Rising Number of Local Deer, Geese." *Montana Standard*, April 18, 2021. mtstandard .com/news/local/urban-wildlife-problems-arise-with-rising-number-of -local-deer-geese/article_4fac863d-3575-550c-9a5b-d785d0913f7b .html.

Adams, Kip. Presentation at Deer Impact Assessment and Mitigation Summit. Penn State University Extension, March 25, 2021.

Adams, Kip. Interview with Brian Grossman. *NDA's Deer Season 365* (podcast), October 6, 2021. podcasts.apple.com/us/podcast/hunting-the -whitetail-rut-the-science-and-strategies/id1571320690?i=100053770 8149.

Adhikusama, Briana. "Rockville Reports 21 Deer Culled in Pilot Program." *MOCO 360*, May 5, 2021. bethesdamagazine.com/bethesda-beat /government/rockville-reports-21-deer-culled-in-pilot-program/.

Ainsworth, William Harrison. n.d. *Windsor Castle.* Originally published in 1842. Posted on Project Gutenberg. Accessed March 8, 2023. www .gutenberg.org/files/2866/2866-h/2866-h.htm#link2H_4_0013.

Alam, Rumaan. *Leave the World Behind.* New York: Ecco, 2020.

Anthes, Emily, and Sabrina Imbler. "Is the Coronavirus in Your Backyard?" *New York Times*, February 7, 2022. www.nytimes.com/2022/02/07 /health/coronavirus-deer-animals.html.

Arena, Joe. "Deer Running Amok in Yards, Streets Causing Issues for Local Township." WPXI, February 24, 2020. www.wpxi.com/news

/deer-running-amok-yards-streets-causing-issues-local-township/A5 NDUVTMNBFXZESLBSZGUIWXKQ/.

"Arkansas CWD." n.d. University of Georgia Deer Research Laboratory. Accessed March 2, 2023. ugadeerresearch.org/arkansas-cwd/.

Arluke, Arnold, and Clinton Sanders. *Regarding Animals*. Philadelphia, PA: Temple University Press, 1996.

Armstrong, Philip. *What Animals Mean in the Fiction of Modernity*. London: Routledge, 2008.

Audubon, John James. *The Birds of America*. 1827; repr. New York: Macmillan, 1946.

Badke, David. n.d. "The Medieval Bestiary." Accessed March 8, 2023. bestiary.ca/intro.htm.

Baker, Chris. "Feds to Begin Culling Deer This Week in Syracuse." *Syracuse .com*, December 2, 2019. www.syracuse.com/news/2019/12/feds-to -begin-culling-deer-this-week-in-syracuse.html.

"B&C Member Spotlight—Theodore Roosevelt." n.d. Boone & Crockett Club. Accessed April 12, 2023. www.boone-crockett.org/bc-member -spotlight-theodore-roosevelt.

"B&C World's Record—Atlantic Walrus." n.d. Boone & Crockett Club. Accessed March 8, 2023. www.boone-crockett.org/bc-worlds-record -atlantic-walrus.

Beaver, Dan. "The Great Deer Massacre: Animals, Honor, and Communication in Early Modern England." *Journal of British Studies* 38, no. 2 (1999): 187–216. www.jstor.org/stable/175955.

The New American Bible. Washington, DC: World Catholic Press, 2010.

Bitler, Dara, and Kevin Torres. "Rare Video Shows Mountain Lion Attacking Deer in Pine." *FOX 31*, December 5, 2019. kdvr.com/news/local /wild-video-shows-mountain-lion-attack-deer-in-pine/.

Blossey, Bernd, Paul Curtis, Jason Boulanger, and Andrea Dávalos. "Red Oak Seedlings as Indicators of Deer Browse Pressure: Gauging the Outcome of Different White-tailed Deer Management Approaches." *Ecology and Evolution* 9, no. 23 (December 2019): 13085–103. doi.org /10.1002/ece3.5729.

Bober, Phyllis Fray. "Cernunnos: Origin and Transformation of a Celtic Divinity." *American Journal of Archaeology*, 55, no. 1 (1951): 13–51. doi.org/10.2307/501179.

Bostian, Kelly. "Friends of Deer Named Christmas Mourn After White Deer Turns Up at Processor." *Tulsa World*, January 2013. tulsaworld .com/news/state-and-regional/friends-of-deer-named-christmas -mourn-after-white-doe-turns-up-at-processor/article_40801bf4-69af -11ec-8345-4f589fecdcf4.html.

Bowles, Nellie. "How to Prepare Now for the Complete End of the World." *New York Times*, March 5, 2020. www.nytimes.com/2020/03/05/style /rewilding-stone-age-bushcraft.html.

Braff, Douglas. "Raining Deer? Residents Want Action as Deer Keep Falling to Their Deaths in Pennsylvania." *National Desk*, March 17, 2022. thenationaldesk.com/news/americas-news-now/raining-deer-residents -want-action-as-deer-keep-falling-to-their-deaths-in-pennsylvania.

Braund, Kathryn E. Holland. *Deerskins & Duffels: Creek Indian Trade with Anglo-America, 1685–1815.* Lincoln: University of Nebraska Press, 1993.

Braverman, Irus. "Conservation and Hunting: Till Death Do They Part? A Legal Ethnography of Deer Management." *Journal of Land Use & Environmental Law* 30, no. 2 (2015): 143–99. www.jstor.org/stable/43741164.

"Brother Nature." n.d. YouTube channel. Accessed March 4, 2023. www .youtube.com/channel/UCe9CjAvvRevJRUrC5aU8OHA/videos.

Budiansky, Stephen. *The Covenant of the Wild: Why Animals Choose Domestication.* New Haven, CT: Yale University Press, 1992.

Byrd, William, John Spencer Bassett, and De Vinne Press. *The Writings of Colonel William Byrd, of Westover in Virginia, Esqr.* New York: Doubleday, Page & Co., 1901.

Cambronne, Al. *Deerland: America's Hunt for Ecological Balance and the Essence of Wilderness.* Guilford, CT: Lyons Press, 2013.

Campbell, Joseph. *The Masks of God: Occidental Mythology.* New York: Penguin Books, 1964.

Campbell, Joseph. *The Masks of God: Primitive Mythology.* 1959; repr. New York: Arkana, 1991.

Camuri, Giacomo, Angelo Fossati, and Yoshadhar Mathpal, eds. *Deer in Rock Art of India and Europe.* New Delhi: Indira Gandhi National Centre for the Arts, 1993.

Cantor, L. M., and J. Hatherly. "The Medieval Parks of England." *Geography* 64, no. 2 (1979): 71–85. www.jstor.org/stable/40569087.

Cerulli, Tovar. *The Mindful Carnivore: A Vegetarian's Hunt for Sustenance.* New York: Pegasus Books, 2012.

"*Cervalces scotti.*" n.d. Wikipedia. Accessed February 27, 2023. en.wikipedia .org/wiki/Cervalces_scotti.

Chacón, Daniel J. "Shed Hunting in New Mexico: Turning Antlers into Cash." *Santa Fe New Mexican*, April 2, 2022, updated May 8, 2023. www.santafenewmexican.com/news/local_news/shed-hunting-in -new-mexico-turning-antlers-into-cash/article_ceeb9438-af7b-11ec -ao4e-eb4410199093.html.

Chalasani, Radhika. "Photos: Wildlife Roams During the Coronavirus

Pandemic." *ABC News*, April 22, 2020. abcnews.go.com/International /photos-wildlife-roams-planets-human-population-isolates/story?id =70213431.

Charrière, Georges. *Scythian Art: Crafts of the Early Eurasian Nomads.* New York: Alpine Fine Arts Collection Ltd., 1979.

Chang, Ryan. "Spreading Positivity with Kelvin Peña." *Sandalboyz*, November 29, 2019. sandalboyz.com/stories/kelv-2019.

Clark, Jonathan L. "Uncharismatic Invasives." *Environmental Humanities* 6, no. 1 (May 1, 2015): 29–52. doi.org/10.1215/22011919-3615889.

Clark, Kenneth. *Animals and Men.* New York: William Morrow, 1977.

Clevinger, Garrett. "The Virginian Appalachian Deer Study: Understanding Population Dynamics of Whitetails West of the Blue Ridge." *Newswires*, January 7, 2021. www.einnews.com/pr_news/534180707 /the-virginia-appalachian-deer-study-understanding-population -dynamics-of-whitetails-west-of-the-blue-ridge.

Coleman, C. Vernon, II. "Boosie Badazz Asks Fans for Help Killing Deer on His Property: 'I Need a Deer Hitter.'" *XXL*, July 24, 2021. www .xxlmag.com/boosie-badazz-help-killing-deer/.

Connors, John P. Casellas, and Christopher M. Rea. "Violent Entanglements: The Pittman-Robertson Act, Firearms, and the Financing of Conservation." *Conservation & Society* 20, no. 1 (2022): 24–35. www .jstor.org/stable/27100579.

Conover, M. R. "Numbers of Human Fatalities, Injuries, and Illnesses in the United States Due to Wildlife." *Human–Wildlife Interactions* 13, (2019): 264–76.

Coqueugniot, Hélène, et al. "Earliest Cranio-Encephalic Trauma from the Levantine Middle Palaeolithic: 3D Reappraisal of the Qafzeh 11 Skull, Consequences of Pediatric Brain Damage on Individual Life Condition and Social Care." *PloS One* 9, no. 7 (July 23, 2014): e102822. doi:10.1371/journal.pone.0102822.

"Corn Toxicity in Ruminants (Deer and Elk)." n.d. Michigan Department of Natural Resources. Accessed March 3, 2023. https://www.michigan .gov/dnr/managing-resources/wildlife/wildlife-disease/wdm/corn -toxicity-in-ruminants-deer-and-elk.

Cowen, Rob. *Common Ground: Encounters with Nature at the Edges of Life.* Chicago: University of Chicago Press, 2015.

"Criminal Charges for Violent Monsters Who Tortured Innocent Wildlife." n.d. Change.org petition. Accessed March 6, 2023. www.change.org/p /criminal-charges-for-animal-abusers-who-tortured-innocent-wildlife.

Cronon, William. *Changes in the Land: Indians, Colonists, and the Ecology of New England.* New York: Farrar, Straus and Giroux, 1983.

Cross, Madeleine. "Growing Concerns About Spread of Feral Deer Across Northern New South Wales." Australian Broadcasting Corporation, August 9, 2022. www.abc.net.au/news/2022-08-10/concern-about-feral-deer-spread-through-northern-nsw/101309744.

"Cull of Female Deer to Protect Millions of Trees." *BBC News*, August 31, 2021. www.bbc.com/news/articles/ck7e4qlqllwo.

Cunningham, Keith. *American Indians' Kitchen-Table Stories; Contemporary Conversations with Cherokee, Sioux, Hopi, Osage, Navajo, Zuni, and Members of Other Nations*. Little Rock, AR: August House, 1992.

D'Angelo, Gino. Personal interview with author, August 26, 2021.

Davidson, H. R. Ellis. *Gods and Myths of Northern Europe*. Baltimore: Penguin Books, 1964.

De Alba, Cassandra. *habitats*. Grand Rapids, MI: Horse Less Press, 2016.

"The Decline of Hunting and Fishing." n.d. Wildlife for All. wildlifeforall.us/resources/decline-of-hunting-and-fishing/.

"Deer Breaks into Christ Church Episcopal School in Greenville." *WYFF 4 News*, October 6, 2021. www.wyff4.com/article/deer-breaks-into-christ-church-episcopal-school/37881568.

"Deer Captured After Eluding Police for Several Hours in East Harlem." *FOX 5 New York*, updated May 14, 2020. www.fox5ny.com/news/deer-captured-in-east-harlem.

"Deer Report 2022." n.d. National Deer Association. www.deerassociation.com/wp-content/uploads/2022/02/Final-NDA-DR2022_web.pdf. Accessed March 7, 2023.

"Deer Resources and Information." n.d. Animal Protection League of New Jersey. aplnj.org/wildlife-advocacy/deer-resources-information/. Accessed March 5, 2023.

"Deer Squad—Sundance 2017." *Public Cinema Club*. www.publiccinemaclub.com/deer-squad. Accessed March 4, 2023.

Del Tredici, Peter. *Urban Plants of the Northeast: A Field Guide, 2nd ed*. Ithaca, NY: Comstock Publishing Associates, 2020.

Deloria, Philip J. *Playing Indian*. New Haven, CT: Yale University Press, 1998.

Dennis, Yvonne Wakim, Arlene Hirschfelder, and Shannon Rothenberger Flynn. *Native American Almanac: More than 50,000 Years of the Cultures and Histories of Indigenous Peoples*. Canton, MI: Visible Ink Press, 2016.

Dickinson, Emily. *Final Harvest: Emily Dickinson's Poems*. Selection and introduction by Thomas H. Johnson. Boston: Little, Brown, 1961.

"Did Early Earth Spin on Its Side?" *Astronomy Now*, November 1, 2016. astronomynow.com/2016/11/01/did-early-earth-spin-on-its-side/.

Dillard, Annie. *Teaching a Stone to Talk: Expeditions and Encounters.* New York: Harper Perennial, 1982.

Dizard, Jan E. *Going Wild: Hunting, Animal Rights, and the Contested Meaning of Nature.* Amherst: University of Massachusetts Press, 1999.

Doddridge, Joseph. *Notes on the Settlement and Indian Wars of the Western Parts of Virginia and Pennsylvania from 1763 to 1783, Inclusive, Together with a Review of the State of Society and Manners of the First Settlers of the Western Country.* Albany, NY: Joel Munsell, 1876.

Donaldson, Bridget M., and James J. White, Jr. "Composting Animal Mortality Removed from Roads: A Pilot Study of Rotary Drum and Forced Aeration Compost Vessels." Virginia Transportation Research Council, April 2013. www.virginiadot.org/vtrc/main/online_reports /pdf/13-r8.pdf.

Donaldson, Bridget M., and Kaitlyn E. M. Elliott. "Enhancing Existing Isolated Underpasses with Fencing to Decrease Wildlife Crashes and Increase Habitat Connectivity." Virginia Transportation Research Council, May 2020. www.virginiadot.org/vtrc/main/online_reports /pdf/20-R28.pdf.

Dong, Yan, Guozhong Zhou, Wenjing Cao, et al. "Global Seroprevalence and Sociodemographic Characteristics of *Borrelia burgdorferi sensu lato* in Human Populations: A Systematic Review and Meta-Analysis." *BMJ Global Health* 7 (2022): :e007744. gh.bmj.com/content/7/6 /e007744.

"Don't Feed Deer." n.d. Minnesota Department of Natural Resources. www.dnr.state.mn.us/wildlife/research/health/feeding/deer.html.

Doucleff, Michaeleen. "How SARS-CoV-2 in American Deer Could Alter the Course of the Global Pandemic." *NPR News*, November 10, 2021. www.npr.org/sections/goatsandsoda/2021/11/10/1054224204/how -sars-cov-2-in-american-deer-could-alter-the-course-of-the-global -pandemic.

Dougherty, Craig. "Freak Show Bucks: A Hard Look at Breeding for Antlers." *Outdoor Life*, September 20, 2011. www.outdoorlife.com /photos/gallery/hunting/2011/09/freak-show-bucks-look-genetically -altered-deer/.

Douthat, Ross. "How I Became a Sick Person." *New York Times*, October 23, 2021. www.nytimes.com/2021/10/23/opinion/lyme-disease-chronic -illness.html.

"Driver Impaled by Fence After Hitting Deer in Texas." *KIRO 7*, February 19, 2020. www.kiro7.com/news/trending/driver-impaled-by-fence-after -hitting-deer-texas/ZK6WQN5Y3ZF3TG45TM2ABFYWLM/.

Dunlap, Thomas R. *Saving America's Wildlife: Ecology and the American Mind, 1850–1990.* Princeton, NJ: Princeton University Press, 1988.

Durkin, Patrick. "Is Killing More Deer the Answer to Reducing Tick Diseases?" *MeatEater*, October 23, 2020. www.themeateater.com /conservation/wildlife-management/is-killing-more-deer-the-answer -to-reducing-tick-diseases.

Durkin, Patrick. "Why Fawn Rescues Fail." *MeatEater*, May 9, 2022. www.themeateater.com/wired-to-hunt/whitetail-management/why -fawn-rescues-fail.

Dutta, Sanchari Sinha. "White-tailed Deer Susceptible to SARS-CoV-2 Infection, Study Finds." *News Medical*, January 15, 2021. www.news -medical.net/news/20210115/White-tailed-deer-susceptible-to-SARS -CoV-2-infection-study-finds.aspx.

"Early Life on Earth—Animal Origins." n.d. National Museum of Natural History. Accessed March 27, 2023. naturalhistory.si.edu/education /teaching-resources/life-science/early-life-earth-animal-origins.

Edelblutte, Émilie. "POV: The Secret to Wildlife Conservation Might Be the 'Animal Agency' Approach—Giving Creatures a Role in Their Own Preservation." *The Brink*, March 9, 2022. www.bu.edu/articles/2022 /key-to-wildlife-conservation-might-be-animal-agency-approach/.

Eichler, Lauren, and David Baumeister. "Hunting for Justice: An Indigenous Critique of the North American Model of Wildlife Conservation." *Environment and Society* 9 (2018): 75–90. www.jstor.org/stable /26879579.

Euripides. *Ten Plays by Euripides.* Translated by Moses Hadas and John McLean. New York: Bantam Books, 1981.

Evers, Larry, and Felipe S. Molina. *Yaqui Deer Songs: Maso Bwikam: A Native American Poetry.* Tucson: Sun Tracks and University of Arizona Press, 1987.

"Evolution." n.d. Encyclopedia Britannica. Accessed March 27, 2023. www.britannica.com/science/evolution-scientific-theory.

Farish, Mitchell Grant. "Homespun and Buckskin."

Farmer, S. "Aristocratic Power and the 'Natural' Landscape: The Garden Park at Hesdin, ca. 1291–1302." *Speculum* 88, no. 3 (2013): 644–80. www.jstor.org/stable/43576781.

Farr, Marigo. "Deer Are Threatening America's Forests. Is More Hunting the Answer?" *Grist*, August 16, 2022. grist.org/science/deer-are -threatening-american-forests-is-more-hunting-the-solution/.

Faulkner, Travis. "Junkyard Buck: Here's a Quadruple Drop-Tine Giant with More Junk on His Head Than a Used Car Dealership." *Outdoor*

Life, December 27, 2009. www.outdoorlife.com/photos/gallery/hunting /2009/12/junkyard-buck.

Faulkner, William. *Go Down, Moses.* New York: Vintage International, 1940.

Figura, David. "CNY Village of Pulaski Erecting Statue of Bella, Its Beloved Deer." NYup.com, January 2, 2020. www.newyorkupstate.com /outdoors/2020/01/cny-village-of-pulaski-erecting-statue-of-bella-its -beloved-deer.html.

Figura, David. "Upstate NY Coyote Hunter Talks About His Passion: 'This Is the Best Time of Year to Be Doing It.'" *Syracuse.com*, February 23, 2021. www.syracuse.com/outdoors/2021/02/upstate-ny-coyote-hunter-talks -about-his-passion-this-is-the-best-time-of-year-to-be-doing-it.html.

Flannery, Tim F. *Europe: A Natural History.* New York: Grove Press, 2018.

Fletcher, John. *Deer.* London: Reaktion Books, 2013.

Flores, Dan L. *Coyote America: A Natural and Supernatural History.* New York: Basic Books, 2016.

Foer, Jonathan Safran. *Eating Animals.* New York: Little, Brown, 2009.

Forman, Richard T. T., et al. *Road Ecology: Science and Solutions.* Washington: Island Press, 2003.

Frazee, Brent. "Poachers Steal from Honest Hunters." *Joplin Globe*, December 22, 2019. www.joplinglobe.com/news/lifestyles/brent-frazee -poachers-steal-from-honest-hunters/article_43061284-cbe2-556b -abcd-b288fd09b5fd.html.

Frazer, James George. *The Golden Bough: A Study in Magic and Religion.* 1980; repr. Oxford, UK: Oxford University Press, 1994.

Frye, Bob. *Deer Wars: Science, Tradition, and the Battle Over Managing Whitetails in Pennsylvania.* University Park: Pennsylvania State University Press, 2006.

Gabler, Neal. *Walt Disney: The Triumph of the American Imagination.* New York: Knopf, 2006.

Giles, Abagael. "Vermont's Tick Season Is Now Year-Round, Thanks to Climate Change. Here's How to Protect Yourself." *Vermont Public*, April 8, 2022. www.vermontpublic.org/vpr-news/2022-04-08/vermonts -tick-season-is-now-year-round-thanks-to-climate-change-heres-how -to-protect-yourself.

Gillard, Laurie. "Deer Culling Normalizes Gun Violence." *Wednesday Journal of Oak Park and River Forest*, April 27, 2021. www.oakpark .com/2021/04/27/deer-culling-normalizes-gun-violence/.

Giltner, Scott E. *Hunting and Fishing in the New South: Black Labor and White Leisure After the Civil War.* Baltimore: Johns Hopkins University Press, 2008.

González, Betina. *American Delirium*. Translated by Heather Cleary. New York: Henry Holt, 2016.

Green, Christie. "Blood Bone Oil Water." *Dark Mountain Project* 20 (Autumn 2021): 180–87.

Greene, Jay. "Car Hits Deer Near Sigourney, Sends It Flying into Another Car's Windshield, Kills Driver." *KCRG.com*, February 20, 2020. www.kcrg.com/content/news/Car-hits-deer-near-Sigourney-sends-it-flying-into-another-cars-windshield-kills-driver-568036461.html.

Greene, Miranda Aldhouse. *The Gods of the Celts*. Stroud, UK: Alan Sutton, 1986.

Greenwald, Katherine R., Lisa J. Petit, and Thomas A. Waite. "Indirect Effects of a Keystone Herbivore Elevate Local Animal Diversity." *Journal of Wildlife Management* 72, no. 6 (2008): 1318–21. www.jstor.org/stable/25097697.

Grossman, Lisa. "Fast-Spinning Earth Settles Mystery of Moon's Makeup." *New Scientist*, October 17, 2012. www.newscientist.com/article/dn22393-fast-spinning-earth-settles-mystery-of-moons-make-up/.

Grumet, Robert S. *Voices from the Delaware Big House Ceremony*. Norman: University of Oklahoma Press, 2001.

"Guide to Hunting in Germany." n.d. U.S. Forces Europe Hunting, Fishing, and Sport Shooting Program. Accessed March 6, 2023. ansbach.armymwr.com/application/files/2314/9272/9541/Guide_11_Hunting_Techniques_Red_2014-06.pdf.

"The Gundestrup Cauldron." n.d. National Museum of Denmark, Accessed February 23, 2023. en.natmus.dk/historical-knowledge/denmark/prehistoric-period-until-1050-ad/the-early-iron-age/the-gundestrup-cauldron/.

Hall, Louise. "Animal Crossing: Watch Wildlife Use Sky Bridge to Cross Interstate Safely." *The Independent*, November 26, 2020. www.independent.co.uk/news/world/americas/animal-crossing-bridge-wildlife-bridge-b1762435.html.

Halls, Lowell K., ed. *White-Tailed Deer: Ecology and Management*. Harrisburg, PA: Stackpole Books, 1984.

Hanberry, Brice B. Personal interview with author, June 9, 2021.

Hanberry, Brice B., and Marc D. Abrams. "Does White-Tailed Deer Density Affect Tree Stocking in Forests of the Eastern United States?" *Ecological Processes* 8, no. 30 (2019). doi.org/10.1186/s13717-019-0185-5.

Hanberry, Brice B., and Phillip Hanberry. "Regaining the History of Deer Populations and Densities in the Southeastern United States." *Wildlife Society Bulletin* 44 (2020): 512–18. doi.org/10.1002/wsb.1118.

Harris, Adam Duncan. *Wildlife in American Art: Masterworks from the*

National Museum of Wildlife Art. Jackson, WY: University of Oklahoma Press in cooperation with the National Museum of Wildlife Art of the United States, 2009.

Haworth, Holly. "Bodies of Knowledge." *Orion*, Autumn 2021.

Heffelfinger, Jim. "Covid Virus Discovered in Mule Deer for the First Time." *MeatEater*, April 11, 2022. www.themeateater.com/conservation /wildlife-management/first-covid-19-case-discovered-in-mule-deer.

Herberg, Laura. "Why Do Huron-Clinton Metroparks Shoot the Deer on Their Land?" *WDET.org*, March 3, 2021. wdet.org/2021/03/03/Why -Do-Huron-Clinton-Metroparks-Shoot-the-Deer-on-their-Land/.

Herman, Daniel Justin. *Hunting and the American Imagination.* Washington, DC: Smithsonian Institution Press, 2001.

Hewitt, David G. *Biology and Management of White-tailed Deer.* Boca Raton, FL: CRC Press, 2011.

Hirakawa, Yuki. "Shop Hopes Its Deerskin Goods Focus Minds on Japan's Huge Deer Culls." *Kyodo News*, June 28, 2021. english.kyodonews.net /news/2021/06/34f20991f380-feature-shop-hopes-its-deerskin-goods -focus-minds-on-japans-huge-deer-culls.html.

"A History of British Pub Names." n.d. The History Press. Accessed March 2, 2023. www.thehistorypress.co.uk/articles/a-history-of-british-pub -names/.

Homer. *The Odyssey.* Translated by Robert Fagles. New York: Viking, 1996.

"How Much Are Shed Antlers Worth and How Do You Sell Them?" *Outdoors Mecca*, February 5, 2022. outdoorsmecca.com/how-much-are -shed-antlers-worth/.

Huetter, John. "State Farm: Average Deer Claim Up to $4,341; W.Va. Still No. 1 in Odds of Hitting One." *Repairer Driven News*, October 1, 2018. www.repairerdrivennews.com/2018/10/01/state-farm-average-deer -claim-up-to-4341-w-va-still-no-1-in-odds-of-hitting-one/.

Huijser, M. P., et al. "Wildlife-Vehicle Collision Study: Report to Congress." Federal Highway Administration, August 2008. www.fhwa.dot .gov/publications/research/safety/08034/.

Hunt, John Dixon, and Peter Willis. *The Genius of the Place: The English Landscape Garden, 1620–1820.* Cambridge: MIT Press, 1988.

Hyde, Lewis. *Trickster Makes This World: Mischief, Myth, and Art.* New York: Farrar, Straus and Giroux, 1998.

Jacobson, Esther. *The Deer Goddess of Ancient Siberia.* Leiden, Netherlands: E. J. Brill, 1993.

Jacoby, Karl, et al. *Crimes Against Nature: Squatters, Poachers, Thieves, and the Hidden History of American Conservation*. Berkeley: University of California Press, 2001.

Johnson, Rachel. "Killing Deer Not the Answer to Reducing Lyme Disease, Says HSPH Scientist." Harvard School of Public Health, November 23, 2010. www.hsph.harvard.edu/news/features/kiling-deer-not-answer-reducing-lyme-disease-html/.

Jordan, Robert A., Terry L. Schulze, and Margaret B. Jahn. "Effects of Reduced Deer Density on the Abundance of *Ixodes scapularis* (Acari: Ixodidae) and Lyme Disease Incidence in a Northern New Jersey Endemic Area." *Journal of Medical Entomology* 44, no. 5 (September 1, 2007): 752–57. doi.org/10.1093/jmedent/44.5.752.

Karish, Talesha. Presentation at Southeast Deer Study Group, February 2021.

Karra, Sushma. "Canela the Deer Takes Internet by Storm but Fans Not Happy to See 'Racist' Brother Nature: 'We Did Not Forget.'" *MEAWW*, June 5, 2020. meaww.com/kelvin-pena-brother-nature-tweet-canela-deer-picture-fans-happy-deer-forgot-racist-tweets.

Kashiwagi, Sydney. "City Resumes Year Four of Deer Vasectomies to Cut Population." *SI Live*, December 31, 2019. www.silive.com/news/2019/12/city-resumes-year-four-of-deer-vasectomies-to-cut-population.html.

Kashiwagi, Sydney. "Max Rose Says He'll 'Start Taking Some of These Deer Down Himself' If Controlled Cull Approved." *SI Live*, January 27, 2020. www.silive.com/news/2020/01/max-rose-says-hell-start-taking-down-some-of-these-deer-himself-if-controlled-deer-cull-approved.html.

Keating, Geoffrey. *The History of Ireland*. Originally published c. 1634. Posted on CELT, the Corpus of Electronic Texts, University of College Cork. Accessed March 3, 2023. celt.ucc.ie/published/T100054/text040.html.

Kelety, Josh. "Ahead of Trump Visit, Deer Found Dead Along Border Wall Sparks Outrage." *Phoenix New Times*, August 18, 2020. www.phoenixnewtimes.com/news/ahead-of-trump-visit-wildlife-found-dead-along-border-wall-11488269.

Kenyon, Mark. "4 Most Endangered Whitetail Destinations in America." *MeatEater*, June 3, 2022. www.themeateater.com/wired-to-hunt/whitetail-management/4-most-endangered-whitetail-destinations-in-america.

Kenyon, Mark. "The Whitetail Addict's Dictionary." *MeatEater*, July 1, 2013. www.themeateater.com/wired-to-hunt/whitetail-hunting/the-whitetail-addicts-dictionary.

Kesselheim, Al. "A Walk on the Wild Side: Joe Hutto's Life with Animals."

The Sun, May 2017. www.thesunmagazine.org/issues/497/a-walk-on -the-wild-side.

Kevin, Brian. "The Man Who Killed Every Deer on Monhegan." *DownEast*, November 2014. downeast.com/arts-culture/hunt-management/.

Kinver, Mark. "Roe Deer Numbers 'Changing Woodland Ecosystems.'" *BBC News*, January 2, 2013. www.bbc.com/news/science-environment -20713190.

Kirk, Rylee. "Oh Deer! Deer Smash Through Window at iSmash in Syracuse." *Syracuse.com*, November 16, 2021. www.syracuse.com/news/2021/11 /oh-deer-deer-smashes-through-window-at-ismash-in-syracuse.html.

Kitagawa, Chiori. "On the Presence of Deer in Ancient Egypt: Analysis of the Osteological Record." *Journal of Egyptian Archaeology* 94 (2008): 209–22. www.jstor.org/stable/40345868.

Knox, Matt. Personal interview with author, August 2019.

Kraker, Dan. "As Anglers and Hunters Drop Out, DNR Seeks More Sustainable Funding." *MPR News*, December 14, 2021. www.mprnews .org/story/2021/12/14/as-anglers-and-hunters-drop-out-dnr-seeks -more-sustainable-funding.

Kroening, Tim. "Woman Attacked by Deer Was a Victim of Neighbors Who Fed It." *Pikes Peak Courier*, March 29, 2021. gazette.com /pikespeakcourier/woman-attacked-by-deer-was-a-victim-of-neighbors -who-fed-it-wild-about-teller/article_4501af40-86b5-11eb-99cf -9325b60767a3.html.

"The Lakota Emergence Story." n.d. Video presentation by Sina Bear Eagle. Wind Cave National Park. Accessed February 27, 2023. www.nps .gov/wica/learn/historyculture/the-lakota-emergence-story.htm.

Lalonde, Maria Cristina. "You Can Harvest Roadkill for Food If You Live in One of These States." *Wide Open Eats*, November 18, 2020. www .wideopeneats.com/all-the-states-where-you-can-legally-harvest-roadkill -for-food/.

Landers, Jackson. *The Beginner's Guide to Hunting Deer for Food*. North Adams, MA: Storey Publishing, 2011.

Lang, Lenora, and Andrew Lang. *The Orange Fairy Book*. New York: Dover Publications, 1906.

Langland, William. *The Vision of Piers Plowman*. London: J. M. Dent and E. P. Dutton, 1978.

Lapham, Heather A. *Hunting for Hides: Deerskins, Status, and Cultural Change in the Protohistoric Appalachians*. Tuscaloosa: University of Alabama Press, 2005.

Larussa, Tony. "Panel of Experts Outline McCandless' Deer Management

Plans." *Trib Live*, January 20, 2021. triblive.com/local/north-hills/panel-of-experts-to-outline-mccandless-deer-management-plans/.

Lawrence, D. H. *Etruscan Places*. 1932; repr. New York: Viking Press, 1957.

Levi, Taal. "Deer, Predators, and the Emergence of Lyme Disease." *PNAS*, June 18, 2012. www.pnas.org/doi/10.1073/pnas.1204536109.

Levin, Rachel. "Instagram's Most Fascinating Subculture? Women Hunters." *Outside*, September 8, 2020. www.outsideonline.com/outdoor-adventure/exploration-survival/women-hunters-instagram-rihana-cary-amanda-caldwell/.

"Little Deer and Mother Earth." n.d. Video presentation by Marilou Awiakta. *PBS LearningMedia*. Accessed March 5, 2023. www.pbslearningmedia.org/resource/natam.arts.drama.littledeer/native-american-culture-little-deer-and-mother-earth/.

Lucas, Richard W., Roberto Salguero-Gómez, David B. Cobb, Bonnie G. Waring, Frank Anderson, William J. McShea, and Brenda B. Casper. "White-Tailed Deer (*Odocoileus virginianus*) Positively Affect the Growth of Mature Northern Red Oak (*Quercus rubra*) Trees." *Ecosphere* 4, no. 7 (2013): 84. dx.doi.org/10.1890/ES13-00036.1.

"Lyme Disease." n.d. Pennsylvania Game Commission. Accessed March 4, 2023. www.pgc.pa.gov/Wildlife/WildlifeHealth/Pages/LymeDisease.aspx.

"Lyme Disease-Causing Ticks Have Increased in Maine." *Mount Desert Islander*, April 9, 2022. www.mdislander.com/maine-news/health-news/lyme-disease-causing-ticks-have-increased-in-maine.

Mac Cana, Proinsias. *Celtic Mythology*. Feltham, UK: Hamlyn, 1970.

Macdonald, Fleur. "As England's Deer Population Explodes, Some Propose a Mass Cull." *New York Times*, July 3, 2021. www.nytimes.com/2021/07/03/world/europe/uk-deer-cull.html.

Machemer, Theresa. "By Creating a 'Landscape of Fear,' Wolves Reduce Car Collisions with Deer." *Smithsonian*, May 26, 2021. www.smithsonianmag.com/smart-news/wisconsin-counties-wolves-see-fewer-collisions-between-cars-and-deer-180977819/.

Makkai, Adam, ed. *In Quest of the "Miracle Stag": The Poetry of Hungary*. Chicago: Atlantis-Centaur, 1996.

Mallapaty, Smriti. "COVID Is Spreading in Deer. What Does That Mean for the Pandemic?" *Nature*, April 26, 2022. www.nature.com/articles/d41586-022-01112-4.

Malloy, Kevin, Derek Hall, and Richard Oram. "Prestigious Landscapes: An Archaeological and Historical Examination of the Role of Deer at Three Medieval Scottish Parks." *Eolas: The Journal of the American*

    Society of Irish Medieval Studies 6 (2013): 68–87. www.jstor.org/stable
    /26193962.

Mann, Charles C. *1491: New Revelations of the Americas Before Colum-
    bus*. New York: Vintage Books, 2005.

March, Chris. "Shock as Severed Deer Head Found Dump at St. Michael
    and All Angels Church in Lyndhurst." *New Milton Advertiser & Ly-
    mington Times*, May 6, 2021. www.advertiserandtimes.co.uk/news
    /savage-callous-and-disgusting-severed-deer-head-dumped-9198101/.

Mark, Aaron. *Deer*. New York: Dramatists Play Service, 2016.

Marshall, John. "Climate Change Could Turn Nova Scotia into a Tick
    Hot Spot." *Saltwire*, April 8, 2022. www.saltwire.com/atlantic-canada
    /lifestyles/climate-change-could-turn-nova-scotia-into-a-tick-hotspot
    -100716362/.

McDonald, J. Scott, and Karl V. Miller. *A History of White-Tailed Deer
    Restocking in the United States 1878 to 2004*. Athens: University of
    Georgia, 1993.

McKay, J. G. "The Deer-Cult and the Deer-Goddess Cult of the Ancient
    Caledonians." *Folklore* 43, no. 2 (1932): 144–74. doi:10.1080/0015587X
    .1932.9718435.

McNally, Bob. "A CWD Outbreak at a Captive Deer Farm in Wisconsin
    Is Creating Problems in 7 States." *Outdoor Life*, September 28, 2021.
    www.outdoorlife.com/conservation/cwd-outbreak-wisconsin-deer
    -farm/.

McNally, Bob. "Whitetail Doe with Fawn Chases Down Woman, Sends
    Her to Hospital." *Outdoor Life*, June 21, 2021. www.outdoorlife.com
    /hunting/whitetail-attacks-woman-hospital/.

McShea, William J., H. Brian Underwood, and John H. Rappole. *The Sci-
    ence of Overabundance: Deer Ecology and Population Management*.
    Washington, DC: Smithsonian Books, 1997.

Merchant, Carolyn. *Earthcare: Women and the Environment*. New York:
    Routledge, 1996.

Mighetto, Lisa. *Wild Animals and American Environmental Ethics*.
    Tucson: University of Arizona Press, 1991.

Miner, Curt. "Hardhat Hunters: The Democratization of Recreational
    Hunting in Twentieth Century Pennsylvania." *Journal of Sport History*
    28, no. 1 (2001): 41–62. www.jstor.org/stable/43609831.

"Monhegan's Special Hunt." n.d. Island Institute. Accessed March 2,
    2023. www.islandinstitute.org/ii-solution/monhegans-special-hunt/.

Montgomery, Sy. *The Soul of an Octopus: A Surprising Exploration into
    the Wonder of Consciousness*. New York: Atria Books, 2015.

Moore, Antonio. "Who Owns Almost All America's Land?" *Inequality.org*, February 15, 2016. inequality.org/research/owns-land/.

Moore, Marianne. "The Rigorists," in *The Complete Poems of Marianne Moore*. London: Faber and Faber, 1943.

Moreland, John, and Dawn Hadley (with Ashley Tuck and Milica Rajic). "Beyond the Pale." Chap. 8 in *Sheffield Castle: Archaeology, Archives, Regeneration, 1927–2018*. York, UK: White Rose University Press, 2020. doi.org/10.2307/j.ctv16kkwpd.13.

Morris, Eric M. "Why We're Failing to Recruit African American Hunters (and How to Fix It)." *Outdoor Life*, Updated April 20, 2021. www.out doorlife.com/story/hunting/how-to-recruit-african-american-hunters/.

"Motorists Reminded to Use Caution to Avoid Deer-Vehicle Collisions in Fall." n.d. Forest Preserve District of DuPage County. Accessed March 4, 2023. https://dupageforest.prowly.com/158739-drivers-reminded-to -use-caution-to-avoid-deer-vehicle-collisions-in-fall.

Nash, Roderick Frazier. *Wilderness and the American Mind*, 5th ed. New Haven, CT: Yale University Press, 2014.

"National Survey of Fishing, Hunting, and Wildlife-Associated Recreation." U.S. Fish and Wildlife Service, 2016. www.census.gov/content /dam/Census/library/publications/2018/demo/fhw16-nat.pdf.

"NDA Position Statements." National Deer Association. Last updated October 4, 2021. deerassociation.com/conserve/position-statements/.

Nelson, Richard. *Heart and Blood: Living with Deer in America*. New York: Vintage Books, 1997.

Nijhuis, Michelle. "Don't Cancel John Muir. But Don't Excuse Him Either." *The Atlantic*, April 12, 2021. www.theatlantic.com/ideas/archive /2021/04/conservation-movements-complicated-history/618556/.

Novak, A. M. "Not Your Trophy: Deer Imagery in Jordan Peele's *Get Out*." Skye Von (blog), March 22, 2017. skyevon.com/blog/2017/3/26 /not-your-trophy-deer-imagery-in-jordan-peeles-get-out.

Ox Ranch. n.d. Accessed March 6, 2023. www.oxhuntingranch.com.

The Papers of George Washington, Colonial Series, vol. 5, *5 October 1757–3 September 1758*, ed. W. W. Abbot. Charlottesville: University Press of Virginia, 1988.

The Papers of George Washington, Revolutionary War Series, vol. 1, *16 June 1775–15 September 1775*, ed. Philander D. Chase. Charlottesville: University Press of Virginia, 1985.

The Papers of George Washington, Revolutionary War Series, vol. 5, *16 June 1776–12 August 1776*, ed. Philander D. Chase. Charlottesville: University Press of Virginia, 1993.

Patoski, Joe Nick. "Which Side of the Fence Are You On?" *Texas Monthly*, February 2002. www.texasmonthly.com/the-culture/which-side-of-the -fence-are-you-on/.

Peattie, Donald Culross. *A Prairie Grove*. New York: Literary Guild of America, 1938.

Perdue, Theda. *Cherokee Women: Gender and Culture Change, 1700– 1835*. Lincoln: University of Nebraska Press, 1998.

"Pet Deer Kills Man and Injures Wife in Rural Australia." *AP News*, April 17, 2019. apnews.com/article/d04477ib29ff49079c0836529a416d22.

Peterson, Tony J. "The Real Benefit of Shed Hunting." *MeatEater*, February 9, 2022. www.themeateater.com/wired-to-hunt/whitetail-scouting /the-real-benefit-of-shed-hunting.

Piotrovsky, Boris, Liudmila Galanina, and Nonna Grach. *Scythian Art*. Oxford: Phaidon Press, 1987.

Pollack, Alison. "What Slime Knows." *Orion*, Autumn 2021. orion magazine.org/article/what-slime-knows/.

Poltrock, Heather. "Teen Attempting to Move Deer from Roadway, Struck, Killed in Birnamwood." *SWAW-TV*, December 20, 2019. www.wsaw .com/content/news/Teen-attempting-to-move-deer-from-roadway -stuck-killed-in-Birnamwood-566374961.html.

"Population of Wisconsin, 1820–1990." n.d. Wisconsin Historical Society. Accessed March 27, 2023. www.wisconsinhistory.org/Records/Article /CS1816.

"Position Statements of the Boone & Crockett Club." n.d. Accessed March 6, 2023. www.boone-crockett.org/position-statements-boone -and-crockett-club.

Powell, Earl A. *Thomas Cole*. New York: Harry N. Abrams, 1990.

Price, Lisa. "A New Trend—Late Born Fawns." *Times News* (Lehighton, PA), March 13, 2020. www.tnonline.com/20200313/a-new-trend-late -born-fawns/.

"Program Data Report G 2020." n.d. USDA Animal and Plant Health Inspection Service. Accessed March 10, 2023. www.aphis.usda.gov/aphis /ourfocus/wildlifedamage/pdr/?file=PDR-G_Report&p=2020: INDEX:.

Purdy, Jedediah. *After Nature: A Politics for the Anthropocene*. Cambridge, MA: Harvard University Press, 2015.

Putnam, Rory. *The Natural History of Deer*. Ithaca, NY: Comstock Publishing Associates, 1988.

Putnam, Rory, et al. "Identifying Threshold Densities for Wild Deer in the U.K. Above Which Negative Impacts May Occur." *Mam-*

mal Review, 2011. www.holyrood-parliament.scot/S5_Environment
/Meeting%20Papers/Mammal_Review_173_Threshold-densities.pdf.

Pyle, Howard. *The Merry Adventures of Robin Hood*. New York: Charles
Scribner's Sons, 1883.

Rackham, Oliver. *The History of the Countryside*. London: J. M. Dent,
1986.

Rahman, Khaleda. "'Destruction Everywhere' as Deer Crashes Through
Oklahoma Home: 'You Probably See More Blood Than You Do Floor.'"
Newsweek, November 28, 2019. www.newsweek.com/destruction
-deer-crashes-oklahoma-home-1474574.

Rawinski, Tom. Presentation at Deer Impact Assessment and Mitigation
Summit, Penn State University Extension, University Park, PA, March
30, 2021.

Rawlings, Marjorie Kinnan. *The Yearling*. 1938; repr. New York: Scribner,
1985.

"Recipes." n.d. *MeatEater*. Accessed March 7, 2023. www.themeateater
.com/recipes?ingredients=venison.

Reilly, Ryan J. "Cowboys for Trump Co-Founder Ditches Plan to Ride
Horse to His Jan. 6 Trial." *NBC News*, March 21, 2022. www.nbc
news.com/politics/justice-department/cowboys-trump-co-founder
-ditches-plan-ride-horse-jan-6-trial-rcna20606.

"Reversing Mule Deer Declines." n.d. National Wildlife Federation. Accessed March 27, 2023. www.nwf.org/Our-Work/Wildlife-Conserva
tion/Mule-Deer.

"Right to Hunt, Fish, and Harvest Wildlife." n.d. Congressional Sportsman's Foundation. Accessed March 3, 2023. congressionalsportsmen
.org/policies/state/right-to-hunt-fish.

Roach, Margaret. "The Elusive Deer-Proof Garden." *New York Times*,
May 5, 2021. www.nytimes.com/2021/05/05/realestate/the-elusive-deer
-proof-garden.html.

Roach, Mary. *Fuzz: When Nature Breaks the Law*. New York: W. W. Nor-
ton, 2021.

Roberts, Taylor. "How Kelvin Peña Became Brother Nature." *Paper*,
December 16, 2019. www.papermag.com/kelvin-pena-brother-nature
-2641583122.html.

Rosenberger, Jacalyn P., B. Bynum Boley, Adam C. Edge, Cheyenne J.
Yates, Karl V. Miller, David A. Osborn, Charlie H. Killmaster, Kris-
tina L. Johannsen, and Gino D'Angelo. "Satisfaction of Public Land
Hunters During Long-term Deer Population Decline." *Wildlife Society Bulletin* 45 (4), 2021, 608–17. ugadeerresearch.org/wp-content

/uploads/2022/01/Wildlife-Society-Bulletin-2021-Rosenberger
-Satisfaction-of-Public-Land-Hunters-During-Long%E2%80%90term
-Deer-Population.pdf.

Rubin, Paul. "A Young Woman Believes She Would've Died If She'd Continued Treatment for Supposed Lyme Disease from Chandler Clini-
cians." *Phoenix New Times*, May 5, 2011. www.phoenixnewtimes.com
/news/a-young-woman-believes-she-wouldve-died-if-shed-continued
-treatment-for-supposed-lyme-disease-from-chandler-clinicians
-6448432.

Rupasinghe, Ruwini, and Beatriz Martinez Lopez. "Changing Climate
Changing Diseases." *Cosmos*, April 13, 2022. cosmosmagazine.com
/earth/climate/animal-to-human-diseases-more-common/.

Schmidt, Daniel. "How Many Deer Hunters in the United States?" *Deer and
Deer Hunting*, July 27, 2020. www.deeranddeerhunting.com/content
/blogs/dan-schmidt-deer-blog-whitetail-wisdom/how-many-deer
-hunters-in-the-united-states.

Schulz, Kathryn. "'Bambi' Is Even Bleaker Than You Thought." *New
Yorker*, January 17, 2022. www.newyorker.com/magazine/2022/01/24
/bambi-is-even-bleaker-than-you-thought.

Seelye, Katharine Q. "Phyllis Marchand, Face of Disputed Deer-Culling
Program, Dies at 81." *New York Times*, April 7, 2021. www.nytimes
.com/2021/04/07/nyregion/phyllis-marchand-dead.html.

Serpell, James. *In the Company of Animals.* New York: Basil Blackwell, 1986.

Sheldon, William G. "A History of the Boone and Crockett Club: Milestones
in Wildlife Conservation," 1955. ScholarWorks at University of Montana, Manuscript Collections. scholarworks.umt.edu/cgi/viewcontent
.cgi?article=1000&context=sheldon.

Shepard, Paul. *The Others: How Animals Made Us Human.* Washington,
DC: Island Press, 1996.

Shepherd, Lynx. "101 Things to Do with a Deer." *Bulletin of Primitive
Technology*, Spring 2000, 7.

Shepherd, Nan. *The Living Mountain.* Edinburgh, Scotland: Canongate,
2011. Originally published Aberdeen University Press, 1977.

Siemer, William F., Daniel J. Decker, and Tommy L. Brown, eds. *Human
Dimensions of Wildlife Management in North America.* Bethesda,
MD: The Wildlife Society, 2001.

Singer et al. v. The Township of Princeton, Superior Court of New Jersey
Appellate Division, Docket No. A-3114-02T3, 2004.

Smalley, Andrea L. "'They Steal Our Deer and Land': Contested Hunting
Grounds in the Trans-Appalachian West." *Register of the Kentucky*

Historical Society 114, no. 3/4 (2016): 303–39. www.jstor.org/stable /44980553.

Smith, Casey. "Climate Change Means More Mice—Natural Reservoirs for Tick Disease." *Portland (Maine) Press Herald*, June 28, 2022. www.pressherald.com/2022/06/28/climate-change-means-more-mice -natural-reservoirs-for-lyme-disease/.

Smola, Travis. "High Fence Hunting Ethics Check: Examining the Practice and Who Really Benefits from It." *Wide Open Spaces*, December 10, 2021. www.wideopenspaces.com/ethics-check-is-high-fence-hunting-actually -a-brilliant-business-idea/.

Smout, T. C. *Nature Contested: Environmental History in Scotland and Northern England Since 1600*. Edinburgh, Scotland: Edinburgh University Press, 2000.

Snyder, Gary. *Regarding Wave*. New York: New Directions, 1970.

The Song of Roland. Translated by Dorothy L. Sayers. New York: Penguin Books, 1957.

Stafford, William. *The Way It Is: New and Selected Poems*. St. Paul, MN: Graywolf Press, 1998.

Stange, Mary Zeiss. *Woman the Hunter*. Boston: Beacon Press, 1997.

Stapleton, Leeann. "Wisconsin Hunters Go Viral for Helping Free Tangled Bucks Instead of Killing Them." *ABC 7 Chicago*, January 7, 2021. abc7chicago.com/wisconsin-hunters-tangled-bucks-viral-video /11473025/.

Stein, Emma. "'I Thought I Was Going to Die': Woman Attacked by Deer in Front Yard, Saved by Son." *Detroit Free Press*, October 16, 2021. www .freep.com/story/news/local/michigan/2021/10/16/woman-attacked -deer-front-yard-saved-son/8489817002/.

Stuart, Tessa. "Severed Deer Head on Campus, Rumors of Violence Preceded Michigan School Shooting." *Rolling Stone*, December 1, 2021. www .rollingstone.com/culture/culture-news/michigan-school-shooting -threat-snapchat-1265408/.

Swan, James A. *In Defense of Hunting*. San Francisco: Harper San Francisco, 1995.

Swann, Brian, and Arnold Krupat. *Recovering the Word: Essays on Native American Literature*. Berkeley: University of California Press, 1987.

Sweeney, Karen. "Deer Changes Recommended After Victorian Man Killed by Pet." *9 News*, August 24, 2022. www.9news.com.au/national/deer -attack-changes-recommended-after-man-killed-victoria/2e25d466 -d2c3-450a-b2e9-4b6c8d31f4de.

"The Sword and Surveying-Instruments of Washington." *Appleton's Jour-*

nal: A Magazine of General Literature 3, no. 43 (January 22, 1870): 102–103. https://quod.lib.umich.edu/m/moajrnl/acw8433.1-03.043/108:7.

Tamarkin, David, and Maggie Hoffman. "The Planet on the Plate: Why Epicurious Left Beef Behind." *Epicurious*, April 26, 2021. www.epicurious.com/expert-advice/why-epicurious-left-beef-behind-article.

"Teen Charged in Viral Deer Torture Video Pleads Guilty, Gets Probation and 200 Hours of Community Service." *CBS News Pittsburgh*, May 11, 2020. www.cbsnews.com/pittsburgh/news/alexander-smith-deer-torture-video-guilty-plea/.

Telford, Sam R., III, "Deer Reduction Is a Cornerstone of Integrated Deer Tick Management." *Journal of Integrated Pest Management* 8, no. 1 (January 2017): 25. doi.org/10.1093/jipm/pmx024.

"Theodor de Bry's Engravings of the Timucua." n.d. Florida Memory. Accessed March 12, 2023. www.floridamemory.com/discover/historical_records/debry/.

Thomas, Elizabeth Marshall. *The Hidden Life of Deer: Lessons from the Natural World.* New York: HarperCollins, 2009.

Thompson, Stith. *Tales of the Northern American Indians.* Bloomington: Indiana University Press, 1966.

Thoreau, Henry David. *The Journal, 1837–1861.* Edited by Damion Searls. New York: New York Review Books, 2009.

"Top 25 Horror Movies." *Time*, October 29, 2007. entertainment.time.com/2007/10/29/top-25-horror-movies/slide/bambi-1942-2/.

Tsing, Anna Lowenhaupt, et al., eds. *Arts of Living on a Damaged Planet: Ghosts of the Anthropocene; Monsters of the Anthropocene.* Minneapolis: University of Minnesota Press, 2017.

Turner, John W., Jr., and Allan Rutberg. "PZP-22: Multi-Year Reversible Contraception for Wild Horses and Deer." Originally presented August 18, 2020. Bobstiber Institute for Wildlife Fertility Control. www.wildlifefertilitycontrol.org/webinar-pzp22/.

Tymkiw, Liz, J. L. Bowman, and W. G. Shriver. "Effect of Deer Density on Breeding Birds in Delaware." In *Proceedings of the Thirteenth Wildlife Damage Management Conference*, ed. J. Boulanger. 71–73. Saratoga Springs, NY: Thirteenth WDM Conference, 2009.

"United States Population Chart." n.d. OER Services. Accessed March 2, 2023. courses.lumenlearning.com/suny-ushistory2os2xmaster/chapter/united-states-population-chart/.

"The Urban Wild: Animals Take to the Streets Amid Lockdown." *The Guardian*, April 22, 2020. www.theguardian.com/world/gallery/2020/apr/22/animals-roaming-streets-coronavirus-lockdown-photos.

"U.S. Deer Population Trend." n.d. Deer Friendly. Accessed March 2, 2023. www.deerfriendly.com/decline-of-deer-populations.

"U.S. Wildlife Damage." National Agricultural Statistics Services, May 3, 2002. downloads.usda.library.cornell.edu/usda-esmis/files/gt54kn01b /8910jx33w/hx11xh98r/uswd-05-03-2002.pdf.

VerCauteren, Kurt C. "The Deer Boom: Discussions of Population Growth and Range Expansion of White-Tailed Deer." USDA—Wildlife Services Staff Publications, 2003, 15.

"Viral Deer Euthanized After Continually Wandering into Utah Neighborhood." *ABC 10 News San Diego*, January 11, 2022. www.10news.com /news/national/viral-deer-euthanized-after-continually-wandering-into -utah-neighborhood.

"Virginia Passes Second Bill to Protect Wildlife Corridors." *Wildlands Network*, February 24, 2021. wildlandsnetwork.org/news/virginia-passes -second-bill-to-protect-wildlife-corridors.

Vitebsky, Piers, and Tom Lowenstein. *Mother Earth, Father Sky: Native American Myth*. Amsterdam: Duncan Baird, 1997.

Wagner, Greg. "How to Take a Proper Deer Harvest Photo." *Lincoln (Nebraska) Journal-Star*, November 17, 2019. journalstar.com/outdoors /how-to-take-a-proper-deer-harvest-photo/article_a04a95dd-e0fd -54ca-bc1b-735f62c38af1.html.

Waller, D. M., and N. J. Reo. "First Stewards: Ecological Outcomes of Forest and Wildlife Stewardship by Indigenous Peoples of Wisconsin, USA." *Ecology and Society* 23, no. 1 (2018): 45. doi.org/10.5751 /ES-09865-230145.

Wallingford, Bret. Presentation at Deer Impact Assessment and Mitigation Summit. Penn State University Extension, University Park, PA, March 25, 2021.

Walton, Richard Elton. "The World's Largest Organism Is Slowly Being Eaten by Deer." Phys.org, November 24, 2021. phys.org/news/2021-11 -world-largest-slowly-eaten-deer.html.

Warren, Louis S. "Animal Visions: Rethinking the History of the Human Future." *Environmental History* 16, no. 3 (2011): 413–17. www.jstor .org/stable/23049819.

"Welcome to Fripp: History." n.d. *Fripp Island*. Accessed March 4, 2023. frippislandliving.com/welcome-to-fripp/history/.

Wenning, Ron. "What's All the Fuss About Deer Antlers?" *Standard-Journal* (Milton, PA), October 7, 2020. www.standard-journal.com /article_11ce45ec-7365-5d48-a4c0-617515b88faf.html.

White, Richard. *The Roots of Dependency: Subsistence, Environment, and Social Change Among the Choctaws, Pawnees, and Navajos.* Lincoln: University of Nebraska Press, 1983.

"White-Tailed Deer." n.d. Historic Jamestowne. Accessed February 27, 2023. historicjamestowne.org/visit/plan-your-visit/wildlife/white-tailed-deer/.

Whitman, Walt. "An American Primer" (draft). Walt Whitman Papers in the Charles E. Feinberg Collection: Literary File 1841–1919; Prose 1841–1892; 1855–1861. Manuscript/Mixed Material. Library of Congress. www.loc.gov/item/mss1863000859/.

Whitney, Gordon Graham. *From Coastal Wilderness to Fruited Plain: A History of Environmental Change in Temperate North America, 1500 to the Present.* Cambridge, UK: Cambridge University Press, 1994.

Wilder, Laura Ingalls. *Little House in the Big Woods.* New York: Harper & Row, 1932.

"Wildlife Crossings Pilot Program Fact Sheet." Wildlands Network, November 16, 2021. wildlandsnetwork.org/resources/wildlife-crossing-pilot-program-factsheet.

Willey, Sarah. "MassBiologics Research into Preventive Shot for Lyme Disease Continues to Move Forward." UMass Chan Medical School, May 5, 2022. www.umassmed.edu/news/news-archives/2022/05/mass biologics-research-into-preventive-shot-for-lyme-disease-continues-to-move-forward/.

Willging, Robert C. *On the Hunt: The History of Deer Hunting in Wisconsin.* Madison: Wisconsin Historical Society Press, 2008.

"Woman Dies After Airborne Deer Crashes Through Windshield, Authorities Say." *KIRO* 7, February 19, 2020. www.kiro7.com/news/trending/woman-dies-after-airborne-deer-crashes-through-windshield-authorities-say/4IPK7GILDBCSLGFJEOLVFHSBCE/.

Worster, Donald. *Nature's Economy: The Roots of Ecology.* Garden City, NY: Anchor Press/Doubleday, 1979.

Wu, Katherine J. "Antlers Do What No Other Bones Can Do." *The Atlantic*, August 2, 2022. www.theatlantic.com/science/archive/2022/08/deer-elk-shed-antlers-hunting/671021/.

Wyatt, Thomas. "Whoso List to Hunt." c. 1530s. Posted at Luminarium: Anthology of English Literature. www.luminarium.org/renlit/whosolist.htm.

Yu, Karl. "B.C. Conservation Officers Put Down Fawn Blinded by Pellet Gun on Vancouver Island." *Vancouver Island Free Daily*, December 11, 2019. www.vancouverislandfreedaily.com/news/conservation-officers-put-down-fawn-blinded-by-bb-gun-in-nanaimo/.

List of Illustrations

© Meredith Coe

ERIKA HOWSARE holds an MFA in literary arts from Brown University and has published two books of poetry. She also worked in local journalism for twenty years, covering culture and environmental issues. She teaches writing and contributes reviews and essays to various national outlets. A native of Pennsylvania, she lives in rural Virginia.